Transitioning from an Ethnic to a Multicultural Church

Transitioning from an Ethnic to a Multicultural Church

—— A Transformational Model ——

Byoung Ok Koo

FOREWORD BY
Steven Ybarrola

PREFACE BY
Ruth A. Tucker

WIPF & STOCK · Eugene, Oregon

TRANSITIONING FROM AN ETHNIC TO A MULTICULTURAL CHURCH
A Transformational Model

Copyright © 2019 Byoung Ok Koo. All rights reserved. Except for brief quotations in critical publications or reviews, no part of this book may be reproduced in any manner without prior written permission from the publisher. Write: Permissions, Wipf and Stock Publishers, 199 W. 8th Ave., Suite 3, Eugene, OR 97401.

Wipf & Stock
An Imprint of Wipf and Stock Publishers
199 W. 8th Ave., Suite 3
Eugene, OR 97401

www.wipfandstock.com

PAPERBACK ISBN: 978-1-5326-8082-3
HARDCOVER ISBN: 978-1-5326-8083-0
EBOOK ISBN: 978-1-5326-8084-7

All Scripture quotations, unless otherwise indicated, are taken from the Holy Bible, New International Version®, NIV®. Copyright ©1973, 1978, 1984, 2011 by Biblica, Inc.™ Used by permission of Zondervan. All rights reserved worldwide.

Scripture quotations marked (NLT) are taken from the Holy Bible, New Living Translation, copyright ©1996, 2004, 2015 by Tyndale House Foundation. Used by permission of Tyndale House Publishers, Inc., Carol Stream, Illinois 60188. All rights reserved.

Manufactured in the U.S.A. 12/19/19

To my wife Eun Jin Lee
and my children Sumin and Youngmin

Contents

List of Figures and Tables | viii
Foreword by Steven Ybarrola | ix
Preface by Ruth A. Tucker | xi
Acknowledgments | xvii

1. Introduction | 1
2. Koreans and Korean Churches in the United States | 14
3. Development and Issues of the Multicultural Church Movement | 48
4. Study of Four Multicultural Churches | 90
5. Key Findings | 122
6. The Windmill T-process Model | 152
7. Conclusion | 178

   Appendices | 189
   Bibliography | 199

List of Figures

Figure 1. Transition Processes of Four Multicultural Churches | 121

Figure 2. Basic Steps of Windmill T-Process | 161

Figure 3. Windmill T-Process | 173

List of Tables

Table 1. Basic Information of Four Case Study Multicultural Churches | 91

Table 2. Avenues of Hearing about CFC | 138

Table 3. Factors for Staying at CFC | 143

Foreword

IN 2010 AT THE Lausanne Conference in Cape Town, South Africa, there was a strong emphasis on what came to be known as "Diaspora Missiology." This approach to missions recognizes the current global phenomenon of migration (currently comprising approximately one-seventh of the world's population), and the need to look at what God is doing to accomplish His mission through migration (the *missio Dei*). The booklet that came out of that conference, *Scattered to Gather: Embracing the Global Trend of Diaspora*, was a call for missiologists to study this movement of people. The missiologist Byoung OK Koo has produced a manuscript that is an important contribution to this missiological focus. I served as Byoung's mentor, and through the years that we worked together I was excited to see that he was approaching this diaspora call by focusing on an area that had not been very well addressed in the literature—how a diasporic (sometimes referred to as an immigrant or ethnic) church could shift to become more multicultural in the US-American context.

There have been many studies of the Korean diasporic church in the United States, but Koo's focus is on how Korean immigrant churches can move beyond their own ethnic community to become more multicultural; to better reach out to the "nations" around them. This is an aspect of diaspora missiology that is quite important. Those who established the diaspora missiology paradigm coming out of Lausanne 2010 talk about missions to (i.e., non-Christian immigrants in a particular community), missions through (i.e., reaching out to those within your cultural community, such as Koreans to non-Christian Koreans), and missions beyond (i.e., those moving beyond their diaspora community to be witnesses within the broader community). Koo's manuscript addresses the third, how Koreans can develop multicultural congregations within an increasingly multicultural society. As he states, "The Korean immigrant church has great potential for the evangelization of other minorities" (p. 3).

This book is based on Koo's dissertation research on primarily Korean congregations, but it provides a model by which other Christian diaspora communities, as well as monoracial and/or monocultural congregations from the dominant society, can move from churches that cater mainly to people from their own ethnic/racial and cultural background to congregations that recognize the cultural diversity around them and see it as a missional imperative to reach out to these culturally different "others." Koo's "Windmill T-Process" model is based on what he gleaned from the scholarly literature as well as what he learned by doing primarily qualitative research among four churches that had moved from being mainly monocultural to multicultural. This model focuses on the process of moving from a largely monocultural to a more multicultural congregation, and consists of two parts. The first deals with foundational elements necessary for establishing a multicultural church, such as "checking for feasibility, casting vision, becoming independent, adopting a non-ethnic church name, and relocating;" and the second deals with sustaining these churches once established by "serving the neighbor, refreshing the vision, diversifying leadership, promoting cultural intelligence, and having multicultural worship teams" (p. 152). Koo richly articulates and illustrates the main elements of each of these parts.

In the end, this study should assist churches to see what they need to do to reach out to a more multicultural society and thereby understand how they can be used by God to reach the "nations."

Steven Ybarrola, PhD

Professor of Cultural Anthropology
Asbury Theological Seminary

Preface

ONE OF MY BEST students during my career as a seminary professor was Byoung Ok Koo. Diligent and insightful, he was a pleasure to mentor. Now, with his diligence and scholarship shining through, he has written a fine book that anyone desiring a biblical model for church outreach should read carefully. A critical component in a biblical approach takes seriously Christ's command to reach people from every tongue and tribe and nation—including those in our own neighborhoods. And here is where Koo offers critical discernment.

He points out that fewer than six percent of American churches are multi-cultural, a term loosely defined with a low standard. One might imagine that to rank as multi-cultural no more than fifty percent of the congregation and leadership should be dominated by one cultural group, as in Caucasian Americans. But, as Koo points out, the standard generally used is eighty percent.

A number of other scholars have published articles and books on the need for churches to become multi-cultural, but Koo takes this concept a step further. He is challenging ethnic minorities to do this. As a Korean who has studied in America and become an astute observer of American churches, he challenges Korean Americans and other minorities to step up to the plate and take the lead.

After all, such population groups know what it is like to experience—or to suffer—the difficulties and indignities of minority status. These experiences, of course, can make the case for such outreach unappealing. Do Korean Americans who often face cultural barriers six days a week really want to abandon an established comfort zone on Sundays? But Koo gives them no slack.

But even if a church with great purpose seeks to become multicultural, its efforts require hard work—indeed, always a work in progress. Thus the question: Why would minorities desire a multi-cultural congregation? I recall well the case of Dr. Denise Isom, an associate professor at Calvin College in Grand Rapids, Michigan.

Dr. Isom, like all faculty members, was required to find a church home in the Christian Reformed denomination or one of its approved sister denominations with similar doctrine. She appealed the ruling, explaining that she did not feel at home in a white church, the very kind of environment in which she worked every day at the college. The administration pointed out that there were multi-cultural churches in the city. Such an environment, however, would require a conscious effort to blend cultures. She wanted one day a week to worship while setting aside such concerns. She knew she had found a spiritual home when she first visited the nearby black Messiah Missionary Baptist Church.

The Calvin College Board, however, denied her appeal for an exemption. That was reason enough for her to turn in her resignation. Her situation is not altogether different from other minority individuals who work in a Caucasian culture. Is it too much to ask, they wonder, to worship with their own people on Sunday? The Apostle Paul no doubt would respond that it's not too much to ask. So also Koo.

Apart from emotional strain and a host of other difficulties, a minority congregation would seem to be a natural sponsor of multi-cultural worship. White American Evangelicals appear to be far less a natural match. Indeed, serious soul searching is a necessary first step. Is the congregation willing to set aside bias to understand the minority cultures it is seeking to reach? American political alliances are potentially a disabling factor. In recent years the Republican party and Evangelicals have become deeply entwined—even more so since the election of Donald Trump.

Thus, for a white Evangelical church to reach out to African Americans, there are major hurdles to jump. I say this in part from my own experience, having lived for nearly three decades in an integrated neighborhood, my son enrolling in mostly black schools, and my teaming up in business with an African-American woman. Black Christians in our neighborhood were unabashedly Democrats. Billie, my business partner, was a Bible study leader in her church and in many respects a *conservative* Christian who joined fellow believers who filled two busses headed for Washington D.C. for Barak Obama's inauguration. Were white Evangelicals loading busses heading in the same direction? Yes. Eight years later for another Presidential inauguration.

Political, social, economic, religious and artistic factors, combined with a heritage of slavery and Jim Crow laws are part and parcel of African-American understandings. They know better than any other minority how racism has infected every aspect of American life. Until we recognize this, ministry across color lines should be put on hold.

Years ago in one of my seminary courses, I was teaching a segment on racism. I began class that afternoon, with the comment that grabbed the attention of my students: *There is racism in this classroom.* I stood before my all-white, mostly male students and slowly looked around the room. *I know there's racism here in this classroom and in this seminary.* Again a pause, perhaps some students wondering if I had heard a comment one of them had inadvertently made. Then I said: *I know there's racism in this room because I am here.* I talked about institutional racism, and then I made it personal, pointing a finger at myself.

I've recently heard certain white politicians use the phrase: *I don't have a racist bone in my body.* Nonsense. The statement alone shows lack of understanding of both institutional and personal racism. And not a white majority culture alone. To a lesser degree, all minorities are infected by racism, most commonly aimed at ones they deem lesser than themselves.

Another form of demeaning those who are in our sights for church growth, whether minorities or not, is the premise that we as Christians are exclusively the givers; our targets are the receivers. It starts with the assumption that we are the owners of Truth, and they are the recipients. From there it extends to other aspects of ministry. Effective outreach, we are taught, involves service such as inviting neighbors to a free picnic dinner, with games and prizes for the children. But there is a reverse side of this "outreach"—that of inviting neighbors to serve. If the church is sponsoring a nearby cleanup of the creek, invite the whole neighborhood to participate. The same with a Habitat house. Even softball and worship teams are church functions for the unchurched. Imagine the potential outcome of inviting a teenager to play his guitar on the worship team, or inviting her to join the liturgical dance troupe.

I remember reading about a small-town church that served the community by staging a live nativity scene every evening beginning two weeks before Christmas. Lacking teenage girls one year, an elderly woman was conscripted to play Mary. How sad. Surely there were teens in town who might have been honored to fill the roll. And whoever said Mary ought to be played by a white girl? Might a black or Hispanic or Korean teen have the perfect skin color to play the role of Mary?

Too often churches insist outsiders become insiders before they are called upon to serve. This I contend is backwards ministry. Inviting outsiders to serve is a key step in bringing them into the church community. And it is also a critical factor in retention. Often churches pay more attention to bringing in newcomers (whether multi-cultural or not) than retaining those who are on the fringes or in the process of leaving. In fact, a rapidly growing population is referred to as "nones," those whose religious affiliation is "none." This faction is now equal to the size of Evangelicalism itself. And all churches are affected. Some "nones" have consciously abandoned the faith; others have simply drifted away. Koo points out that Korean immigrant churches face a serious "silent exodus"—that of "younger Koreans leaving church and faith during/after college."

In some respects, this category is a cultural subset in itself and deserves multi-cultural concepts utilized in church outreach. It is all too tempting to hassle a young person for absence at worship service. Far better to invite participation on the softball team, potluck dinners, service projects, coaching a neighborhood basketball team or teaching crafts for Vacation Bible School. A judgmental attitude is a sure way to keep such individuals outside the circle of the church community.

Without retention of youth and young adults, church growth, including multi-cultural outreach, is stymied. But even with a healthy church community, multi-cultural growth is hard work that requires years, sometimes decades, to accomplish. But difficult as this may be, Koo also discusses the "pull factor" that multi-cultural churches have today. Many people, including mixed-race couples, are seeking a community of believers that is not segregated on Sunday morning. Koo's volume fills a critical gap in the literature. His case studies offer insights on both successes and pitfalls of such ministry.

One of the most profound examples Koo offers of transformational multi-cultural outreach features a Korean immigrant church, Emmanuel Church of Philadelphia (ECP), formed in 1968. By the 1990s, although members were prospering financially, the neighborhood was not. Then the unthinkable happened: "In 1993, a Korean deacon was shot and killed in the church parking lot by two African-American teenagers." It would not have been surprising had the church relocated to a safer area, and that is exactly what some members wanted to do.

The pastor however, supported by elders, wondered if this terrible incident might have been a wakeup call. His words were prophetic: "we have all this money and we drive BMW, Mercedes, we come here every week and we don't do anything for this poor community." In the years that followed the church sought to heal relationships with their closest neighbors, sponsoring college scholarships for graduating seniors, tutoring classes, trips to summer camps, and community festivals. Today the church and its daughter church have further strengthened the surrounding community by offering homeless and medical ministries.

Have these caring ministries transformed the church into a healthy multi-cultural Christian community of believers? No, not in this case. But

Koo concludes, "it definitely has led members to open their arms widely to reach out to everyone."

Times are changing. Today greater numbers of Christians are condemning racism and white supremacy. Minorities and migrants are on their minds, a trend that makes Koo's book all the more relevant.

Although Calvin College has not issued a public apology to Denise Isom since the 2008 episode relating to her being forced out, the school has made progress in this realm. So also, the Christian Reformed Church (CRC), a denomination that only decades ago was almost exclusively Dutch. In an August 2019 statement it publicly condemned hate speech and actions and, among other strong words, called on all its members:

> to stand up against racism and acts of white supremacy. We ask them to speak up against words of misogyny and of hatred toward immigrants. We ask them to be proactively anti-racist, proactively anti-sexist, and to proactively promote the dignity of all people.

It is interesting that one of Koo's case studies comes right out of this denomination. Madison Square CRC began in 1914 as an outreach ministry of a Dutch-speaking church to reach out to non-Dutch neighbors. For that church it was no doubt a bit of a cross-cultural experience. Decades pass, now in the 1960s, a staff member seeks to do multi-ethnic outreach, particularly to African Americans. Church members were opposed, and it was decided that it was better to "not contact them, than to take them into a hostile environment." But soon the Dutch residents were leading the caravan of white flight. Now with a renewed focus on the changing neighborhood, black families slowly began joining, then a black pastor who, three years later resigned. Why? It was "due to the racism he encountered in the upper leadership of the CRC denomination."

Today Madison Square is a large thriving multi-cultural congregation with more than one campus. It is "racially well-mixed both in the pews and on the stage (with whites, blacks, Hispanics, and Asians present)." Koo knows it well, having found his church home there while he was a seminary student. It is a model for other churches—and a miracle of sorts. Here in Southeast Grand Rapids is a wonderfully colorful flower garden—a garden fertilized by the foul dung of racism and white flight.

Ruth A. Tucker, Ph.D.

Author, *From Jerusalem to Irian Jaya:*
A Biographical History of Christian Missions

Acknowledgments

I GIVE PRAISE, HONOR, and thanksgiving to God, who has been with me all the time. Writing a book is a difficult journey, but it still has been a great blessing in that the more I recognize my limitations, the more I sense God's limitless grace in the process. One of the ways God makes impossible things possible is to surround me with his people, only some of whom are mentioned here.

Above all, I am truly indebted and thankful to my mentor, Dr. Steven Ybarrola, professor at Asbury Theological Seminary, for his insightful advice, encouragement, and friendship amid his struggle with thyroid cancer and leukemia. His sacrificial instruction made this book possible. Often I think of his humble and loving attitude as I teach my students at Reformed Graduate University. Also, it was a great blessing to meet Dr. Ruth A. Tucker in 2004 at Calvin Theological Seminary. A well-known scholar and bestselling author of many books, including *From Jerusalem to Irian Jaya: A Biographical History of Christian Missions*, she has given me encouragement, love, and invaluable advice.

I am indebted to the senior/lead pastors of the case study churches who helped me in many ways: Rev. David Beelen of Madison Square Church, Rev. Min Joshua Chung of Covenant Fellowship Church, Rev. Joshua Kang of Lakeview Church, and Rev. Dwight Yoo of Renewal Presbyterian Church. I would especially like to express my deep appreciation to Rev. David Beelen, who sowed an interest in the multicultural church in me as a member of his church while studying at Calvin Theological Seminary; he graciously gave me many opportunities to learn from him and his ministry.

I want to acknowledge extraordinary friendships with both Dr. Robert Hughes and Dr. Andy Ponce; they prayed for and helped me by providing proofreading with valuable comments. Their friendship and practical help shine in my heart. With many people's prayer and help, Reformed Graduate

University thankfully supported me to have a six-month research break in this long process of publication.

I am grateful to my parents-in-law, Kyuwoong Lee and Hyun Sook Yoon, for their spiritual, emotional, and financial support. I am so thankful to my two sisters, Heekyoung Lee and Hwajin Koo, who have always been supportive. With much prayer, my parents, Kwang Kwang Koo and Sunje Cho made this journey possible by taking care of my two children, as well as doing all the housework, while Eun Jin and I studied. Their sacrificial love remains in my heart and will be there forever. In closing, my deepest gratitude goes to my eternal friend and wife, Dr. Eun Jin Lee, and my two loving children, Sumin and Youngmin, who are always encouraging and patient and prayerful. Eun Jin beautifully reflects Proverbs 31: "Many women do noble things, but you surpass them all."

1

Introduction

My interest in multicultural congregations emerged from my personal experiences at Madison Square Church (Madison hereafter) in Grand Rapids, Michigan while I was attending Calvin Theological Seminary between 2004 and 2007. In one of my memories of this church, there is a crying woman whom I will never forget.

The woman cried when my wife told her that she was pregnant. It was right after the Sunday worship service in the crowded church lobby where there was no space to move. When my wife found her and informed her of the pregnancy, she immediately started to shout and leap for joy like a child, unconcerned with the reactions of the people around her. She then prayed with tears. It seemed she could not be more joyful for such a great unexpected gift. The woman was Caucasian, around sixty years old, intelligent, tall, and a well-dressed church member. She was a prayer servant in the church and had known that we were praying for a baby. So after my wife had two miscarriages in the six years after we married, the pregnancy was a miracle for us.

My wife and I joined Madison shortly after our arrival in the United States in 2004. It was the first time in my life to observe and experience a multicultural church.[1] My initial goal was only to see an American church. I did not imagine that I would instead become a member of a multicultural church that would give me a picture of what the heavenly gathering will be like after Christ's return.

There is one other significant occasion that also caused me to think deeply about multicultural churches—this time about the ability of Korean churches to reach out to non-Koreans. Shortly after I arrived at Asbury Theological Seminary in 2007, God led me to serve a Korean immigrant church (Korean Presbyterian Church of Cincinnati: KPCC) as

---

1. Madison Square Church consists of 65 percent of Caucasians, 15 percent African Americans, 15 percent Hispanics, and 5 percent others.

its educational pastor. Because KPCC was a small church with about 30 Sunday worshippers, there were only four students in my children's Sunday school program. These students often missed Sunday worship, sometimes leaving me with no students at all. It seemed there was no opportunity for growth in my Sunday school because the church's members had no children except those four students, and the congregation was located in a community which had no Korean neighbors.

Under these circumstances, God filled us with a desire to reach out to the non-Korean children in our community. Because my Sunday school class was conducted in English, expanding our outreach beyond the Koreans of the church seemed reasonable. When we went out to get to know some of our neighbors, we met two Nepali teenagers on the street. We invited them to church, and they started to come the next week. Soon after, whenever the church would hold special worship services such as at Thanksgiving, Christmas, and Easter, or a picnic, the number of Nepali attendees would often outnumber the Korean members of the congregation. As a result, the Korean church members learned how to joyfully serve these Nepalese neighbors through a combination of Word and deed. The children's Sunday school grew to have about 20 to 25 Nepali students and a few parents every Sunday. However, when an existing Nepali church decided to move to within close to our congregation, KPCC and the Nepali church decided together to merge the (Nepali) children's Sunday school into the Nepali church, so that the children could worship and learn in their own heart language. KPCC implemented this decision in the late Spring of 2012; however, unexpectedly almost all of the Nepalese children decided not to go to the Nepali church.

In spite of my sweet memories at Madison and the blessings of the Nepali ministry at KPCC, I can see that there are several challenges facing the church in America with regard to multicultural ministry.

Challenge of Korean Immigrant Churches

Most Korean Protestant churches in the United States are oriented only toward reaching out to other Koreans, forming a Christian ethnic ghetto, and are not effective in reaching out to non-Koreans despite being a part of a globalized multicultural society; they do not know how to do this well, even though they are often located in multi-ethnic neighborhoods and are called to serve all nations.

While minority populations are growing explosively and are becoming more and more diverse in terms of people and their cultures in the United States, most churches focus on their own ethnic groups, and relatively few churches strategically reach out to others of different ethnic/racial backgrounds.[2] Korean immigrant churches are no exception.

The US Census for the year 2010 showed that within the 308.7 million total US population, the minority population was 111.9 million (36percent).[3] According to the US Census Bureau, minorities, rather than non-Hispanic and single-race whites, will become the numerical majority by 2042.[4] Diversity is a reality that we cannot avoid. According to the Pew Forum on Religion and Public Life, less than 6 percent of American churches are multicultural (defined as churches where one single ethnic or racial group does not exceed 80 percent of the total membership). In other words, most churches are not ready to embrace people of other ethnicities and may not even want to. The problem is, while Christians are focusing only on reaching people of their same ethnic/racial backgrounds, many unchurched others are in "blind spots" in the evangelization of a globalized United States. For instance, only 45 percent of Asians in the United States are Christians.[5] Specifically, of the Asian Christian population, only 27 percent are Protestant.[6] Asians, in general, represent the least Christianized group in the United States. Like Asians, other minorities, too, need to become the focus of more concern in terms of evangelism. According to ARIS (American Religious Identification Survey), de-Christianization is also found among whites as "the rapid proportionate growth of the Nones [no stated religious preference, atheist, or agnostic] among whites was a 1990s phenomenon while the fast decline in white Mainline Christians is a more recent trend."[7]

Nevertheless, the Korean immigrant church has great potential for the evangelization of other minorities. Unlike other Asian groups, over 70 percent of Koreans are active church attenders in America.[8] In 2018, Korean immigrant churches numbered 4,454, and they are considered to

2. DeYoung et al., *United by Faith*, 2; DeYmaz and Li, *Ethnic Blends*, 24; Yancey, *One Body*, 15. There are 7.5 percent mixed religious congregations in America. However, for Christian congregation only 5.5 percent are racially mixed.

3. U.S. Census Bureau, "Overview of Race and Hispanic Origin: 2010," 17–18. Except for Hispanic, there are 9 million (3percent) other races such as American Indian, Alaska Native, Native Hawaiian, mixed races and so on.

4. "Minorities expected to be majority in 2050," *CNN*, August 13, 2008.

5. The Pew Forum, *U.S. Religious Landscape Survey*, 43.

6. The Pew Forum, *U.S. Religious Landscape Survey*, 43.

7. Kosmin and Keysar, *American Religious Identification Survey*, 15.

8. The Pew Forum, *Asian Americans*, 16; Kwon et al., *Korean Americans and Their Religions*, 87; Kim, *A Faith of Our Own*, 23, 159; Min and Kim, "Ethnic and Sub-ethnic Attachments," 762; Hurh and Kim, "Religious Participation," 20; Kim and Kim, "Revival and Renewal," 292.

be among the growing churches in America.[9] In addition, Korean Christians have a strong zeal for mission and evangelism as Korean immigrant churches have typically emphasized foreign missions and have supported missionaries strongly.

Korean immigrant churches are growing, but they are also known for their ethnic detachment. They seldom try to evangelize local unchurched people of other ethnicities due to Korean immigrants' maintaining their ethnicity and culture through the social interactions gained from their participation in Korean immigrant churches.[10] This frequent participation is a result of these churches providing for Koreans' practical and spiritual needs. This provision for needs has caused Korean-centered tendencies in these churches. These ethno-centric tendencies can be characterized by extraordinary in-group commitment. Korean-American Christians put enormous energy and resources into their ethnic churches, but they are indifferent to other ethnic groups outside their churches.[11] Most Korean churches only try to reach out to non-Christian Koreans.

Demographic shifts due to immigration and globalization challenge Korean immigrant churches. To obey the Great Commission's call to make disciples of all nations, they must change to become outwardly focused. The crucial question, then, is *how might Korean churches in America maximize their capacity to reach and integrate non-Koreans into their faith communities?*

My hypothesis is that by studying congregations that transitioned from being mono- to multi-cultural, one may find valuable insights and use those insights to formulate principles that would help other mono-cultural churches make this same transition.

---

9. Suh, "*Mijunkuk Haninkyohoi 4,544* [4,454 Korean Churches in USA]," *Christian Today*, January 21, 2018.

10. Min, "Immigrants' Religion and Ethnicity," 36.

11. The 1997–1998 Presbyterian Racial and Ethnic Panel Studies shows that 78 percent of Korean Presbyterians attend Sunday worship service every week, compared to 49 percent of Latino, 34 percent of African American, and 28 percent of Caucasian Presbyterians. [Min and Kim, "Intergenerational Transmission," 269] Also, the 1997–1998 Queens Survey reveals that 44 percent of Indian immigrants and 41 percent of Chinese immigrants attend a church worship at least once a week. [Min, "Immigrants' Religion and Ethnicity," 41] In terms of financial commitment, according to the 1997 Ethnic and Racial Panel Survey, "[t]he majority of Koreans (62percent) contributed $2,000 or more in regular giving to their current congregations in the previous year. Only 35 percent of African Americans, 26 percent of Hispanics, and 40 percent of Caucasians report giving that much." [Kim and Kim, "The Ethnic Roles," 82]

Delimitations

I have two delimitations in my research. First, although there are many multicultural churches in the United States, I will mainly focus on English-speaking Korean-initiated multicultural congregations. For the sake of comparison, however, I will also include one Dutch-initiated multicultural church as well.[12] Second, even though there are several kinds of Christian churches in the United States, I will limit my study to Protestant multicultural churches.

Definition of Key Terms

When discussing multicultural churches, many people, including scholars, use "multiethnic," "multicultural," and "multiracial" interchangeably to describe a church's diversity. However, the different emphases and meanings should be clarified for a study which seeks to examine this phenomenon in depth and with precision.

(1) *Multiethnic Church*: The term "multiethnic church" is a local church that combines different ethnic groups. The focus of a multiethnic church is ethnic diversity. It can have multiple racial groups, but racial diversity is not necessary.

(2) *Multiracial Church*: "Multiracial church" is a local church consisting of multiple races and in which "no one racial group is 80 percent or more of the people."[13] This definition implies that a multiracial congregation includes multiethnic and multicultural members.

Even though "multiracial church" implies diversity within a congregation, there are many situations in which churches may be multiethnic but not multiracial. For example, Koreans, Filipinos, Japanese, and Chinese may all attend the same church, but they are all categorized as the same "race"—i.e., Asian—in the context of the United States. Therefore, such a congregation would be culturally diverse but not multiracial.

(3) *Multicultural Church*: "Multicultural church" is a local church, consisting of multiethnic people, pursuing multiculturalism as its foundation. To make it clear, I define "multicultural church" in two ways. First, following

---

12. I intentionally use the term 'congregation' because some churches have multicultural/multiethnic EM (English-speaking) congregations along with their ethnic congregations. In my study I will study multicultural churches as well as multicultural congregations.

13. DeYoung et al., *United by Faith*, 76. According to DeYoung et al., "Mathematically, assuming people randomly meet twenty others in the congregation, each person has a 99 percent chance of meeting someone of another race."

DeYoung et al., the number of church members from the dominant ethnic group does not exceed 80 percent of a congregation's total population.[14] Second, the multicultural church values equality in cultural, ethnic and racial diversity and pursues integration rather than assimilation. The term "multicultural" implies the presence of ongoing intentional efforts to maintain unity in diversity. I will use the term "multicultural church" for my study because it can include both ethnic and racial differences, and because it is the most compatible with my theoretical framework of "multiculturalism."

(4) *Korean-Initiated Multicultural Church*: I define a Korean-initiated multicultural church (KIM church) as a multicultural local church that has at least one of the following three distinctions: 1) Korean congregants are dominant in number, 2) leadership is dominated by Korean leaders such as pastors, elders, or council members who have authority in the decision-making process, and 3) the church originated from a Korean church.

(5) *Minority*: The word "minority" in relation to human populations overlaps with the image of a subordinate people group confronting a dominant majority. In the American context, minority "is commonly used to describe persons who are not white." [15] In many cases, minorities have limitations in language, job opportunities, political power, etc. However, in this paper which focuses on the church context, I will use the word "minority" to refer to a person or people group who are in a subordinate position to the dominant population, which among three of the case study churches is Korean.

Multiculturalism and Yancey's 7 Principles

In order to come to a strong understanding of the function of multicultural churches in a multicultural context, it is important to fully grasp the core concept of multiculturalism. In addition, to help us understand the dynamics of multiculturalism within churches, George Yancey's seven principles of multiracial churches provide a strong basis for this study focusing on Korean-American churches in multicultural contexts.

Multiculturalism

Many scholars have pointed out the importance of culture in evangelism, an issue that the church has had to address from its very beginning (e.g., Acts 15). For instance, through his research in India, Donald McGavran

14. DeYoung et al., *United by Faith*, 2–3; Yancey, *One Body*, 15.
15. Mulder, *Learning to Count to One*, 13.

discovered that people often choose not to become Christians because of cultural and sociological barriers, rather than for theological and religious reasons.[16] Because of the significance of these barriers, George Hunter argues that the church should approach unchurched people through culturally appropriate forms.[17] He later defines this approach as "cultural relevance" in evangelism and writes that effective churches adapt to the target population's culture in areas such as language, music, and aesthetics.[18]

Also significant, crucial changes in perspectives on culture can also be found in the recognition of diversity itself as a form of culture. In considering the importance of multiculturalism in evangelism, Guder et al. state that, along with independent cultures, "multiple cultures" also exist in communities in the North American context.[19] In this situation, multiculturalism is primarily considered to be a movement and also "a conceptual framework for challenging the cultural hegemony of the dominant ethnic group . . . in the United States and the United Kingdom."[20] There are many different understandings and forms of this multiculturalism.[21] Nevertheless, there are two common emphases which often arise: equality and integration.

First, multiculturalism pursues *equality* in cultural diversity. This value is exemplified in one high school principal's statement to his students in 1996 that "as an American, you don't have to divorce yourself from your cultural history. What's so good about America is we try to respect the rights and privileges of people different from us, and teach our children to respect people's cultural integrity."[22] Minorities do not need to give up their cultures; rather, people need to learn to respect each culture, because people pursue equality between different cultures under this understanding of multiculturalism.

Second, multiculturalism emphasizes *integration* between individuals and people groups who have different cultures. According to Kathleen

16. Lausanne Committee, "LOP 1: The Pasadena Consultation." Also, according to Lewis R. Rambo's sequential stage model for understanding religious conversion, culture is an important factor during the first stage of the model, and it continues to have an influence in all conversion stages. [Rambo, *Understanding Religious Conversion*, 1993)].

17. Hunter, *Church for the Unchurched*, 68.

18. Hunter, *The Apostolic Congregation*, 31.

19. Guder, *Missional Church*, 45.

20. Turner, "Anthropology and Multiculturalism," 412.

21. For example, Turner discusses the contradiction between critical and difference multiculturalism. See Turner, "Anthropology and Multiculturalism," 412. Also, John Rex emphasizes egalitarian multiculturalism with an emphasis on equality. See Hutchinson and Smith, *Ethnicity*, 243.

22. Lopez, "Hispanics see security in citizenship," 2.

Garces-Foley, before the 1980s Roman Catholics in the United States pursued cultural pluralism (which caused separation among different cultures) in their posture toward immigrants. However, during the 1980s and 1990s, Catholics gradually moved toward multiculturalism, with its emphasis on integration, and adopted a slogan of "Unity in Diversity."[23] Catholic Bishops, in a letter written in the United States in 2000, clarified the importance of this integration, saying, "It is not a call for 'assimilation' or the disappearance of one culture into another, but for continuing cooperation in pursuit of the common good and with proper respect for the good of each cultural tradition and community."[24] In contrast, according to Garces-Foley, evangelicals during this time period were often ignorant about racial reconciliation and integration, even after the Civil Rights movement and the change of immigration law in 1965.[25] While evangelicals emphasized evangelism more, their ideology remained that of ecclesial homogeneity. However, since the 1990s, several diverse evangelical churches have argued that "evangelism must be cross-cultural in order to fulfill the commandment to preach to all nations."[26] Nonetheless, evangelicals stress the identity of the born-again Christian regardless of cultural and ethnic diversity.[27]

Also, regarding integration, John Rex asserts that the depth of such integration is crucial in fostering multiculturalism. He says, "[T]he nature of the relationships between minority groups and national societies on the political level must be moral. The individuals who negotiate with one another do not simply have an external relationship with each other; they become united in their consciences and their pursuit of justice."[28] Therefore, the existence of merely superficial external relationships is not an authentic form of multiculturalism; the level of integration must be deepened through intentional, continuous efforts.

George Yancey's 7 Principles of Multiracial Churches

George Yancey provides an additional analytical lens in *One Body One Spirit*, which is helpful for my study. He proposes seven general principles for building multicultural churches: inclusive worship, diverse leadership,

---

23. Ortiz and McGlone, *To Be One*, chap. 8. The title of Catholic bishops' letter in 2000 was *Welcoming the Stranger Among Us: Unity in Diversity*.
24. Ortiz and McGlone, *To Be One*, chap. 8.
25. Garces-Foley, "Catholic and Evangelical Integration," 20–21.
26. Garces-Foley, "Catholic and Evangelical Integration," 21.
27. Garces-Foley, "Catholic and Evangelical Integration," 22.
28. Hutchinson and Smith, *Ethnicity*, 245.

an overarching goal, intentionality, personal skills, location, and adaptability.[29] "Inclusive worship"[30] means that a multicultural church embraces diverse cultural elements in its worship such as different worship songs, racially diverse worship leaders, and even different preaching style. "Diverse leadership"[31] means that a multicultural church tends to have diverse leadership on staff, or even in lay leadership, which reflects the diversity of the congregation. "An overarching goal"[32] is what a multicultural church primarily pursues, as Yancey found that becoming a multicultural church was not the primary goal of those multicultural churches. Instead, he found that having an overarching goal like "winning souls" also helps the church to maintain cultural diversity, when the church intentionally reaches out to diverse people through the goal. The fourth principle is "intentionality;"[33] it takes significant intentionality for a church to become multicultural and then to maintain its multicultural atmosphere. Next, Yancey asserts that since a multicultural church can have additional interpersonal challenges, often due to cultural misunderstandings, pastors and other leaders need outstanding sensitivity and "personal skills."[34] In addition, the geographical "location"[35] of multicultural churches also tend to play an important role in their being multicultural, as the demographics of their surrounding neighborhoods have an impact. Finally, Yancey's principle of "adaptability"[36] means that a multicultural church has to have the ability to properly respond to the multicultural challenges which the church encounters, such as language barriers for the first-generation immigrants, how to deal with numerical minorities, and interrelations between leadership skills and adaptability.

All in all, even though I do not necessarily depend upon these theories, it will guide my studies what I need to focus especially on my case studies. Also, I will see how both the two core elements of multiculturalism—equality and integration—and Yancey's seven principles are related to the transition processes of the four multicultural churches and their ministries.

---

29. Yancey, *One Body*, 65–151.
30. Yancey, *One Body*, 71–84.
31. Yancey, *One Body*, 85–97.
32. Yancey, *One Body*, 99–107.
33. Yancey, *One Body*, 108–117.
34. Yancey, *One Body*, 118–127.
35. Yancey, *One Body*, 128–137.
36. Yancey, *One Body*, 138–151.

Research Methodology: Case Study

To answer the research questions[37], I studied four multicultural churches as field-based case studies, which functioned as the primary research methodology. Four churches were identified which had more than twenty percent of their members representing different (i.e., non-majority) ethnic or racial groups in the church. Three were Korean-initiated multicultural churches and one was a Dutch-initiated church, studied for the sake of comparison and contrast: Covenant Fellowship Church (Urbana-Champaign, Illinois), Lakeview Church (Chicago, Illinois), Renewal Presbyterian Church (Philadelphia, Pennsylvania), and Madison Square Christian Reformed Church (Grand Rapids, Michigan).

I followed the general rules, principles, and terms of Robert K. Yin[38] in these case studies, supplemented with Russell Bernard's anthropological methodology,[39] utilizing three sources of evidence: documentation, interviews, and direct-observation.

Documentation

For these case studies, I was able to collect church publications such as annual reports, which provided demographic and statistical data regarding the churches' ethnic/gender/generational makeups, as well as their changes and growth. I also gathered mission statements, Sunday bulletins, and monthly and yearly publications which indicated the direction which the churches/congregations were pursuing and their practical applications in their ministries. In this regard, Madison Square Church, which is the oldest church (turning 100 years old in 2014), provided an abundance of documents, including statements and guidelines that showed how the church strategically developed its multicultural ministry. I was also able to obtain several research papers on Madison's history that had been written by seminarians, which were valuable for understanding its long history.

---

37. I have five questions for this study: 1) By what processes do churches become multicultural in the United States? 2) What difficulties do Korean-initiated multicultural (KIM) churches face in relation to reaching out to unchurched non-Koreans? 3) What factors attract non-Koreans to visit a KIM church? 4) What factors cause non-Korean visitors to stay in a KIM church? 5) Based on these discoveries, what are the lessons that the Korean immigrant church can learn and apply for reaching out to non-Koreans?

38. Yin, *Case Study Research*.

39. Bernard, *Research Methods in Anthropology*.

One of these documents is provided in an appendix section in order to help church leaders understand these case study churches' efforts to develop their multicultural character so that they can apply what they learn to their own ministries.

Interviews

Interviews were conducted in three different ways: face-to-face, phone, and e-mail.[40] In terms of interview style, I used semi-structured interviews, which is the best style to use when the interviewer "won't get more than one chance to interview someone"[41] in person. This was particularly necessary for the interviews with senior/lead pastors and staff members which were conducted when I visited the case study churches. I used three sets of questions based on the interviewee's status in order to maximize the effect of the interview. I also found that interviewing through e-mail provided valuable information, particularly when used to ask complementary questions to follow up on first responses. Interviewees often gave more detailed answers with useful descriptions or explanations that were helpful for seeing the whole picture when the interviewer raised these complementary questions.

I conducted thirty-nine interviews, eleven of which were conducted with pastors and staff, and twenty-eight with lay people. I interviewed pastors, staff, and lay leaders/long-term members who were a part of the churches during their transition period from being monocultural congregations to becoming multicultural. I also interviewed newer congregants who joined the church after its transition toward becoming a multicultural church. Each of the interviews lasted between forty minutes and two-and-a-half hours, and they were conducted in various locations, including private homes, churches, coffee shops, and restaurants. Interviews were recorded and transcribed for accurate analysis, using pseudonyms for specific quotations or references, except for in the cases of pastors and staff members.

Direct Observation

For this study, I participated in multiple-day events such as retreats and revival meetings in all three KIM churches. Participating in these events was helpful not only for observing the multicultural atmosphere and characteristics of the case study churches but also for building rapport, which was beneficial when I needed to contact and interview through phone calls

40. Bernard, *Research Methods in Anthropology*, 203.
41. Bernard, *Research Methods in Anthropology*, 205.

or e-mails later. I also attended Sunday worship services and small group meetings to observe their worship styles and music, and to hear their sermons, focusing on how each church displays its multicultural character throughout the services. In addition, I observed different meetings such as a teaching team meeting and a pastoral care meeting that showed how church leaders manage and develop diversity in ministry.

Why This Study Is Important

This study works to help fill a gap in the existing research regarding minority-dominant multicultural churches in the United States, specifically regarding those which are Korean-initiated. Many American multicultural churches with predominantly white populations are mainly concerned with racial reconciliation with the African-American community. Accordingly, many resources are available dealing with these types of white-dominant multicultural churches. However, resources concerned with minority-dominant multicultural churches are scant. Thus, this study contributes to the body of knowledge regarding Korean-initiated multicultural churches in America by identifying and summarizing their characteristics and developing terminology to describe them.

The second reason why this study is important is that it provides a model transition process, named the Windmill T-process, to help monocultural/monoethnic churches that want to become multicultural churches. There are many minority churches with leaders who want to move toward becoming a multicultural church, especially under the circumstances of being a minority in white-dominant America. This study will help them to move forward in that process.

The third reason why this study is valuable is that it will give insights to Korean immigrant church leaders on how to reach out and take care of their congregants' non-Korean family members. Regardless of their pursuit of multiculturalism, almost all Korean churches in America have unchurched, non-Korean family members from interracial/ethnic marriages. Unfortunately, most Korean immigrant churches are not effective in this area. I hope that findings from this study can provide new ideas for Korean and other minority church leaders who are looking for answers to this problem.

The fourth reason why this study is significant is that it provides insight into the relationships between multicultural churches and evangelism. Whereas many scholars have published books about multicultural churches, no one has addressed specifically the interrelation between multicultural churches and evangelism. Even though there are limits to its insight in this area, this study touches on the issue of evangelism in the multicultural church. Through this study, I describe what factors first draw different racial/ethnic people to a church and what factors cause them to stay in the church. These pull and stay factors will help Korean or other ethnic minority church leaders to reach out to all nations beyond ethnic/racial identity.

Finally, although it will take time, this study will also map a route for Korean churches in Korea to effectively reach out to the growing non-Korean population in Korea.

2

Koreans and Korean Churches in the United States

Potential Emerging Leaders for the Multicultural Church Movement

EVEN THOUGH THE HISTORY of Korean immigration to the United States is relatively short when compared to the history of immigration among other Asian-Americans, Korean-Americans are one of the most significant minorities in the United States. Korean-Americans, who form a significant part of the Asian-American community, have an increasingly important role in shaping the future of American Christianity. In *A Different Mirror: A History of Multicultural America*, Ronald Takaki, a third-generation Japanese-American, claims that Asian-Americans are indeed active participants in American history, though they have often been considered as "strangers," "heathen," "exotic," and "unassimilable."[1] He also points out that in recent years Asian-Americans have received significant attention as "the Model Minority."[2] A nationwide survey in 2010 revealed that most Christian denominations in the United States are now declining in membership, except for the Roman Catholic Church.[3] In addition, for the last two decades, immigration has impacted the growth of religious pluralism in the United States.[4]

---

1. Takaki, *A Different Mirror*, 7.

2. Takaki, *A Different Mirror*, 414–417. "Model Minority" is a term used to portray a financially and educationally successful image of Asian-Americans as a minority group in the United States.

3. According to the survey by National Council of Churches, most Christian denominations such as Southern Baptist Convention, The United Methodist Church, Evangelical Lutheran Church in America, Presbyterian Church (USA) and many other denominations show continuous declines in membership.

4. Lindner, "The New Immigrant Church," 16–18.

Nevertheless, Korean churches in most denominations are in fact growing, and over seventy percent of Koreans in the United States are churchgoers.[5] In *The Next Evangelicalism*, Soong-Chan Rah also points out the significance and potential of the second-generation immigrants due to their bicultural character, their strong spiritual heritage, and, their consequently being uniquely well-equipped to carry the gospel within today's dramatic demographic changes.[6] Rah asserts that second-generation immigrants bring hope and will play a significant role in the American church's crisis. Likewise, as one of the more active immigrant groups, Korean-American Christians in the United States can be considered the new "relief pitcher" for turning around Christianity in the United States.

Therefore, in this chapter, I will discuss Koreans and Korean churches in the United States. First, I will examine the history of Korean Christianity as a background for understanding Korean churches in America. Even though several religions have influenced Koreans for far longer than Christianity, this chapter will focus on early Christianity in Korea, because it was the catalyst for Korean immigration to America. Second, this chapter will examine the history of Korean immigration, with a particular focus on how Protestant missionaries influenced the early Korean immigrants, which caused Korean-Americans to develop a passion for the church. Even though Christianity was a newly received religion, with a minimal number of believers (less than 1 percent) when Korean immigration to the United States began, it powerfully affected Korean-Americans and their lives in America from the beginning. Third, I will discuss the characteristics and challenges of Korean immigrant churches in the United States. Koreans' extraordinary zeal for the church and its mission present great potential to change and further American Christianity, even though the number of Koreans is relatively small.

The History of Korean Christianity

In 1984, churches throughout Korea celebrated the 100th anniversary of Korean Christianity. This date was based on the records of the first American missionary to Korea, Horace Newton Allen (a North Presbyterian missionary and medical doctor from the United States), who arrived on September 20, 1884.[7] In 1885, several denominations sent additional

---

5. The Pew Forum, *Asian Americans*, 16; Kim, *A Faith of Our Own*, 23, 159; Kwon et al., *Korean Americans and Their Religions*, 87; Min and Kim, "Ethnic and Sub-ethnic Attachments," 762; Hurh and Kim, "Religious Participation," 20; Kim and Kim, "Revival and Renewal," 292.

6. Rah, *The Next Evangelicalism*, 180–199.

7. Park, *Hankook Gidok Kyohoisa I*, 369; Kim, "Korean Immigrants," 54.

missionaries, including Horace Grant Underwood from the North Presbyterian Church and Henry Gerhard Appenzeller from the Methodist Church (April 5), Mary F. Scranton from the Methodist Church (May 1), and J. W. Heron from the North Presbyterian Church (June 21).[8] However, as shown throughout Christian history, God had been at work among Koreans even long before the first American missionary arrived in Korea.

Some scholars have suggested that Nestorianism was the first form of Christianity to be introduced to Korea.[9] E. A. Gordon, an English archeologist, was the first person who asserted that Nestorianism was introduced to Korea during the Shilla Dynasty.[10] Stephen Neill says, "Until the fall of the T'ang Dynasty, Nestorian Christians had a significant influence in China."[11] Nestorians brought the Gospel along the silk roads to Central Asia, arriving in central China by 635.[12]

Several historians agree that Nestorianism was introduced to the Shilla Dynasty in Korea through the influence of the close relationship between the Shilla Dynasty and the T'ang Dynasty of China.[13] In this regard, Gordon suggested several items and symbols showing characteristics of Nestorianism as evidence. These emerged from her research around 1910, when she stayed in Korea for about four years and researched the probability that Nestorianism had existed in Korea in centuries past.[14] Gordon found a statue of a mother holding a baby and Nestorian-style stone crosses and patterns in a Buddhist temple in Korea. According to Deuk-Hwang Kim, *Kyungkyo* (Nestorianism) was introduced to the Shilla Dynasty in the late eighth century.[15] Even though we need more concrete proof in this regard, it suggests that God had worked among Koreans long before they realized his activity.

In the early seventeenth century, *Chonju-Silui* ("The Doctrine of the Lord of Heaven"), written in Chinese by Matteo Ricci in 1603, was introduced to the Chosun Dynasty (1392–1897) of Korea.[16] In this time period, Catholicism was considered by Koreans to be a kind of Western philosophy.

---

8. Park, *Hankook Gidok Kyohoisa I*, 369.
9. Kim, *Hankook Kyohoisa*, 40–43.
10. Park, *Hankook Gidok Kyohoisa I*, 82.
11. Bevans and Schroeder, *Constants in Context*, 137.
12. Neill, *History of Christian Mission*, 81.
13. Park, *Hankook Gidok Kyohoisa I*, 82; Kim, *Church Growth in Korea*, 85.
14. Park, *Hankook Gidok Kyohoisa I*, 8.
15. Kim, *Hankook Kyohoisa*, 40.
16. Min, *Hankook Gidok Kyohoisa*, 50–51; Kim, *Hankook Kyohoisa*, 52.

Later, many Koreans became Catholic believers and were persecuted and martyred up until 1876.

In 1832, the first Protestant missionary, Karl Gutzlaff, a German who was working for a Dutch missionary society, visited Korea as a translator for the British East India Company.[17] Even though he tried to evangelize Koreans, they were indifferent to his efforts, and the government prohibited his mission work because of the *Shoekuk Jungchek* ("locked-country policy") of the Chosun Dynasty of Korea.

The second Protestant missionary who visited Korea was Robert Jermain Thomas from the Church of England. He came to China as a missionary sent by the London Mission Society in 1863.[18] He had become interested in Korea when he heard that Korean Catholics were greatly persecuted. In 1865, Thomas visited Korea and distributed the Bible. He visited Chosun again as an interpreter on an American trading ship, the General Sherman. When the government ordered the ship to leave the country, the captain of the ship ignored the order and instead arrested several Chosun soldiers. In addition, the Americans fired at and killed twelve Chosun citizens who observed the arrest and protested against the captain's illegal misbehavior.[19] In the meantime, the General Sherman became stuck in the river and was shot at by the Chosun army. As a result, people on the ship, including Thomas, were arrested and executed. Thus, almost immediately after Thomas reached the land of Korea in order to distribute Bibles to Koreans, he was executed by the Korean army. In other words, Thomas became the first Protestant martyr for Korea in 1866.[20] Nevertheless, the Bible influenced some Koreans toward faith.

Soon after, a series of late-nineteenth-century treaties with Western countries changed the political situation, and missionaries' safety became guaranteed. Two years following the 1882 signing of a formal treaty between the Chosun dynasty of Korea and the United States, Horace Newton Allen, a Presbyterian missionary from the United States, arrived in Korea in 1884. In the next year, three other American missionaries, Horace G. Underwood (Presbyterian) and Henry and Ella Appenzeller (Methodists) followed.[21] They founded a Western-style hospital, in addition to schools and churches. Missionaries translated the Bible into Hangul, a language which is more accessible than Chinese (at least in its written form) to the

17. Kim, *Hankook Kyohoisa*, 66–67.
18. Kim, *Hankook Kyohoisa*, 67.
19. Min, *Hankook Gidok Kyohoisa*, 91.
20. Kim, *Hankook Kyohoisa*, 67–69; Hurh, *The Korean Americans*, 22.
21. Hurh, *The Korean Americans*, 22–23.

grass roots population, which in turn contributed to mass literacy.[22] This is how Christianity was introduced to Korea and laid a foundation for Korean immigration to the United States. Now I will discuss a brief history of Korean immigration to the United States.

History of Korean Immigration in the United States

To help clarify the history of Korean immigration to the United States, I will divide this history into four periods with several subcategories. Many scholars[23] tend to separate this history into three periods, based on radical changes in context and numbers. Won Moo Hurh, for instance, in *The Korean Americans*, divides Korean immigration history to the United States into three waves: the first-wave of immigration from 1903 to 1905, the second-wave from 1951 to 1964, and the third-wave of immigration from 1965 to present.[24] On the other hand, some other scholars prefer to divide it into a greater number of segments. For instance, in "Korean Population in the United States, 2000," Eui-Young Yu, Peter Choe, and Sang Il Han use four distinct periods, and Gil Pyo Lee categorizes it into six periods.[25] The common choice among these scholars, however, is to include a prelude period, which is based on the first treaty between Korea and the United States.

The Prelude Period: 1882–1902

The prelude period began in 1882 when the diplomatic relationship between the United States and the Chosun dynasty of Korea was established through a document known variably as the Korean-American Treaty, the Treaty of Amity and Commerce, and the Chemulpo Treaty.[26] In this period, there were four different groups of Korean immigrants to America: government officers (diplomats), political exiles, students, and merchants. Soon after the Chemulpo Treaty was signed in May 1882, the first five diplomats, including Min Young Ik, the first Korean ambassador, came to the United States in July. Their arrival was the beginning of a significant movement of Koreans coming to the United States. Next, in 1885, after *Gapsinjeongbyeon*[27] failed,

22. Kwon et al., *Korean American and Their Religions*, 7.
23. Hurh, *The Korean Americans*; Kim, *Bridge-Makers*; Min, *Koreans' Immigration*.
24. Hurh, *The Korean Americans*, 36–47.
25. Yu et al., "Korean Population;" Lee, "Traditional to Missional Church."
26. Hurh, *The Korean Americans*, 36.
27. *Gapsinjeongbyeon* is a 3-day failed coup in December 1884 led by a group of reformers who wanted to initiate rapid change within the Chosun Dynasty of Korea.

a few political exiles came to the United States.²⁸ For example, Philip Jaisohn (Korean name: Seo, Jae-Pil) came to the United States in 1885 as a political exile and became the first Korean naturalized as an American.²⁹ He became the first Korean-American medical doctor but returned to Korea in 1896 to reform Korea. Eventually, he returned to the United States, where he died in in 1951. In 1888, according to Hurh, a small number of Korean students came to America.³⁰ In 1899, some ginseng merchants started to come to America, but the number of people was minimal. These ginseng merchants were interestingly recorded as Chinese by the USA immigration office.³¹ As a result, the first Korean correctly recorded as a Korean by the immigration bureau was Doo-Pyo Ryu, a ginseng merchant who came through Hong Kong on January 9, 1901. Cumulatively, by 1902 the total number of Koreans in America was estimated at less than fifty.³²

The First Wave of Korean Immigration: 1903-1950

The first wave of major Korean immigration began in 1903 when the first organized migration of Korean laborers to Hawaii was initiated, and it ended in 1950 when the Korean War began. This period can be divided into three stages by means of distinctive historical events.

Immigration to Hawaiian Sugar Plantations (1903–1905): The first Korean immigrants to Hawaii between 1903 and 1905 were mostly semi-skilled or unskilled male workers from large inland cities and port cities such as Seoul, Chemulpo (Incheon), Pusan, Wonsan, and Chinnampo.³³ With regard to education and religion, seventy percent of them were literate, and forty percent were Christian.³⁴ In this short period, the total number of immigrants reached up to nearly 7,200.³⁵ Among them, only ten percent of these Korean immigrants were female. This unbalanced Korean population later caused another round of Korean immigration, the so-called "picture brides immigration," in which generally much younger Korean women came to the United States to marry unknown Korean male immigrant workers by seeing their pictures.

28. Kim, *Korean-American Methodism*, 28.
29. National Association of Korean Americans, "Korean Immigration to the U.S."
30. Hurh, *The Korean Americans*, 36.
31. Kim, *Korean-American Methodism*, 28.
32. Hurh, *The Korean Americans*, 36.
33. Kim, *Bridge-Makers*, 4.
34. Kwon et al., *Korean American and Their Religions*, 13.
35. Min, *Koreans' Immigration*, 2; Kwon et al., *Korean American and Their Religions*, 9.

This first Korean immigration had some pull and push factors. The pull factors of Korean immigration to the United States, specifically to Hawaii, were several. First, the fundamental reason why Hawaiian sugar plantations needed more foreign workers was an increasing demand for sugar in the world.[36] Second, the Chinese Exclusion Act in 1882 led to a demand for alternative cheap labor forces from other countries besides China. Even though the influx of a large number of Chinese laborers to the United States began in the mid-1800s during the Gold Rush, the 1882 Chinese Exclusion Act banned further recruitment from China.[37] Third, Hawaiian sugar plantation owners wanted to bring Korean workers to mitigate the power of Japanese laborers.[38] As a result of the Chinese Exclusion Act, large numbers of Japanese laborers began migrating in 1885 to Hawaii and became the dominant laborers on Hawaiian sugar plantations by the beginning of the twentieth century. The problem was, as the sugar plantations depended on Japanese workforces more and more, Japanese workers frequently went on strike.[39] In addition to these pull factors, three push factors were found in Korea: economic, political, and religious reasons. First, economic calamities and a particularly severe famine provided the primary reasons for immigration to Hawaii. A second reason was political instability. Before the Japanese occupation took place in 1910, Japan had already exerted pressure on the Korean government. Under the darkening shadow of Japanese colonialism and imperialism, some Koreans chose to leave their home country in order to find political freedom. Third, since Christianity was still new and rare in Korean peninsula at the time, some Korean Christians boarded the immigration ship to find religious freedom.

Based on the records of the US Immigration Bureau, the number of Korean immigrants increased from 564 Koreans in 1903 to 1,907 Koreans in 1904 and reached up to 4,929 Koreans by 1905.[40] However, this first immigration wave to the Hawaiian sugar plantations came to an end in 1905. With that year's signing of the Protectorate Treaty between Japan and Korea, Japan forced the Korean government to forbid Korean immigration to Hawaii in order to protect its own workers there.[41] In February 1906, in addition to this ban, the Korean government also lost its right to manage emigration, as it was placed under the jurisdiction of the Japanese

---

36. Hurh, *The Korean Americans*, 36.
37. Min, *Koreans' Immigration*, 2.
38. Min, *Koreans' Immigration*, 3.
39. Min, *Koreans' Immigration*, 2–3.
40. Ryu, *Christ United Methodist Church*, 26–27.
41. Ryu, *Christ United Methodist Church*, 26; Min, *Koreans' Immigration*, 3.

consulates.⁴² These shifts caused the initiation of the Koreans' anti-Japanese movement in the United States.

Between 1906 and 1924, about 2,000 Koreans came to the United States. Among them, picture brides for former male immigrants constituted the largest group. Between November 1910 and October 1925, nearly 1,100 picture brides (951 to Hawaii and 115 to the mainland) came to the United States.⁴³ The average age of the picture brides was seventeen years old.⁴⁴ There are many stories about the picture brides. Bong-Youn Choy, a well-known scholar on Korean American history, describes their situation as follows:

> A majority of the picture brides were much younger than their bridegrooms. This was the beginning of the comedy as well as the tragedy in the lives of early Korean immigrants. The young brides were under the impression that their chosen mates would be exactly what their pictures depicted. Unfortunately, many men sent deceivingly young pictures of themselves. The girls thought the men's age would not be too different from their own. When the ship carrying the picture brides arrived in Honolulu, the bridegrooms, dressed in their best suits, greeted them at the dock. According to eyewitnesses, some of the brides fainted because their bridegrooms were so old and much uglier than they expected. Some of the brides were bewildered and cried "*Aigo omani,*" which means "O dear me, what shall I do?" A few of the brides refused to land, and some of them returned to their homeland.⁴⁵

Since not enough picture brides came, about 3,000 Korean men, who were deeply influenced by Confucianism, remained bachelors, and 104 Korean men married non-Koreans.⁴⁶

In the same period, between 1910 and 1924, approximately 540 political refugees entered the United States by way of China and Europe without passports.⁴⁷ Also during this period, 289 Korean students bringing passports issued by the Japanese government arrived.⁴⁸ These groups of political

42. Min, *Koreans' Immigration*, 3.
43. Kim, *Bridge-Makers*, 4.
44. Hurh, *The Korean Americans*, 37.
45. Choy, *Koreans in America*, 88–89.
46. Kim, *Bridge-Makers*, 4; Hurh, *The Korean Americans*, 38.
47. Yu et al, "Korean Population," 1; Min, *Koreans' Immigration*, 4.
48. Yu, "Korean Population in the United States," 2.

refugees and students were highly educated and committed to the Korean independence movement which opposed Japanese colonization.[49]

Bringing to an end the first wave of Korean immigration, the United States' Immigration Act of 1924 (The Johnson-Reed Act) limited immigration quotas by national origins and completely excluded all immigrants from Asia. Thus, between 1924 and 1945, no Korean immigrants were allowed into the United States. Accordingly, the U.S. Immigration and Naturalization Service did not compile the number of Korean immigrants until 1948.[50] Also, Korea gained its independence from Japan in 1945, most political refugees and students returned to Korean in order to play leading roles in government and universities.[51]

The Second Wave of Korean Immigration: 1951–1964

The second wave of Korean immigration to the United States began during the Korean War when American intervention took place. Immediately after acquiring independence from Japan in 1945, Korea began to suffer from the hegemonic struggle between the United States and the Soviet Union, one which resulted in the division of the country in 1948 between two political entities—South Korea, supported by the United States and North Korea, supported by the Soviet Union. As a result of the influence of a large number of American servicemen during the consequent Korean War, three groups of Korean immigrants emerged: GI brides, war-orphans, and students. In terms of the numbers, 6,500 brides, 6,300 war-orphans, and 6,000 students entered into the United State between 1951 and 1964.[52] In this period, the number of Korean immigrants grew gradually.

The War Brides Act of 1947 made it possible for American servicemen to bring their Korean wives and children to the United States until the McCarran-Walters Immigration and National Act of 1952 superseded it. The latter allowed immigration and naturalization to all wives and minor children of U.S. servicemen, regardless of race.[53] The notable difference between the first and second waves of Korean immigration is in the sex ratio: the sex ratios of the first wave of Korean immigrants showed 10 males to 1 female,

49. Yu et al, "Korean Population," 1.
50. Yu, "Korean Population in the United States," 2.
51. Min, *Koreans' Immigration*, 4.
52. Yu, "Korean Population in the United States," 3. Pyong Gap Min estimates the number of Korean immigrant between 1950 and 1964 approximately 15,000. See Min, *Koreans' Immigration*, 5.
53. Lee, *Orientals*, 162; Wolgin and Bloemraad, "'Our Gratitude to Our Soldiers,'" 29–31.

whereas the ratio of the second wave represented 1 male to 3.5 females.[54] Nevertheless, in this second wave of immigration, Korean students, who came for graduate education, were mostly male. One more characteristic of this student group was that "the vast majority of them found professional occupations, especially as professors, in the United States after completing their graduate education."[55] Since they had lived in predominantly white communities with little contact with other Koreans, their children were heavily assimilated to American society, losing their ethnic identity.[56]

The Third Wave of Korean Immigration: 1965–Present

The Immigration and Nationality Act of 1965, which abolished the national origin quota system, dramatically changed the climate of Korean immigration and its numbers. According to Pyong Gap Min, a Korean-American sociologist, "More than 95 percent of Korean Americans consist of post-1965 Korean immigrants and their children."[57]

Within the policies established by the Immigration Act of 1965, three mechanisms determined those who were eligible for immigration to the United States: 1) family reunification, 2) occupational immigration, and 3) refugees and other categories by special measures.[58] Based on this change in criteria, family members of U.S. citizens or that of permanent residents—such as spouses, children, parents, and siblings—were able to easily immigrate to the United States.

Although the original intention of such family union immigration was to encourage immigrants from Europe, in reality, the number of European immigrants declined following its implementation. In contrast, the number of Asian immigrants increased by about six times by the mid-1970s.[59] Specifically, two groups of Koreans mainly benefited: 1) wives of American servicemen and 2) students and professional workers in America who became permanent residents. For example, between 1953 and 1980, about 15,000 Korean students came to America, but about 90 percent of them did not return to Korea.[60] In this regard, Reimers's description provides a clue as to how the Immigration Act of 1965 affected Korean/Asian immigration:

54. Hurh, *The Korean Americans*, 39; Min, *Koreans' Immigration*, 6.
55. Min, *Koreans' Immigration*, 6.
56. Min, *Koreans' Immigration*, 6.
57. Min, *Koreans' Immigration*, 7.
58. Min, *Koreans' Immigration*, 25.
59. Hurh, *The Korean Americans*, 39.
60. Hurh, *The Korean Americans*, 40.

> While finishing his studies, he [an Asian student] finds a job, gets Labor Department certification, and becomes an immigrant. Once an immigrant he uses the second preference to bring over his spouse and children. A few years later the new immigrants, and his spouse, become citizens and are eligible to sponsor their brothers and sisters under the fifth, the largest and most popular preference, or to bring their nonquota parents. Needless to say, the brothers and sisters, once immigrants, can also use the second preference to bring in their spouses and children and expand the immigrant kin network still further when they become citizens. No wonder the 1965 law came to be called the brothers and sisters act.[61]

As a result of the Immigration Act of 1965, the number of new Korean immigrants per year increased dramatically in the years which followed and reached 30,000 per year in 1976. It was a big change because the number of Korean immigrants in 1965 was only 2,165. The number of over 30,000 per year was maintained until 1990. As a result, between 1976 and 1990, Korea was ranked the third largest immigration source country in the United States, after Mexico and the Philippines.[62]

As to the reason for the phenomenal increase of Korean immigrants to the United States, Min suggests five push and pull factors in "Koreans' Immigration to the U.S: History and Contemporary Trends."[63] The first and foremost reason behind Korean immigration was an economic hardship. Koreans' per capita income increased from only $251 in 1970 to $1,355 in 1980. Nevertheless, this figure was about 1/8 of Americans' per capita income in 1980. In addition, an extreme lack of job opportunities led to an average 28 percent unemployment rate for male college graduates in Korea from 1965 to 1980.[64] Second, political insecurity and lack of freedom, especially between 1960 and 1987, also contributed to large numbers of Koreans' immigration to the United States. Third, the political tension between South Korea and North Korea also influenced Korean immigration. Fourth, a college education was another important factor as extreme competition for admissions and high tuition costs caused many Koreans to come to the United States. Finally, exceptionally strong political, military, and economic ties between Korea and the United States made extensive Korean immigration to the United States possible. Due to these strong relations, South Korea

61. Reimers, *Still the Golden Door*, 94.
62. Min, *Koreans' Immigration*, 8.
63. Min, *Koreans' Immigration*, 8–12.
64. Lee, "From Traditional to Missional Church," 14; Yoon, "Analysis of Korean Immigrants," 67.

was the second highest country of origin for U.S. immigration among Asian countries between 1975 and 1990.[65]

The Withdrawal and Rebound Period: 1991–Present

Since 1991, Korean immigration to the United States has become unstable. In 1991 and 1992, there were significant reductions in the number of Korean immigrants per year, from 32,301 (in 1990) to 19,359 (in 1992). As the 1990s progressed, this declining trend continued and reached 12,840 in 1999. Since the Immigration Act of 1990 increased the overall number of annual immigrants to the United States to 675,000, the decline of Korean immigration in the years which followed seems to be an anomaly.

Why did Korean immigration to the United States decline in the 1990s? Min presents four reasons.[66] First, an improved South Korean economy played an important role in holding back Korean immigration to the United States. For instance, Korean per capita income changed from nearly $6,000 in 1990 to about $10,000 in 2000. The improved economy of Korea attracted even American-educated professionals. Second, '*Minjoohwa*' (democratization) provided better political conditions. Third, due to the improved economic condition in Korea, the number of international marriages between Korean women and American servicemen declined too. Fourth, Koreans began to become more aware of the hardships which Korean immigrants often faced in the United States. The mass media allowed Koreans to become familiar with the difficulties that Korean immigrants to the United States faced as they attempted to adjust to life in America. In addition, the 1992 Los Angeles riots, with their more than 2,000 Korean victims, were greatly publicized in Korea.

However, Korean immigration began to increase again starting in 2000, with the exception of 2003 (12,512). Min suggests two main reasons for this renewed increase.[67] First, the financial crisis of 1997, during which Korea borrowed money from the International Monetary Fund (IMF), caused many Koreans to lose their jobs, which resulted in a high unemployment rate in Korea; this situation caused many Koreans to seek employment in other countries like the United States. For example, between 1998 and 1999, Samsung Electronics laid off approximately 10,000 employees. Min describes the impact in this way:

65. Min, *Koreans' Immigration*, 10.
66. Min, *Koreans' Immigration*, 12–13.
67. Min, *Koreans' Immigration*, 13–15.

> According to Korean real estate agents, a large number of people who had lost their jobs in Korea came to the United States in 1999 and the ensuing years to find jobs in Korean-owned stores or even to explore the possibility of starting businesses. Many of these temporary residents seem to have changed their status as permanent residents in later years.[68]

Another contributing factor is a dramatic increase in the number of temporary Korean residents in the United States due to globalization. In recent years, many Koreans have visited the United States for various reasons such as study, internships, training, sightseeing, family visits and so on. Many of them stay beyond their original intended period and become permanent residents.

According to Min, this notable change in Korean immigration in the United States took the form of an increase in temporary residents who then became "status adjusters."[69] Based on statistics provided by the Immigration and Naturalization Service, the percentage of status adjusters among the total number of Korean immigrants has gradually grown since 1988, reaching a high point where 81 percent of Koreans who became permanent residents in a year did so by adjusting from their temporary statuses. This 81 percent figure is exceptionally high compared to the total number of immigrants to the United States (59 percent) and all Asian immigrants (56 percent).[70] It seems that when compared to immigrants from many other nations in recent years, Koreans have more often come to the United States on a temporary basis at first, and then decided to stay.

Lastly, addressing the overall context, it is important to point out that even though the number of Korean immigrants reached a level of approximately 12,000 to 26,000 from 2000 to 2016, this figure is a relatively small number compared to other countries. Korea is far behind other Asian countries with significantly larger populations such as China, India, and the Philippines. Even countries such as Vietnam are in front of Korea in terms of the number of immigrants coming to the United States.

---

68. Min, *Koreans' Immigration*, 14.

69. Min, *Koreans' Immigration*, 16–18. "Status adjusters" are those who apply to become permanent residents of the United States after initially entering the country as temporary residents.

70. Min, *Koreans' Immigration*, 18.

Distinctions and Challenges for Korean Churches in the United States

If the history of full-scale Korean immigration is relatively short and the number of Korean and Korean-Americans is not large compared to other ethnic groups, how can Korean-Americans be considered a potential emerging leader for the multicultural church movement in the United States? Before discussing this potential of Korean Christians and their churches in the United States, acknowledging the characteristics and challenges of Korean immigrant churches will provide a better understanding of their potential in the development of American Christianity in the twenty-first century. Thus, in this section, I will discuss four distinctions and challenges that Korean immigrant churches in the United States encounter: mission-initiated immigration, high affiliation and strong in-group commitment, church-centered Korean community, and a generation gap which causes a silent exodus.

Missionary-Initiated Immigration

From the beginning of Korean immigration to the United States, God has had a plan for Koreans in his mission for the ages to come.

Unlike in the past religious situation of Korea that was dominated by Confucianism, Buddhism, and Shamanism, God led Korean Christians in the late twentieth century to become the center of Korean immigration to the United States. Even when Confucianism and Buddhism were still major religions in Korea, the first official[71] Korean immigration to the United States became possible through two American missionaries' active contribution. This Christian initiation was very meaningful for three reasons: first, the Christian population was less than 1 percent of the total population of Korea in 1903; second, the time of missionaries' residency was only two decades; third, missionary initiated immigration influenced Korean immigrants in the United States to be church-centered. According to records, the number of Christians in Korea was 530 in 1895 and 7690 in 1900, out of a total population of 12 million. In terms of the number of believers, the Christian population of Korea did not grow significantly until the late 1960s.

---

71. Korean immigration to Hawaii was the first official immigration in Korean history. Even though there were considerable numbers of Koreans who moved to China or Russia in the late nineteenth century, these were not government-approved official immigrations.

During the time when the Korean government did not allow Korean emigration, an American missionary, Horace Newton Allen, played a crucial role in promoting Korean immigration to the United States. This was possible because Allen was officially appointed as the American Minister to Korea from 1897 to 1905.[72] Using his position of influence, he persuaded King Kojong to allow Koreans to go to the sugar plantations in Hawaii as a way of saving people from a severe famine.[73] As a result, the Korean government officially allowed immigration to Hawaii. Even after the Korean government's official announcement of this possibility, the role played by another American Methodist missionary, George Heber Jones, was crucial. When people hesitated, Jones, the senior pastor of Naeri Methodist Church of Incheon, encouraged people to go to Hawaii for a better life. The first Korean immigrant group (121 people) left Incheon port on December 22, 1902, but only 102 Koreans out of 121 arrived in Hawaii in 1903 because some failed the physical examinations in Japan. The number of the first Korean immigrants (102) is exactly the same as the number of passengers of the Mayflower who came to America for religious freedom in 1620.[74] This was meaningful for their spiritual journey for the days to come in this new country. Even though the first group was not many, the total number of Korean immigrants increased to over 7,000 in three years. According to Ryu, the number of Korean immigrants was 1,133 Koreans in 1903, 3,434 Koreans in 1904, and 2,659 Koreans by July of 1905; a total of 7,226 Koreans immigrated to Hawaii.[75] Of the total 6,048 were men, 637 women, and 541 children.

High Affiliation and Strong In-Group Commitment

Many scholars agree that religion plays a significant role in the daily lives of post-1965 Korean immigrants.[76] For these immigrants to the United States,

72. Lee and Patterson, *One Hundred Years*, 37–38.

73. Allen "persuaded the Korean emperor to grant an emigration franchise to a friend (to pay off a political debt) by falsely stating that his friend was an official of the American government and that, by giving him the franchise, the emperor would strengthen ties between Korean and the U.S. government. And Allen did this knowing that neither the State Department nor the Korean emperor would be the wiser." Lee and Patterson, *Korean-American Relations, 1882–1982*.

74. Kim, *Korean-American Methodism*, 34–35. Some historians recorded the number of the first Korean immigrants as 101. However, according to Hong Ki Kim, more historical resources indicate the number as 102.

75. Ryu, *Christ United Methodist Church*, 26.

76. Kwon et al., *Korean American and Their Religions*, 71; Hurh and Kim, "Religious Participation," 20.

Christianity, especially Protestantism, is the most dominant and influential religion. Specifically, three measures of the importance of Christianity in their lives ought to be noted 1) weekly church attendance, 2) the amount of time Koreans spent at church each week, and 3) financial contributions. When compared with other racial and ethnic groups, the extent of Koreans' weekly church participation is exceptionally high. The 1997–1999 Presbyterian Racial and Ethnic Panel Studies shows that 78 percent of Korean Presbyterians attend Sunday worship services every week, compared to 49 percent of Latino, 34 percent of African-American, and 28 percent of Caucasian Presbyterians.[77] Since most Korean immigrants are affiliated with Christianity and approximately half of Korean Protestant Christians are Presbyterians, Kwang Chung Kim and Shin Kim insist, limited samples of Presbyterian churches are not a serious problem in analyzing Korean immigrants' religious lives.[78] Also, the 1997–1998 Queens Survey revealed by comparison that 44 percent of Indian immigrants and 41 percent of Chinese immigrants attend a church worship at least once a week.[79]

In addition to this high weekly church attendance (on Sunday mornings), Koreans also spend more time altogether in church than any other ethnic/racial group. Based on the 1997–98 Presbyterian Panel Studies, 54 percent of Koreans spent six hours or more at church gatherings per week, whereas among other racial and ethnic populations only 40 percent or less did so (40 percent of Caucasians, 39 percent of Hispanics, and 36 percent of African-Americans).[80]

Third, Koreans' financial commitment to their churches is also notable. According to the 1997 Ethnic and Racial Panel Survey, "[t]he majority of Koreans (62 percent) contributed $2,000 or more in regular giving to their current congregations in the previous year. Only 35 percent of African Americans, 26 percent of Hispanics, and 40 percent of Caucasians report giving that much."[81] Furthermore, 27 percent of Koreans gave over $5,000 to the church, whereas 11 percent of Caucasians, 8 percent African Americans, and 6 percent of Hispanics did so.

Also significant for this study, unlike Koreans' strong commitment to their churches, research shows that a relatively small portion of Korean immigrant Christians participates in other activities in their communities.

77. Min and Kim, "Intergenerational Transmission of Religion and Culture," 269; Kwon et al., *Korean American and Their Religions*, 82.
    78. Kwon et al., *Korean American and Their Religions*, 77.
    79. Min, "Immigrants' Religion and Ethnicity," 41.
    80. Kwon et al., *Korean American and Their Religions*, 82.
    81. Kwon et al., *Korean American and Their Religions*, 82.

According to the survey, 70 percent of Koreans did not spend even one hour to help people or their community to be a better place to live. In contrast, 42 percent of Caucasians, 38 percent of Hispanics, and 33 percent of African-Americans did spend time serving the community.[82] Also, Koreans give relatively little money to organizations other than their churches. Nearly 20 percent of Koreans donated no money for nonreligious reasons, while 4 percent of Caucasians, 5 percent of African-Americans, and 15 percent of Hispanics did so.[83]

Church-Centered Korean Community

Another characteristic of Korean immigrants in the United States has been that Korean immigrant churches have always been the center of the Korean-American community. However, the degree of church-centeredness among Koreans in the United States is much higher than any other immigrant groups. Unlike other Asian groups, approximately 75 percent of Koreans actively attend church in America.[84] For instance, there is a popular saying, "When the Chinese go abroad, they open a restaurant. When the Japanese go abroad, they start a factory. When the Koreans go abroad, they start a church."[85] Several factors account for why Korean immigrants have become church-centered.

First, from the very beginning, Korean Christian immigrants were worship-centered. During the first voyage for Korean immigrants, two church leaders of Naeri Methodist Church in Incheon led worship services on board the ship. Not long after the settlement in the Kahuku-Waialua area of Hawaii, Korean Christians of the first and the second immigration ships started informal worship, probably sometime in March 1903.[86]

Second, not only was church the first organization that Korean immigrants started after they arrived, but these Korean Christians also helped other Korean immigrants to cope with their unexpected hardships in a strange place. Because of the difference between immigrants' expectations and reality, Korean immigrants had to deal with a great amount of hardship. In *A History of Christ United Methodist Church, 1903–1988*, Ryu describes

---

82. Kwon et al., *Korean American and Their Religions*, 83.

83. Kwon et al., *Korean American and Their Religions*, 83.

84. Min and Kim, "Ethnic and Sub-ethnic Attachments," 762.

85. Chai, "Generation," 297. This is one version of common saying among Koreans, but the emphasis is always in Koreans' church-centeredness. See Kim, *Bridge-Makers*, 7.

86. Lee Murabayashi, "Korean Ministerial Appointments," 8.

the miserable lives of Korean workers in Hawaii.[87] Except for 30 minutes for lunch, Korean workers were not allowed to even stand up. Luna, a foreman at a Hawaiian sugar plantation, called people by number and managed them by whips. Their weary lives and the unfamiliar environment caused many Korean immigrants to suffer from homesickness or turn to debauchery through alcohol and prostitutes. Since Korean Christian leaders believed that the Christian faith was the ultimate way to save fellow Korean workers from their hardships, they established Korean immigrant churches to help others overcome mental, social, and spiritual crises.[88] The first organized church in Hawaii was the Kahuku-Waialua Korean Church (informal), but the first formally established church was on Oahu Island in 1903. A few months later, Korean Christian immigrants organized the Korean Evangelical Society (the Korean Evangelical Mission)[89] in Honolulu and had the first worship service on November 10, 1903.[90] Two years later, the Korean Evangelical Mission received regular church status in April 1905.[91]

Third, Korean immigrants vigorously established churches as one of their major adaptation strategies, because churches met not only spiritual needs but also other needs by functioning as community social centers.[92] In this regard, the church has provided invaluable social services and help to members in matters such as healthcare, citizenship classes, translation, jobs, housing, and even business.[93] Therefore, many non-Christian Korean immigrants began participating in the Korean church as soon as they arrived in the United States.

Fourth, Korean churches provide a secure and comfortable place where Koreans gather together regularly and have fellowship with each other. Every Sunday most Korean churches provide lunch for fellowship time so that members can eat together and share their lives freely. A few months ago, for instance, I had a chance to visit a newly planted Korean church in New Jersey. Since the church does not have their own building,

---

87. Ryu, *Christ United Methodist Church*, 27–33.

88. Ryu, *Christ United Methodist Church*, 32–33.

89. Hyung Chan Kim and Duk Hee Lee Murabayashi mentioned it as the Korean Evangelical Society, but Ryu mentioned it as the Korean Methodist Mission. Since the time and initiators (Chung Soo Ahn and Byeng Kil Woo (later known as Byung Koo Yoon)) are same, it seems it was originally called as the Korean Evangelical Society and then later changed to the United Methodist Mission.

90. Ryu, *Christ United Methodist Church*, 34.

91. Lee Murabayashi, "Korean Ministerial Appointments," 9.

92. Hurh and Kim, "Religious Participation," 20; Kang, *Socioculturally Constructed Multivoiced Self*, 1; Kim, *A Faith of Our Own*, 23.

93. Kim, *A Faith of Our Own*, 23–24; Hurh and Kim, "Religious Participation," 21.

they have Sunday worship at 1:30 pm. After the worship, they have a fellowship time at 3:00 pm not because of hunger but because of a strong desire to have a time together. During this time, they exchange valuable information regarding jobs, children's education, health issues, and so on. This is also crucial because it makes it possible to run other programs in the afternoon such as various Bible study classes, choir practice, various meetings, and so on. In addition, some Koreans only get to eat Korean foods at this time during the week.

Fifth, the church bestows social status on members who otherwise experience anonymity in the new country, by providing titles and positions in the church such as elder, deacon, and committee chairman. In Korea people usually call others by their titles and last names as an expression of respect. *SaJangNim* (an owner or a president of business), *SaMoNim* (a business owner/president's wife), and *SunSangNim* (a teacher) are most popular titles, even for those who are not really presidents/business owners or teachers. In fact, studies show that many Korean immigrants experience a downward slide in their social positions after immigration to the United States, even though many of them were middle class, well-educated citizens in their home country.[94] Therefore, the desire for recognition by Korean immigrants is often fulfilled by appointments as elders and deacons in the Korean church. In addition, most Korean churches have non-ordained deacons who are annually appointed by the church. In this regard, Jung Ha Kim points out how Korean churches in the U.S. successfully function to help wounded and marginalized Koreans:

> In short, one can conclude that, as an ethnic "minority" group in the United States, Korean-Americans experience both a sense of loss of their social identities through "desocialization" (bar-Yosef, 1968) and homogenization (Hurh, 1977) in the host society and a sense of ethnic solidarity based on a commonly shared struggle to maintain their native culture and ethnic pride. Among many Korean-American institutions based on ethnic solidarity, one institution in particular seems to be quite successful in healing the pains of the desocialized people and simultaneously ensuring a sense of personal worth and group identity. That institution is the Korean-American church in the United States.[95]

Sixth, most Korean immigrant churches play a crucial role in preserving Korean culture and passing on ethnic identity to future generations.

94. Kim, *A Faith of Our Own*, 24; Hurh and Kim, "Religious Participation," 29.
95. Kim, *Bridge-Makers*, 14.

Thus, Korean churches celebrate traditional Korean holidays such as New Year's Day, Korean Independence Day, *Chuseok* (Korean Thanksgiving) by wearing *hanbok* (traditional costumes), eating traditional foods, and playing traditional games. Also, many Korean churches run a Korean school for teaching Korean language and culture. For this function, the Korean government supports Korean schools all over the world through the Overseas Koreans Foundation (OKF). According to OKF, there were 1,011 Korean schools in the United States in 2007. Among them, conservatively speaking, over 80 percent of Korean schools in the United States were run or supported by Korean churches.[96]

The Generation Gap and Silent Exodus

Although Korean churches in the Unites States have experienced continuous growth, there has been a problem of second-generation Korean-Americans leaving the church. In "Silent Exodus," Helen Lee issues a warning concerning the crisis of losing the next-generation of Korean-American Christians.[97] In 1994, Peter Cha estimated that about 90 percent of Korean-Americans do not attend church after college.[98] Likewise, a study of Korean-Americans in the New York area found that only 5 percent of second-generation Korean-Americans stay in the church after college, whereas about 75 percent of first-generation parents participate in the church.[99] Since these estimations were observed about two decades ago, there could be some changes in the degree of the problem since that time. In fact, Pyong Gap Min and Dae Young Kim provided different survey data conducted in the New York and New Jersey area, which indicated that as of 1998 approximately two-thirds of 1.5- and second-generation Koreans attend a church, even after college—54 percent Protestant and 11 percent Catholic.[100] Nevertheless, most scholars admit that first-generation Korean churches need to be concerned with the generation gap in the church. In "Silent Exodus," Lee indicates three main problems in relation to the second-generation in first-generation dominant immigrant churches: 1) the language barrier, 2) leadership distribution, and 3) cultural preferences. Second-generation Korean-Americans desire to

---

96. Overseas Koreans Foundation, *"2007 Jaewoi Hangulhakkyo Hyunhwang* [2007 Overseas Korean School List]."

97. Lee, "Silent Exodus," 50–53.

98. Warner and Wittner, *Gatherings in Diaspora*, 300.

99. Warner and Wittner, *Gatherings in Diaspora*, 300.

100. Min and Kim, "Intergenerational Transmission of Religion and Culture," 266–268.

attend a church where English is the primary language in ministry. However, there is a dilemma in that they do not want to attend a Caucasian church either. In leadership matters, since second-generation Korean Christians grew up in a more democratic environment, rather than a hierarchical one, they want to have leadership equality in church participation. Also, second-generation Korean-Americans prefer multiethnic and multicultural settings, whereas first-generation Korean-Americans strongly want their churches to maintain a monocultural Korean distinction.

The Potential of Koreans and Korean Churches in the United States

As discussed in the previous section, even though Korean churches in the United States have some problems, it is clear that Koreans' commitment to the church and ministry is outstanding. Based on this commitment, this study will examine what kinds of potential Korean Christians and Korean churches in the United States have in relation to the multicultural church movement.

Hidden Opportunity behind Identity Crisis

Identity crisis is a common, but crucial, ongoing problem of minority immigrants. Korean-Americans are not an exception. In fact, it can be harsher for Korean-Americans than other immigrants because of the high homogeneity of Korean ethnicity in Korea, and its long-standing history. In this regard, Jung Ha Kim succinctly but precisely describes,

> Hurh (1977) observed the sense of identity loss among Korean immigrants. Korean immigrants' loss, he maintains, is due to the hegemonic tendency of the host culture to lump all Koreans and other unfamiliar and seemingly "exotic" Asian groups together as a culturally homogeneous group. From Korean immigrants' perspectives, this tendency of the dominant culture in the United States is derogatory, and ignores their much treasured Korean culture, which is distinctively different from all the rest of Asia. Quite naturally, then, ethnic solidarity among Korean immigrants serves as a necessary social device to ensure their own ethnic community.[101]

---

101. Kim, *Bridge-Makers*, 1.

In addition, it does not matter what kind of position or economic status Korean immigrants have, because it is a problem of race and ethnicity. For instance, we can find this typical identity issue in a personal reflection of Sang Hyun Lee, who was an international student but later became a professor in the United States:

> However long I stayed in this country [America], I seemed to remain a stranger, an alien. And this condition of being a stranger appeared to have two dimensions: the experience of being in between two worlds, the Korean and the American, belonging to both in some ways, but not wholly belonging to either. The other element in my feeling as a stranger was the sense that I as a non-white person may never be fully accepted by the majority of the dominant group in this country.[102]

Identity crisis is not solely the problem of the first-generation Korean immigrants, but also of the later-generation Korean-Americans, although the forms of second- and later-generation's identity crises can be different. For second-generation immigrants, English is their first language, and they are more culturally identified with the dominant American culture. "Some Korean Americans grow up denying their Korean heritage in order to fit in, only to become drawn into activities and organizations that emphasize that heritage when they arrive at college."[103] The result is a crisis of identity. According to Josephine Kim, a Nationally Certified Counselor and a lecturer at Harvard Graduate School of Education, because of this identity crisis, Korean-American students are at risk of "suicidal tendencies, depression, anxiety, perfectionism, low self-esteem, body image issues, substance abuse, and identity confusion."[104]

Although there are some high positioned Korean descendants in the mainstream of the United States, there are still invisible obstacles, the so called "glass ceiling." According to Deborah Woo of the United States Glass Ceiling Commission and her federal publication "The Glass Ceiling and Asian Americans," she proves the underrepresentation of Asian-Americans in management in the areas of private business, industry, government, and in both public and private institutions of higher education.[105]

Nevertheless, Korean immigrants' identity crises in America can be an opportunity for new possibilities. In Chinese, the word crisis is *wee-ki*[106]

102. Lee, "Pilgrimage and Home, 55.
103. Blagg, "The Culture of Counseling."
104. Blagg, "The Culture of Counseling."
105. Woo, "The Glass Ceiling and Asian Americans."
106. Korean pronunciation of 危機.

(危機), which is a compound word made up of the characters for danger and opportunity. In fact, many scholars recognize the potential of marginality. According to Jung Ha Kim, "The concept of 'marginal man' was first presented by Robert E. Park in 'Human Migration and the Marginal Man' (1928) and was defined as 'the man who stands on the border or margin of two cultural worlds but is fully a member of neither.'"[107] This concept was elaborated by several scholars such as Everett V. Stonequist (1935), Alfred Schutz (1944), Everett C. Hughes (1949), and D. Riesman (1954), and developed by Sang Hyun Lee and Jung Young Lee.[108] In "Pilgrimage and Home in the Wilderness of Marginality: Symbols and Context in Asian American Theology" in *Korean Americans and Their Religions*, Sang Hyun Lee, based on his own journey in the United States, proposes embarking on a "pilgrimage," by which he means, "the willingness to face up to one's marginality and to join with other strangers in the margins."[109] This pilgrimage perspective provides hope because this "pilgrimage . . . prepares them [marginalized people] for an experience of the reality of the household of God that God is building for all humankind."[110]

Sang Hyun Lee also sees the potential of pilgrim theology for Korean-American Christians as "the calling to make the Christian church more truly universal than it typically is in America."[111] Likewise, in *Marginality: The Key to Multicultural Theology*, Jung Young Lee focuses on Asian-Americans like Koreans, Chinese, and Japanese as examples of marginal peoples in the United States and asserts that marginality has the possibility to transform the world, which Lee considers power-oriented. According to Lee, pilgrimage "is an invitation for all to meet in the margin as fellow strangers."[112] Furthermore, marginal people have potential because "the margin is the locus which the spirit of God fills with mighty power."[113] This concept has similarities to the perspective of the stranger in Miroslav Volf's "Exclusion and Embrace: Theological Reflections in the Wake of 'Ethnic Cleansing.'"[114] Therefore, the authentic church should be a community for marginal people and provide services advancing reconciliation. As Lee emphasizes,

107. Kim, *Bridge-Makers*, 16.
108. Kim, *Bridge-Makers*, 16.
109. Kwon et al., *Korean American and Their Religions*, 68.
110. Kwon et al., *Korean American and Their Religions*, 68.
111. Kwon et al., *Korean American and Their Religions*, 5.
112. Kwon et al., *Korean American and Their Religions*, 69.
113. Lee, *Marginality*.
114. Volf, "Exclusion and Embrace." Based on biblical reflection on ethnic cleansing in Croatia, Volf insists the need of embrace others based on biblical figures such as Abraham and Jesus. It is possible through self-recognition of strangers in this earth.

Korean-American Christians have potential and an accompanying calling to reach out to the diverse population groups in globalized America.

Transnationalism among Korean Diaspora in the United States

Considering the more recent changes in the pattern of Korean immigration to the United States, mostly coming through naturalization in recent years, temporary residents like international students are a primary source of Korean immigrants in the United States. The reason why Korean immigrants are becoming more and more important in the United States is in the power of transnationalism.

According to Mike Rynkiewich, diaspora is "[o]ne of the newest areas in anthropology and related disciplines."[115] Who is the diaspora? *Diaspora* is a noun form of the Greek verb *diaspeirein* (means scatter; Acts 8:1, 4; 11:19), which is now used to indicate a dispersed people group. According to Rynkiewich, diaspora has three main distinguishing characteristics: "[A] diaspora community is composed of people who (1) have migrated from a homeland and settled in a new place, (2) have taken the time and trouble to form a separate community there, and (3) still maintain connections with the homeland."[116] Among many diaspora groups, Koreans are one of the most widely scattered ethnic groups in the world. As of 2011, the Korean diaspora is more than 7 million people in 175 countries.[117] In addition, according to Min Young Jung, a veteran missionary and a vice president of Wycliffe Bible Translators International, the Korean diaspora might be the most similar ethnic group to Jews in both 1) the homogeneity of ethnicity, culture, and language, and 2) the exclusiveness and closeness in culture.[118] As a result, Koreans in the United States show extraordinarily strong attachment and loyalty to the home country, Korea. To evaluate the level of ethnic attachment without bias, Pyong Gap Min, a sociologist, studied three Asian immigrant groups—Korean, Chinese, and Indian—who have similar immigration history in the same area, New York and New Jersey.[119] Whereas Indians and Chinese are characterized by high degrees of sub-ethnic divisions based on their religion, place of origin (and national origin), and language,

---

115. Rynkiewich, *Soul, Self, and Society*, 207.

116. Rynkiewich, *Soul, Self, and Society*, 207.

117. Overseas Koreans Foundation, "*Jaewoi Dongpo Hyunhwang* [Status of Overseas Koreans]."

118. Jung, "*JunRyakjuk Sunkyojawon.*"

119. Min, "Ethnic Sub-ethnic Attachment," 759.

Koreans show relatively high homogeneity.[120] This impacts their loyalty to their homeland. For instance, when they were asked which team they would support if the US team were to compete against a Chinese, Indian, or Korean team in an Olympic game like soccer or cricket, the difference between the three ethnic respondents was revealing. While 90 percent of Koreans replied that they would definitely support Korea, only 52 percent of the Indians and 40 percent of the Chinese stated that they would support their respective teams.[121]

However, the real importance of the Korean diaspora in the United States and the similarity between Korean and the first-century Jewish diasporas lies in their God-given mission. According to anthropologist Ybarrola, "diasporas and transnationalism are intimately related."[122] In fact, Koreans in the United States have gained transnational characteristics by given circumstances. As to the transnational identity of Korean-Americans, Helene K. Lee writes,

> In the home, Korean often was the primary language, the family ate Korean food and observed Korean holidays and customs such as taking their shoes off as they entered the home, bowing greetings to family friends and relatives and stressing the importance of the family. Some (begrudgingly) attended weekly Saturday school to improve their Korean reading and writing skills at a Korean church with other second-generation Korean Americans. At the same time, many were encouraged outside of the home to be more "American." As a result, many second-generation Korean Americans became adept . . . to [a] "switching of cultural codes" between their Korean and American lives by adapting language, physical appearance and behaviors to the context they were in.[123]

According to Lee, not only do Korean diasporas have transnational characteristics, but the transnational characteristics can be a powerful tool for reaching out to non-Koreans in the multicultural society of America. Lee's description of a typical Korean family in the United States gives us a clue for understanding how in-group focused Korean-American Christians can also have transnational characteristics due to generational differences between first and second-generations. Whereas the Apostle Paul intentionally tried to have a transnational identity in order to win as many non-believers as

---

120. Min, "Ethnic Sub-ethnic Attachment," 760.
121. Min, "Ethnic Sub-ethnic Attachment," 775–776.
122. Ybarrola, "Anthropology, Diasporas, and Mission," 83.
123. Lee, "Transnationalism and 'Third Culture Kids," 4–5.

possible (1 Cor. 9:19–22), Korean-Americans, especially second-generation, have gained it naturally.

Along with the Koreans' transnational characteristics, Korean immigrants' close affiliation with Christianity and their extraordinarily strong commitment to mission work leverage their potential in the development of American Christianity. According to Overseas Koreans Foundations, as of 2011, the United States has the second largest Korean diaspora in the world (2,176,998; 30 percent of total), second only to the Korean diaspora in China (2,704,994; 37 percent of total). However, the number of Korean churches in the USA made up 95 percent of the total Korean immigrant churches in the world, with over 70 percent Christianization.

Within American theological seminaries, one sees a good number of the next-generation of Korean-American leaders enrolled, a fact which increases even more the expectations regarding the potential which their multicultural/transnational identity presents in a globalized America. Unlike most denominations that encounter difficulties in finding enough pastors or seminarians from new generations, Koreans are still overflowing seminaries in both Korea and America. According to *Christianity Today*, Tim Stafford reports that many seminaries have a great number of Asian citizens or Americans of Asian descent—22 percent at Fuller Theological Seminary, 25 percent at Talbot School of Theology, 9 percent at Trinity Evangelical Divinity School, and even 40 percent at the San Jose campus of Western Seminary.[124] In fact, Korean-Americans comprise the largest nonwhite group in American evangelical seminaries.[125] Furthermore, second-generation Koreans are also more actively involved in college campus ministry.[126] This shows how important it is to them to challenge and transform American Christianity.

Running for Mission and American Christianity

Korean Christians and Korean churches in the United States have been traditionally characterized by an in-group focus in their church life. However, this is beginning to change, and many are now actively working for both mission work and for shaping American Christianity. In this section, I will discuss the reasons why Korean-Americans are becoming active participants in reshaping American Christianity with this mission emphasis.

124. Stafford, "The Tiger in the Academy."
125. Kim, *A Faith of Our Own*, 5; Kim and Kim, "Revival and Renewal," 292.
126. Kim, *God's New Whiz Kids?*, 69; Kim, "Second-Generation Korean American Evangelicals," 20–21.

Mission-Oriented Koreans

Mission-Oriented Korean Churches: Korea is well-known as the second largest missionary sending country after the United States. In 2018, the Korean church in Korea had 21,378 overseas missionaries in 146 countries.[127] Since the Korean immigrant church in the U.S. is closely connected to the Korean church in Korea, Korean churches in America also have an enormous passion for mission work. Even though there is no concrete data about missions of Korean churches in the United States, Rebecca K. Kim and Sharon Kim's research in "Revival and Renewal: Korean American Protestants Beyond Immigrant Enclaves" provides tangible examples of how Korean immigrant churches become involved in missions in and out of the United States.[128]

According to Rebecca Kim and Sharon Kim, for example, World Mission Church (WMC), one of the oldest and largest Korean churches in Los Angeles, has attempted to reach out to underprivileged non-Korean communities and is recognized as one of the most socially engaged immigrant churches in the L.A. area. Pastor Park, a first-generation Korean pastor at WMC, explains:

> We try as best as we can given our limitations in language and cultural commonality to use our resources to serve others. For firemen and policemen, we have a special scholarship fund for their children. We also have a special scholarship fund for children of the Neighborhood Association. We give these scholarships out annually. We try continually to develop a good relationship with our neighbors.[129]

Also, whenever other countries have encountered natural disasters, WMC has provided generous financial donations. For example, WMC donated approximately three million dollars when the earthquake took place in El Salvador in January of 2001. Grace Korean Church is another good example. Rebecca Kim and Sharon Kim describe it as follows:

> At Grace Korean Church in Fullerton (California), one of the largest Korean churches in the United States, the entry way of the church serves as a photo gallery that highlights the work of 208 missionaries serving in 47 countries like Bangladesh, Vietnam, Sweden, and Italy. Inside the church's new "Vision Center" with a 3,000 seat auditorium, there is a sign on a giant board that reads "Mission is prayer. Mission is warfare. Mission is martyrdom."

---

127. Moon, "Missions from Korea 2019."
128. Kim and Kim, "Revival and Renewal," 296–306.
129. Kim and Kim, "Revival and Renewal," 293.

Demonstrating their seriousness about missions, half of Grace Korean Church's budget is set aside to support mission work.[130]

Like Grace Korean Church and World Mission Church, there are many Korean churches that are passionate about missions in the United States.

KOSTA (Korean Students in America): Along with the growing importance of the Korean church in the United States, the geopolitical locus of the United States strengthens the potential of Koreans and their churches within it. KOSTA is a good example. In 1986, two Korean pastors started a retreat for Korean international students in America named KOSTA. During that year, about 200 students participated in this meeting, but it continually grew and became one of the most well-known and influential retreats for Korean college and graduate students. Specifically, the geopolitical importance and the role of the United States for Koreans can be explained through the contributions of KOSTA. First, even though it aimed to meet the spiritual needs of Korean students in America, who wished to integrate knowledge and faith mainly for service in their home country of Korea, KOSTA has helped provide mission-minded Christian leaders for the church in America as well. For instance, Tae Pyong Kim, a former UPS executive, a reverend, and a KOSTA fixture who has attended it continually from the beginning, currently serves as a vice president of Chesapeake Reformed Theological Seminary.[131] Many KOSTANs (participants of KOSTA) are serving the church in the United States in such an important position like him. Second, the target participants of KOSTA diversified from solely international students to diverse groups including adults, 1.5- and second-generation immigrants and the youth, and the vision of KOSTA broadened too.[132] In many cases, Korean immigrant churches encourage their congregations to take part in KOSTA and attend it as a group. KOSTA, therefore, contributes toward revitalizing Korean immigrant churches. Third, KOSTA expanded its focus from the home country, Korea, to beyond Korea's borders, and incubated a vision for both Korean and non-Korean diasporas in the United States.[133] Now KOSTA USA[134] is

---

130. Kim and Kim, "Revival and Renewal," 296.
131. Kim, "*Pyongsindosayeok Kimtaepyongmoksa*."
132. KOSTA, "*KOSTA Ran?*"
133. KOSTA, "Korean Student Diaspora."
134. Even though KOSTA started in the United States in 1986, it spread out to other countries such as France, Italy, Germany, Japan, Canada, New Zealand, China, Japan, Korea, and so on. Also there are KOSTAs for the youth. So now KOSTA has added the area/nation name at the end like KOSTA USA.

praying to be used as a glorious instrument for non-Korean Diaspora students scattered in the United States.[135]

KWMC: Korean World Mission Conference (KWMC) is another example of how the Korean church in America serves as a center for world missions among Koreans. With the strong support of Billy Graham, Korean churches in North America played a leadership role in launching a worldwide Korean mission conference focused on accomplishing the Great Commission. As a result, KWMC, held every four years like the Olympics, had its first meeting at Wheaton College in 1988 when Korea hosted the Seoul Olympics. Since then Korean churches in the United States have actively led a mission movement for the Korean diaspora through KWMC. In 2008, the 6th KWMC had about 5,100 attendants from all over the world such as missionaries, pastors, lay leaders, and young adults interested in missions. No doubt, there is a high number of English-speaking next-generation Koreans within this group. For example, at its 5th conference, KWMC provided a separate English conference at the same time for about 1,000 next-generation English-speaking Koreans.[136] Through this meeting, English-speaking Korean pastors agreed to hold a biennial regional mission conference for English-speaking Koreans in North America. In 2012, 6,000 participants including 700 missionaries attended Korean World Missionary Fellowship from all over the world.

GKYM: The other example which shows that God is raising Korean immigrants in the U.S. for his mission is the Global Korean Young Adult Mission (GKYM) Festival, which is non-denominational. In 2008, GKYM was initiated by first-generation Korean pastors in North America for Korean-speaking young adults, just as KOSTA initially focused on Korean international students in the United States. However, in 2009 the GKYM conference opened up to second-generation Korean-Americans as well. According to GKYM, the "GKYM is a mission movement that seeks to mobilize the next-generation for world missions." As to why God calls second-generation Korean-Americans, Joel Kim a second-generation Korean-American pastor says,

> God has given them [diaspora Korean Americans] such good opportunities to study and to be educated. They have the bicultural experience. They have the bilingual experience, which allows them to even be more missional. So we want to really understand that as a gift of God. One of the key aspects that GKYM emphasizes is the fact that if the unreached are

---

135. KOSTA, "Korean Student Diaspora."
136. See www.kwmc.com.

remaining unreached then we cannot see the fulfillment of the Great Commission.[137]

In other words, with the innate, extraordinary passion and zeal for missions, Korean-Americans (especially second-generation), as Korean descendants, are more missional than many other Christians, making use of their bilingual ability and bicultural experience.

Since 2008, GKYM festivals have been held in various places in North America in order to prepare Korean young adults for missions. The characteristics of GKYM are two: 1) focusing on Korean young adults in North America, who have bi/multi-lingual skills and abilities to adapt to other cultures, 2) high rate of mission commitment among participants. According to a report, 786 Korean young adults committed their lives as long-/short-term missionaries out of total 2,723 participants in the Rochester 2011 GKYM festival.[138]

Move Beyond Ethnic Enclaves

In spite of a common criticism that Korean Churches work only for co-ethnic group Koreans, in reality, Koreans and Korean churches in the United States move beyond their ethnic boundaries. Among many, here I will discuss two large-scale examples: University Bible Fellowship (UBF) and the Jesus Awakening Movement for America/All Nations (JAMA).

UBF: UBF was founded in 1961 by a Korean Presbyterian pastor (Samuel Lee: 1931–2002) and an American missionary (Sarah Barry: 1930–present) in order to raise disciples of Jesus by planting a life-giving spirit among college students. "Bible Korea, World Mission," was the prayer topic from the beginning.[139] UBF contributes to world evangelism by raising lay missionaries and sending them throughout the world. Thus, America has become one of the mission fields for UBF missionaries.

According to Korean UBF's 2008 statistics, the number of UBF Korean missionaries in North America amounted to about 700. A report called "2012 Korean Overseas Missionary Status," given by KWMA, shows that the influence of UBF, the second largest missionary sending agency, has grown in both the number of missionaries and countries, from 1,405 missionaries/80 countries in 2008 to 1,722 missionaries/92 countries in

137. GKYM Chicago '12 Promotional Video.

138. Kim, "*Segye Hanin Chungnyun Sunkyochookje.*" According to the report, except for 786 missionary commitments, there are 1,379 participants who decided to take part in mission with financial and prayer support.

139. UBF, "Origin and Purpose."

2011.[140] Working with about a hundred "native" non-Korean leaders, UBF missionaries in North America have had some success in the conversion and discipling of Americans. UBF missionaries' evangelistic approach to the native population of the United States and their view on the United States in relation to missions and evangelism are simple and straight forward. According to Rebecca Kim and Sarah Kim,

> [T]he United States is viewed as a prime mission field. It is believed that raising disciples in America can lead to significant strides in the preaching of the gospel and the sending out of missionaries across the globe. Moreover, America is viewed as a nominally Christian nation that has lost its way and is in need of spiritual revival. With this view, Korean missionaries from UBF immigrate to the United States for campus evangelism. Entering the country through family, work and student visas, they go out to college campuses in Chicago, New York, Los Angeles, and other cities, asking students, particularly white students, in accented English 'Would you like to study Bible?'[141]

After the simple question, UBF missionaries' zeal, hard work, and sacrificial shepherding (parent-like care) have made their mission work possible in a cross-cultural environment.

JAMA: Jesus Awakening Movement for America/All Nations (JAMA) was birthed by a handful of Korean Americans' burning prayer for revival in the United States in 1993. John C. Kim, a Korean-American retired professor and the founder and president of JAMA, has been the center of this spiritual awakening movement. According to his testimony, when he was thirty-seven years old, he was expected to die because of a liver problem. John C. Kim says,

> [In] 1976, I was given a terminal diagnosis by three doctors because of my liver . . . And then my stomach became pregnant like 9-month pregnant woman. There's no way that I could have survived. During that time God convicted me you are dying because of your toxins in your soul; rather than toxins in your blood, which is physically killing you.[142]

Through the encounter with God and the long process of thorough repentance and healing, John Kim got a vision for America and its revival. Because

---

140. KWMA, "*2012 Hankuk-Sunkyosa PasongHyunHwang* [2012 Korean Missionary Statistics]."

141. Kim and Kim, "Revival and Renewal," 305.

142. http://www.catalystspace.com/catablog/full/catalyst_voices_-_dr._john_c._kim_from_jama/ (accessed March 20, 2012).

of his personal experience of healing and personal revival, JAMA emphasizes repentance and prayer. JAMA seeks God's healing and revival in the United States in three ways: a large national conference (New Awakening), an intercessory prayer conference, and a leadership development program (GLDI).[143] For Korean-Americans JAMA is well-known as a nationwide, large-scale summer retreat especially for second-generation Korean-Americans. Even though young second-generation Korean-Americans are the main target group of JAMA, the scope of participants is broadening, and the primary concern of the conference is not Korean-Americans or their churches, but this land of America and its revival. In JAMA's homepage, there are eleven items of prayer listed for America with the title of "Prayer Topics for this Nation." For example, it says "Please fervently pray for our nation. Would you include these prayer topics not only during your personal prayer time but also during times of corporate prayer? 1. Pray that God will bring repentance and awakening to this nation."[144] While the prayer topics begin and end with prayer asking for awakening in this land (America), the prayer topics include prayer for the local, state, and federal government, elected public servants, Christians, local churches, and so on. A testimony of a female student, who attended JAMA's New Awakening 2011 conference, shows how JAMA influenced her to participate in God's work for the United States. Juhyen Seo says,

> [T]hrough JAMA's New Awakening 2011 conference I've had a change of heart. I now realize why I was not able to see the dreams and visions that God had planned for me . . . I used to cry out to God asking for help so that He would meet my needs. Now my prayers are not about what I need but are of repentance to my Heavenly Father, asking Him to "even now" use all the gifts and blessings He's given to me to *bring revival to this land*.[145]

Aside from GKYM and JAMA, there are other large and small conferences, meetings, and gatherings—activities working together for the revival of the United States with Koreans as a chosen part of this revival. While maximizing the benefit of being in the United States as a world power in the twenty-first century, Korean immigrant churches also play a significant role

---

143. http://www.jamaglobal.com/wp/what-is-jama/ (accessed March 20, 2012).

144. http://www.jamaglobal.com/wp/prayer-topics-for-this-nation/ (accessed March 20, 2012).

145. http://www.jamaglobal.com/wp/new-awakening-2011-testimony/ (accessed March 20, 2012) [emphasis is mine].

in discipling, networking and mobilizing Koreans and Korean churches in the U.S. to fulfill the Great Commission.

Conclusion

This chapter shows the potential and importance of the Korean-American Christians and their churches for the spread of the gospel in the twenty-first century by considering immigration history, their characteristics, and challenges. God called Koreans to the United States through political and economic hardships and prepared Korean immigrant churches not for the sake of Koreans, but for all nations in God's mind. Koreans in the United States established a church-centered community with an exceptionally high degree of affiliation with Christianity. Their marginal identity provided an opportunity to embrace and serve others, as Jesus did, in this strange place. Besides, the locus of the United States and its centrality in politics, economy, society, culture, and transportation made it possible for Korean-Americans and their churches to play a significant role in renewing American Christianity. Now Korean Christians and their churches have gradually started to understand God's given potential in them. Koreans and their churches in the United States have conceived a vision to dedicate themselves to American Christianity in order to bring the progress of the gospel. It is a calling, which is holy and historic.

However, it does not mean that everything is positive. Korean Christians and Korean immigrant churches have encountered hardships and have had to deal with them wisely. While Korean immigrant churches are growing and many second-generation Korean-Americans lead campus ministries, some scholars have observed a "silent exodus" of younger Koreans leaving church and faith during/after college. Although Korean Christians have had high affiliation with Christianity, the ingrown characteristics of Korean-American Christians should be changed. In fact, Koreans and Korean churches in the United States have now begun to recognize their unique identity and their mission to serve American and all nations. In this regard, the generational distinction between first and second-generation immigrants makes a big difference. With their bilingual ability and bicultural experience, along with their extraordinary passion for missions, second-generation Korean American Christians are uniquely well-equipped to lead the development of American Christianity as emerging leaders.

To accomplish God's good will, Christians need to focus on God's vision for others through one's life and community. For Koreans in the United States, there is great potential to be a blessing for others and American Christianity if they choose the right things and the right direction in every situation where they face challenges.

3

Development and Issues of the Multicultural Church Movement

IN RECENT YEARS MANY scholars and Christian leaders have focused on the issue of diversity in the church, specifically the development of, and issues related to, multicultural (normally multi-ethnic and multiracial) churches. This does not mean that the multicultural church is a new ecclesial model. From the first century, there have been multicultural churches such as those in Ephesus and Antioch. Nevertheless, until fairly recently theologians and church leaders did not deal with the issues surrounding multicultural churches, not because they were opposed to the idea but because multicultural churches were rare. However, one of the effects of globalization has been the scattering of people through migration, causing individuals to live together with those who are from different countries and cultures. This has led scholars, church leaders, and lay people alike to have to deal with this diversity within the context of the church in the United States, one of the most diverse countries in the world.

In this chapter, I will discuss how the understanding of race, ethnicity, and their related issues have developed and changed in relation to the multicultural church and its movement, and give an overview of the multicultural church movement from its beginning to its current stage of development, as well as its future direction.

Historical Background of the Multicultural Church Movement

Before the multicultural church movement emerged in the United States over the last few decades, several historical events preceded it which had profound effects on the ways that people of different cultures, ethnicities, and races related with one another in the United States. These historical events took place primarily in relation to racism and social responses to it. This section will highlight three which shaped American Christianity and race relations: nineteenth-century racial theology, the use of science to justify racism, and the social and political changes surrounding race which occurred in the late nineteenth and twentieth centuries.

Misunderstanding of Racial Difference

Racial theology in the West during the nineteenth century was polarized into two main groups: the monogenic creationists and the polygenic creationists. Proponents of monogenic creationism insisted that God created all of mankind through a single creation and believed that the "Negro" (blacks) came to exist through the "curse of Ham." According to monogenic creationists, though coming to exist through this curse, "the Negro was a descendant of Adam and thus had an immortal soul, a position that allowed whites a measure of racial superiority without contradicting literal, 'orthodox' understandings of the Genesis creation story."[1] Polygenic creationists, on the other hand, principally rejected the "curse of Ham" as a theoretical framework for the origin of the black race and instead supported the theory that God created the "Negro" before Adam and Eve. These understanding of creation thus differed as to whether the black was a human being or a beast.[2]

The Curse of Ham

Since the beginning of the early Colonial period, American race relations have been distorted. Theologians and church leaders supported notions of superiority and inferiority and perpetuated misunderstandings of racial differences through misinterpretation of the Bible. Though the goal of theology is to help us gain a correct understanding of God's will through exegesis of the Bible, sometimes people employ theology in order to justify their wrongdoing. There have been various attempts to justify racial and ethnic superiority through misinterpretation of the Bible, and these attempts became increasingly severe and intentional as the American antislavery movement gained momentum. Stephen R. Haynes insists,

> By the 1830s—when the American antislavery movement became organized, vocal, and aggressive—the scriptural defense of slavery had evolved into the "most elaborate and systematic

---

1. Blum and Poole, *Vale of Tears*, 246.
2. Blum and Poole, *Vale of Tears*, 246.

statement" of proslavery theory, Noah's curse had become a stock weapon in the arsenal of slavery's apologists, and references to Genesis 9 appeared prominently in their publications.³

The curse of Ham in Genesis 9 was at the center of this intentional effort to defend slavery by means of misinterpreting the Bible.

The first Africans arrived in Virginia, in what would later be called America, in August 1619. When the Africans were introduced to early Colonial society, they were considered human beings in need of salvation and, therefore, indentured servants rather than slaves⁴ Peart's explanation is helpful in this regard:

> [W]hen Africans were introduced into early Colonies, their status was changed from slave to indentured servant because of their religious conversion. The Colonial government had purchased twenty Negroes, three of whom were women, from a Dutch frigate and had then distributed these individuals to private settlers. These Africans had been baptized, and according to English law, which governed Virginia, any slave who had converted to Christianity had to be freed. The theory behind this practice was that infidels could be enslaved as a means of communicating the gospel to them, but upon their conversion to Christianity, they had to be freed.⁵

Africans could change their status and be made free after working for three to seven years. The system of indentured servitude, however, changed in the following decades. Whites reinforced the slavery system because blacks were the primary work force in America. In the process, "this text [Genesis 9:18–27] became a standard, central Scripture for the defense of slavery."⁶ According to Edwin M. Yamauchi, "The earliest use of 'Curse of Ham' theory to justify slavery in America dates to the 1670s."⁷ Against abolitionists, Southern writers, often clergymen, proposed three reasons for how this text justifies slavery. Hays succinctly summarizes:

> They argued that, first, the curse was really intended for all of the descendants of Ham rather than just for Canaan, because Ham was not blessed in 9:26–27 and because Ham was the one who committed the offense. Second, 'Ham' means 'black' or 'burnt', thus explicitly referring to the Black race; and third, God

---

3. Haynes, *Noah's Curse*, 8.
4. Priest, *Slavery*, 326.
5. Peart, *Separate No More*, 21–22.
6. Hays, *From Every People and Nation*, 52.
7. Yamauchi, "The Curse of Ham," 55.

commanded that these descendants be slaves to Japheth, who represents the White races.[8]

Based on this logic, the proponents of slavery argued that God ordered the blacks' slavery. For example, Josiah Priest writes, "The servitude of the race of Ham, to the latest era of mankind, is necessary to the veracity of God Himself, as by it is fulfilled *one* of the eldest of the decrees of the Scriptures, namely, that of Noah, which placed the race as servants under other races."[9]

As time went by, the systematic defense of slavery was deepened against abolitionists. In *Divided By Faith*, Michael Emerson and Christian Smith describe how whites, especially Southern Christians, developed their arguments and insisted on the superiority of whites and the justification of slavery respectively. According to Emerson and Smith, before 1865, Southern church leaders proposed key reasons "why Christians should support slavery" by using the Bible. The spectrum of reasons was categorized into four areas: 1) biblical, 2) charitable and evangelistic, 3) social, and 4) political. Many people, including church leaders, used these Bible verses to support slavery:

Biblical Reasons

- Abraham, the father of faith, and all the patriarchs held slaves without God's disapproval (Gen 21:9–10).
- Canaan, Ham's son, was made a slave to his brothers (Gen 9:24–27).
- The Ten Commandments mention slavery twice, showing God's implicit acceptance of it (Ex 20:10, 17).
- Slavery was widespread throughout the Roman world, and yet Jesus never spoke against it.
- Paul returned a runaway slave, Philemon, to his master (Philem 1:2).

Social Reasons

- Just as women are called to play a subordinate role (Eph 5:22; 1 Tim 2:11–15), so slaves are stationed by God in their place.
- Slavery is God's means of protecting and providing for an inferior race (suffering the "curse of Ham" in Gen 9:25 or even the punishment of Cain in Gen 4:12).[10]

---

8. Hays, *From Every People and Nation*, 52.
9. Priest, *Bible Defense of Slavery*, 393–394.
10. Emerson and Smith, *Divided by Faith*, 35.

In the name of faith, church leaders tried to justify their sin of slavery and racism. They believed that blacks were an inferior race that needed slavery for protection.

After the American Civil War, white clergymen continued this way of thinking. For example, in an editorial in the Louisville *Central Methodist* in 1889, editor Richard Rivers stressed that the black "must occupy the position of inferiority" in America, where white and black live together, as "Ham must be subservient to Japheth."[11]

The Negro is a Beast, not a Human Being

While the monogenic creationists supported the theory of the curse of Ham, American polygenic creationists demonstrated more severe discrimination toward the black race based on a misinterpretation of the Bible. According to the polygenic creationists, the black is not a man but a beast. Then, how did the black emerge as the black people of the human race? In 1867, Buckner Payne, publisher and clergyman, published a small book entitled *The Negro: What is His Ethnological Status? Is he the progeny of Ham? Is he a descendant of Adam and Eve? Has he a soul? Or is he a beast in God's nomenclature? What is his status as fixed by God in creation? What is his relation to the white race?* While using the pseudonym "Ariel," Payne insisted that the black was not human but a beast. Interestingly, Payne insisted that there were only two races in the world, white and black. He says, "It will be admitted by all, and contradicted by none, that we now have existing on earth, two races of men, the white and the black."[12] He defines both races as follows:

> [T]he prominent characteristics and differences of these two races as we now find them.
>
> The white race have long, straight hair, high foreheads, high noses, thin lips, and white skins: the olive and sunburnt color, where the other characteristics are found, belong equally to the white race.
>
> The negro or black race, are woolly or kinky-headed, low foreheads, flat noses, thick-lipped, and have a black skin.[13]

Payne's stance of white superiority made the following claims: "The learned men of the past and present age, the clergy and others have assumed as true: 1. That the negro is a descendant of Ham, the youngest son of Noah.

---

11. Smith, *In His Image*, 271.
12. Payne, *The Negro*, Locations 24–25.
13. Payne, *The Negro*, Locations 28–31.

This is false and untrue. 2. That the negro is a descendant of, or the progeny of, Adam and Eve. This is also false and untrue."[14] In other words, the black person was not a human being at all.

Many Christians of that time believed that Ham's name indicated the color of the "Negro," and that Ham was, therefore, the ancestor of the black race. In contrast, Payne suggested several reasons why the theory of the curse of Ham was wrong. First, the curse was given not to Ham but to his youngest son Canaan. Second, the name Ham in Hebrew does not necessarily mean the color black. According to Payne, there are several interpretations of Ham in Hebrew such as sunburnt, swarthy, and dark; black is atypical meaning in the word's usage.[15] If the meaning of Ham had indicated the color of race, Payne argued that "the names of Shem and Japheth should be of equal value, in determining their color."[16] Third, since Noah was a perfect man in God's eyes, it would have been impossible for him to have had a black son with his only wife. Payne says:

> The Bible says of Noah, that he was perfect in his generation. We will not stop to criticise the Hebrew translated "generation," for any English scholar on reading the verse in which it occurs, will see at once, that to make sense, it should have been genealogy. Then Noah was perfect in his genealogy—he was a preacher of righteousness—he was the husband of one wife, who was also perfect in her genealogy; by this one wife, he had three sons, all born about one hundred years before the flood, and all three of them married, before the flood, to women who were perfect also in their genealogies . . . whatever the color of one might be, the others would be the same color—if one were black, all would be black—if one were white, all would be white.[17]

If the Hebrew translation of the word "generation" (in Genesis 6:9) is interpreted as "genealogy," as in the case of one husband and one wife, then children of different colors are impossible. Since scholars had studied where Shem traveled, where his descendants settled, and what countries they occupied, Payne concluded that Shem belonged to the white race. Likewise, since "Japheth's descendants peopled Europe," Japheth was white too.[18] In the same way, since Ham's descendants settled "in Egypt, in India, all over Asia, a portion of Africa and Europe respectively," and "all history in the

14. Payne, *The Negro*, Locations 17–18.
15. Payne, *The Negro*, Locations 98–99.
16. Payne, *The Negro*, Locations 48–49.
17. Payne, *The Negro*, Locations 108–114.
18. Payne, *The Negro*, Location 121.

Bible, and all history outside of the Bible, fully attest," in Payne's criteria, they were members of the white race too.[19] Payne described whites as having long straight hair, high foreheads, high noses, and thin lips. Based on his interpretation of Noah's perfect "genealogy," Payne concluded that their ancestors Adam and Eve must also be white.[20] In other words, Shem, Ham, and Japheth were all white by birth.

While Payne denied the theory of the curse of Ham as a foundation of black slavery, he claimed that the black was a creation of God not as a man but as a beast. Since Adam, Eve, Noah, Noah's wife, and Adam's three children (including Ham) were all white in his understanding, Payne claimed that the only possible reason for the black's presence was that they survived as a beast in the ark. He reasons:

> The Bible tells us that Noah was perfect in his genealogy, and the tenth in descent from Adam and Eve; that, consequently, Adam and Eve were white . . . We have also shown that the negro did not descend from either of the sons of Noah. That he is now here on earth, none will deny; and being here now, this logic of facts proves that he was in the ark, and came out of the ark after the flood; and that it indubitably follows, from the necessities of the case, that he entered the ark as a beast, and only as a beast. Now, it is very plain, from this statement, that as he came out of the Ark, the negro, as we now know him, existed anterior to the flood, and just such a negro as we have now, with his kinky head, flat nose, black skin, etc.[21]

For Payne, blacks were inferior because they were not part of the human race but instead were like the beasts of the field.

Payne also excluded the probability of Ham having a black wife, which could have introduced the black race after the flood. Payne asserted:

> suppose we admit, for the sake of the argument, that Ham was black, and that he was made so by the curse of his father Noah—we say, suppose we were to admit this, then what follows? Ham would have been just such a negro as we now find on earth—admitted; but then he would have been the *only* negro on earth. Where was his negro wife to be had? He could not propagate the negro race, by a cross with the white woman; for that would have produced a *mulatto*, and not the negro, such as we now have. To propagate the negro that we now have on earth,

---

19. Payne, *The Negro*, Locations 283–285.
20. Payne, *The Negro*, Locations 346–347.
21. Payne, *The Negro*, Locations 339–346.

the *man* and the *woman* must both be negroes. Now, where did Ham's negro wife come from? She did not come out of the ark? She was not on earth? Do we not see clearly from this statement of facts, that the assumption of the learned world, even admitting it, destroys itself the moment that we bring it to the test of facts. Under no view of their assumptions can the negro we now have on earth be accounted for.[22]

Therefore, Payne's only possible conclusion for the existence of the black race was that the black survived in the ark as a beast.

How then did the black emerge as the black people of the human race? Payne claimed that the black is an advanced kind of animal with the innate ability to imitate human sound. Perfect imitation of human sound made it possible for the black to communicate with the white. He wrote, "The difference between these higher orders of the monkey [the gorilla, orangutan, baboon, etc.] and the negro, is very slight, and consists mainly in this one thing: the negro can utter sounds that can be imitated; hence he could talk with Adam and Eve, for they could imitate his sounds."[23] However, a severe problem arose when the sons of God took the daughter of men (the black), which is an unforgivable sin. To support this theory, Payne distinguished "the man" (referring to Adam and his descendants) from "man" (referring to the black) in the Bible. When the white had sexual relations with the black, God punished the earth by the flood. Therefore, Payne insisted that "[t]he seed of Adam, which is the seed of God, must be kept pure; it *shall be kept pure, is the fiat of the Almighty.*"[24] For the same reason, God decided "*disapprobation of the negro*, in those various attempts to *elevate* him to *social, political* and *religious equality* with the white race."[25] Furthermore, Payne issued the following warning:

> The first attempt at the social equality of the negro, with Adam's race, brought the flood upon the world—the second, brought confusion and dispersion—the third, the fire of God's wrath, upon the cities of the plain—the fourth, the order from God, to exterminate the *nations* of the Canaanites—the fifth, the inhibition and exclusion, by *express law* of God, of the *flat-nosed* negro from his altar. Will the people of the United States, now furnish the sixth? *Nous verrons.*[26]

22. Payne, *The Negro*, Locations 306–313.
23. Payne, *The Negro*, Locations 370–371.
24. Payne, *The Negro*, Locations 673–674.
25. Payne, *The Negro*, Locations 714–716.
26. Payne, *The Negro*, Locations 720–724.

That is to say, any attempt to enhance the black's status needed to be prevented, otherwise God would again harshly punish the human race. In other words, not only was the white race superior to the black race but the distinction between the white and the black needed to be kept in order to obey God's will.

Scientific Attempts to Justify White Superiority

Many people attempted to prove the black's inferiority in order to insist on the white's superiority in the name of science, especially the sciences of psychology and anthropology.[27] Science was broadly accepted by most white Christians in Europe and in the United States. As a result, the origin of scientific racism, which justifies racial hierarchy through scientific approaches, can be found in a classification of *Homo sapiens* completed by Carolus Linnaeus, a Swedish scientist, in 1758. Linnaeus divided *Homo sapiens* into four types or races: white, red, yellow, and black. Linnaeus characterized "*Homo Europaeu* as gentle and governed by laws, *Homo Asiaticus* as haughty and governed by opinions, *Homo Americanus* as choleric (short-tempered) and regulated by customs, and *Homo Afer* as indolent and governed by caprice (whim)."[28] His hierarchy was the reflection of the political views of his time, but most scientists in America and Europe until the twentieth century accepted and developed Linnaeus's hierarchy in order to uphold the institution of slavery by proving the black's intellectual inferiority. According to Leonard Lieberman, "Until about 1940, mainstream science was consistent about the reality of race and the inferiority of blacks."[29]

There were three most influential examples of scientific approaches. First, scientists asserted the white's intellectual superiority over the black based on skull size. Samuel G. Morton, a Philadelphia physician, collected and measured over 600 skulls from around the world and insisted on racial hierarchy in *Crania Americana* (1839) and *Crania Aegyptiaca* (1849). He ranked races based on skull measurement and determined that the "Caucasoid" was most superior, followed by the "Mongoloid," and asserted that the "Negroid" was the most inferior.[30] J. C. Nott and George Gliddon adopted Morton's method in *Types of Mankind*, published in 1854, and presented his research to the American South in order to justify slavery.[31] These

27. Scupin, *Race and Ethnicity*, 37.
28. Scupin, *Race and Ethnicity*, 38.
29. Scupin, *Race and Ethnicity*, 44.
30. Scupin, *Race and Ethnicity*, 39.
31. Scupin, *Race and Ethnicity*, 39–40.

publications demonstrate the influence of anthropology on racism in the United States, because Morton, Nott, and Gliddon were considered "the nucleus of the American school of anthropology."[32] Even though Morton's approach was scientific, it had two serious sampling errors: uneven sample size and ignorance of the difference between male and female in cranial size. Morton used only three skulls for his Caucasian sample, whereas samples from other races were overrepresented. In addition, although the female cranial size is ten percent smaller than the male's, it seemed Morton was unaware of this difference and used more male skulls for examining Caucasians' brain sizes.[33] When I attended middle and high school in the 1980s, my classmates ridiculed each other based on their head sizes. Many of us told others, "You are smart because of your big head, but I am not because my head is small." We did not know this theory's origin and if it was credible; nevertheless, we often quoted the theory to prove why one was smarter than another.

Second, in the 1900s scientists turned their interests to eugenics, employing this "science" in order to prove the scientific validity of racism. In the 1880s, Frances Galton, the English inventor of the term "eugenics" and a first cousin of Charles Darwin, studied the number of great figures from different races and concluded the British to be the greatest.[34] He defined eugenics as "the study of the agencies under social control that may improve or impair the racial qualities of future generations, either physically or mentally."[35] In 1901, Galton's lecture to the British Anthropological Institute kindled interest and activity even in the United States.[36] In 1904, Charles B. Davenport, an American pioneer scientist in eugenics, organized the Eugenics Record Office (ERO) in Long Island. The supervisor of the ERO, Harry H. Laughlin, researched and interpreted the data that Negroes, Mexicans, and Puerto Ricans were dominant in prison populations, and he believed it was because of racial inferiority.

The Nazi human experimentations of the 1930s and 1940s are the best-known example of eugenics. The more surprising fact, however, is that Americans also adopted eugenics into immigrant policies to various degrees. Changes in immigration policies were on one occasion the result of the direct influence of eugenics, because "Laughlin gave testimony for two days before the congregational committee that wrote the 1924 Johnson

32. Scupin, *Race and Ethnicity*, 39.
33. Scupin, *Race and Ethnicity*, 39.
34. Scupin, *Race and Ethnicity*, 41.
35. Priest and Nieves, *This Side of Heaven*, 41.
36. Scupin, *Race and Ethnicity*, 41.

Act" in order to restrict certain groups of people in immigration policy.[37] In this regard, Eloise Hiebert Meneses succinctly summarized the impact of eugenics on politics as follows:

> Americans too were interested in breeding a better race at the time. Eugenicists' reports to the U. S. Congress resulted in legislation against immigration from countries of "poor stock." The Johnson Act of 1924, for instance, restricted immigration from eastern and southern Europe, where criminal genes supposedly abounded, to 2 percent per country... Between 1911 and 1930, twenty-four states had enacted sterilization laws for "social misfits" and "idiots," identified by their inability to pass intelligence tests. Seventy-five hundred people were forcibly sterilized in Virginia between 1924 and 1972 (Gould 1996, 365). By 1941, sixteen thousand people had been sterilized in California alone, and thirty-six thousand in the nation. The "science" of eugenics was having real social and political impact.[38]

A third example of a false approach in scientific racialism is the so-called IQ (intelligent quotient). Based on the measurement of the heads of students in 1898, the French psychologist Alfred Binet introduced his method of testing human intelligence. The director of the New Jersey Institute for the Feebleminded, Henry H. Goddard, translated Binet's 1908 IQ test into English. He used the test widely and published books in the 1910s to support eugenics with the assertion that the black race is inferior. A resurgence of scientific racialism through the use of IQ tests is found in the publication of the article "How Much Can We Boost IQ and Scholastic Achievement?" in the 1969 *Harvard Educational Review*. In 1994, surprisingly, the misuse of IQ tests was revived again in the publication of *The Bell Curve* by psychologist Richard Herrnstein and political scientist Charles Murray. They stated that IQ tests show a large gap between the bottom and top of society; there is a 10- to 15-point gap between blacks and whites primarily due to genetics. In addition, "poverty, crime, illegitimacy, and welfare dependency are associated with low IQ."[39] These three peaks involving the IQ test show how racialist ideas take a deep root in humans' minds and influence people to justify and practice racism.[40] Even though these kinds of scientific attempts were revealed to be false theories, it took a long time to change Christians'

---

37. Scupin, *Race and Ethnicity*, 41.
38. Priest and Nieves, *This Side of Heaven*, 41.
39. Scupin, *Race and Ethnicity*, 50.
40. Scupin, *Race and Ethnicity*, 46–52.

views on racial issues. People have slowly come to realize that there are racial differences without superiority or inferiority.

Social and Political Changes

Social and political changes in the United States had an enormous impact on American Christianity as it moved toward the reality of a multicultural church. Among many of these changes, three historical events proved to be critical. First, the basic and foundational historical events were the Civil War and the abolition of slavery in 1865. Freedom from slavery as a result of the Civil War caused "a 'mass exodus' of African Americans from white denominations and biracial congregations."[41] This freedom did not draw them to multiracial churches, but rather led them to establish black Protestant denominations, which gave blacks a sense of worth and equality. John Boles's description of this phenomenon provides a better understanding of why the mass exodus of blacks was necessary:

> Of course, that freed persons wanted to leave the biracial churches is a commentary on the less-than-complete equality they had enjoyed in them. Blacks had a strong sense of racial identity, reinforced by their having been slaves and, within the confines of the churches, by their segregated seating. The complete sermons they had heard for years, not just the self-serving words the white ministers directed specifically at them, had engendered in blacks a sense of their moral worth and equality in the sight of God. The biracial churches simultaneously nurtured this sense of moral equality and thwarted it by their conformity to the demands of the slave society . . . Theologically and experientially blacks were ready to seize the moment offered by emancipation to withdraw from their old allegiances and create autonomous denominations. No better evidence of the freedom slaves had not enjoyed in the biracial churches exists than the rapidity with which blacks sought to establish separate denominations after the Civil War.[42]

Instead of superficial togetherness under inequality in biracial churches, blacks chose to leave and establish their own denominations in order to escape the discrimination that still existed in these biracial churches and to avoid racial conflict. In contrast, equality among different people groups is one of the core values of multicultural churches.

41. DeYoung et al., *United by Faith*, 52–53.
42. Boles, ed., *Masters & slaves*, 17.

The Civil Rights movement from the 1950s to the early 1960s can be considered a second historical event which provided pathways to the multicultural church movement. Of course, the Civil Rights movement did not aim to establish multicultural churches. Leaders and black Christian participants of the Civil Rights movement, "called, protested, boycotted, and died for an end to Jim Crow segregation."[43] Emerson and Smith say, "In this case, the goal was freedom from oppression and unequal treatment, at least as expressed through the laws and practices of the South."[44] In this period a great contrast between black and white Christians existed on this race issue. Whereas white Christians resisted personal prejudice and discrimination, they did not recognize systematic social racialization.[45] Emerson's account of Billy Graham's response to the 1963 March on Washington is a good example of how white Christians understood unity and togetherness between the black and the white:

> In response to King's famous "I Have a Dream" speech that his children might one day play together with white children, Graham, who had been invited but did not attend the 1963 March on Washington, said: 'Only when Christ comes again will little white children of Alabama walk hand in hand with little black children.' This was not meant to be harsh, but rather what he and most white evangelicals perceived to be realistic.[46]

Neither the Civil War nor the Civil Rights movement directly contributed to the establishment of multicultural churches. Nevertheless, they were meaningful because they made it possible for blacks to gain freedom and equal rights.

The third important political event was the Immigration Act of 1965. The current demographic composition of the United States is partially the result of American immigration policy. The Immigration Act of 1882 set up qualitative standards to preclude undesirables such as criminals, mental incompetents, the seriously ill, and *Asians* from entering the country.[47] Emerson writes, "Before 1965, more than 90 percent of all immigrants to the United States were from Europe."[48] This predominance of European

---

43. Emerson and Smith, *Divided by Faith*, 45.
44. Emerson and Smith, *Divided by Faith*, 46.
45. Emerson and Smith, *Divided by Faith*, 46.
46. Emerson and Smith, *Divided by Faith*, 47.
47. Ortiz, *One New People*, 30.
48. Emerson, "The Gift of Our Changing Culture." According to Ortiz, "between 1900 and 1965, 75 percent of all immigrants were of European extraction." *One New People*, 31.

immigration was due primarily to the broad exclusion of Asians. In addition, Japanese and Koreans were excluded from U.S. immigration by the influence of the Gentlemen's Agreement of 1907–1908.[49] Then, "[b]eginning in 1921, a series of measures [strove to] block the growing immigration from southern Europe . . . and block all Asian immigrants by establishing a zero quota for them."[50] This exclusion was expanded by the 1924 Immigration Act, which "reaffirmed these prohibitions by banning the admission of persons ineligible for citizenship."[51] In 1960, 88.5 percent of the US population was white and 10.5 percent was black.[52] However, the Immigration Act of 1965 changed the ratio of immigrants to the U.S.: the Hispanic population increased to 16 percent and the Asian population reached 5 percent in 2010.[53] In other words, without the Immigration Act of 1965, only the biracial church or the Asian-absent multicultural church would be possible in the United States.

Theological Foundation of the Multicultural Church Movement

The multicultural church movement is not just a situational response to the present multicultural context. Rather, it is in many ways the result of theological reflection related to the church's calling in a globalized twenty-first-century America. In this section, I will discuss three theological/missiological concepts which are closely connected to the multicultural church movement: the complementarity between particularity and universality, the multicultural ecclesiology of the missional church movement, and the new perspective on the homogeneous unit principle. As the backbone and theological foundation of the multicultural church movement, these concepts working together lead us to a multicultural ecclesiology.

The Complementarity between Particularity and Universality

Having a correct understanding of both the *particularity* of election and the *universality* of God's love for all nations is foundational in pursuing

---

49. Zhou and Gatewood, *Contemporary Asian America*, 156.
50. Schaefer, *Racial and Ethnic Groups*, 93.
51. Zhou and Gatewood, *Contemporary Asian America*, 156.
52. US Census Bureau, "Statistical Abstract of the United States 1961."
53. Emerson, "The Gift of Our Changing Culture."

the multicultural church. It is significant not only for a biblical theology of mission, but it is also necessary for understanding the multicultural church movement. Without a correct understanding of both particularly and universality, we can lose our foundation in pursuing the multicultural church, because they play a key role in establishing the theological basis for a multicultural ecclesiology.

Particularity in relation to election indicates that God chooses a particular people or nation for the sake of accomplishing his purposes. For example, we can read in the Bible that God's will is accomplished through many individuals such as Abraham, Moses, David, and John the Baptist. The Bible also plainly states that God chooses to use some over others. He chose Abraham among many, Isaac not Ishmael, Jacob not Esau, David not Saul, and Israel among many nations. When specific individuals or a group of people are chosen, this choice means that others are excluded. Did the exclusion of an individual or a group of people mean they were rejected? No. Nonetheless, for a long time, exclusion caused both Jews and Christians to misunderstand particularity. The fact is that people were actually considered blessed and privileged if God chose to use them. Lesslie Newbigin asserts that the "scandal of particularity is at the center of the question of missions."[54] As a result, he also brings us to the importance of correctly understanding particularity. In other words, if we misunderstand particularity, we run the risk of assuming that we no longer need to reach out to non-chosen people.

Understanding the particularity of election also requires a correct understanding of universality. Universality in relation to election represents another crucial distinction of God's love and vision for all nations in the matter of salvation. One of the common difficulties in mission and evangelism is the introduction of God's universal love for all because God chose only certain particular people or nations in the Bible. Because of this, Christianity is often considered an exclusive foreign religion and only intended for a particular people such as those in Israel or in the West. Even though many Christians acknowledge the universality of God's love superficially, many do not grasp the fact that it is presented as a major theme throughout the Bible and is God's utmost will.

Universality indicates the wideness of God's reign, which is universal, and also represents the unchanging will of God. He wants to bless and save all people as expressed throughout the Bible from beginning to end. Even though God wants to save all people, universality is different from universalism. James Chukwuma Okoye, a Catholic Old Testament theologian,

---

54. Newbigin, *The Open Secret*, 67.

argues in *Israel and the Nations: A Mission Theology of the Old Testament* that "the Old Testament focuses not only on Israel but also on the world outside of Israel."[55] For example, the story of Abraham in Genesis 12:1–3, which is known as a representative passage revealing particularity, contains the universality of God's vision for all nations as well. Furthermore, Christopher J. H. Wright says, "God's covenant with Abraham is the single most important biblical tradition within a biblical theology of mission and a missional hermeneutic of the Bible."[56]

Since God is the main missionary, He has accordingly called Abram to be the instrument of His blessing to the world. The meaning of being a source or agent of God's blessing to all is significant, though the Abrahamic covenant is much more profound. Okoye insists in this regard,

> Abraham is the physical progenitor of Israel and in blessing Abraham God is conferring the blessing on his descendants, on Israel. Yet God surprisingly links this blessing to blessing for all families of the earth (Khoury 2003, 189). It means that the blessing of Israel consists precisely in being a blessing for all families of earth. The special favors of God to Abraham and his descendants are to make them agents of blessing for all of humankind.[57]

In other words, the Abrahamic covenant is meaningful for three main reasons: 1) the election of Abraham represents God's love for all families of the earth, 2) the covenant shows that particularity (blessing for Israel) is connected to universality (God's love for all humankind), and 3) God's love for all people will be an ongoing process through Abraham's descendants. Therefore, universality is not a new concept which emerges in the New Testament only, but rather "the tension between the universality of the goal (all nations) and the particularity of the means (through you) is right there from the very beginning of Israel's journey through the pages of the Old Testament."[58]

Christopher J. H. Wright also assigns much more space to the discussion of universality in the Old Testament than in the New Testament in his book *The Mission of God: Unlocking the Bible's Grand Narrative*. James Okoye also wrote a single book *Israel and the Nations: A Mission Theology of the Old Testament* to deal with the universality of salvation in the Old Testament.

55. Okoye, *Israel and the Nations*, 4.
56. Wright, *The Mission of God*, 189.
57. Okoye, *Israel and the Nations*, 48.
58. Wright, *The Mission of God*, 222.

To emphasize this point, I will share a few more examples of how the universality of God's love is revealed in the Old Testament. First, in Exodus 19:5–6 God said, "Now if you obey me fully and keep my covenant, then out of all nations you will be my treasured possession. Although the whole earth is mine, you will be for me a kingdom of priests and a holy nation." Even though this is a covenant between God and Israel at Mount Sinai, this text explicitly reveals a universal perspective through the phrase "all nations" and "the whole earth." Second, although it does not explicitly address being a source of blessing for all people and nations, the expression "all the earth *coming to know YHWH*"[59] in the Old Testament (e.g. Joshua 4:24; 1 Samuel 17:46; 1 Kings 8:43) shows the universality of God's vision. Third, in Psalm 72 the psalmist praises and sings to the Lord, saying, "May his name endure forever; may it continue as long as the sun. All nations will be blessed through him, and they will call him blessed" (Psalm 72:17). This verse apparently reveals the Abrahamic universal and mutual blessing by echoing and reminding the hearer of the covenant in Genesis 12:1–3 through the expressions "may his name endure forever," "be blessed" and "call him blessed."

Fourth, another surprising example of universality is found in Isaiah 19:24–25, which says, "In that day Israel will be the third, along with Egypt and Assyria, a blessing on the earth. The LORD Almighty will bless them, saying, 'Blessed be Egypt my people, Assyria my handiwork, and Israel my inheritance.'" Wright mentions his surprise in finding God's universality in this phrase, and confesses, "I find this one of the most breathtaking pronouncements of any prophet, and certainly one of the missiologically most significant texts in the Old Testament . . . The identity of Israel will be merged with that of Egypt and Assyria, such that the Abrahamic promise is not only fulfilled *in* them but *through* them."[60] In Isaiah, these verses God's universal care and love are not ambiguous but clearly apparent. Universality is not written between the lines but distinctly on the surface. According to this text, God will not only bless foreign nations but also choose and use them as an agent of Abrahamic blessing for others. Foreign nations are not outsiders in God's vision but are also considered his chosen ones (my people, my handiwork). With regard to this phrase (Isaiah 19:24–25), Okoye's idea of the "inclusive covenant" coincides with three other Scriptures: Zechariah 14, Isaiah 56:1–8, and Isaiah 66:18–24.[61] Finally, the whole book of Jonah is a good example of universality. In the climax of the story, Yahweh's question

---

59. Wright, *The Mission of God*, 227–29.
60. Wright, *The Mission of God*, 236.
61. Okoye, *Israel and the Nations*, 118–128.

to Jonah, "should I not have concern for the great city of Nineveh?" (4:11) highlights the universality of God's love. According to Andreas J. Kostenberger and Peter T. O'Brien, the question reveals *hesed* (God's covenantal love in Hebrew), which is not limited to Israel.

In addition to the Old Testament, the New Testament too reveals the universality of God's love. From the beginning of the New Testament, Matthew reveals the universality of God's love in the genealogy of Jesus Christ, affirming the Abrahamic covenant. Wright says,

> By combining the Abrahamic and Davidic covenant reminders in this way [the son of David, the son of Abraham (Mt1:1)], Matthew highlights the universal significance of the one who would, as son of Abraham, fulfill what was promised for Abraham's seed (blessing for all nations), and as son of David, would exercise the prophesied messianic reign over all the earth.[62]

In other words, the genealogy of Jesus is not a simple genealogy but a special tool for expressing God's faithfulness to fulfill his covenant for all nations. While this genealogy describes Jesus Christ as a descendant of David and Abraham, it also supports God's universal plan for all nations that God promised through Abraham. As Abraham and Israel are chosen in the Old Testament, the disciples are chosen to be fishers of men (Mark 1:17), and the church is chosen to declare God's wonderful deeds (1 Peter 2:9).

Although Luke was a Gentile as an outsider, he describes his implicit relationship with Abraham through four accounts in the books of Luke and Acts (the healing of a crippled woman on the Sabbath, Luke 13:10–16; the poor beggar Lazarus, Luke 16:19–31; the story of Zacchaeus, Luke 19:1–10; and the healing of the lame man, Acts 3:1–25). In the Bible, God uses healing, transformation, and restoration to demonstrate his love as well as salvation. In the same way, Luke understands these meanings and uses them in his writing to express God's universality. Wright argues, "All of them [four narratives] illustrate the healing, transforming or restoring the power of God and seem designed to affirm that this is part of what receiving the blessing of Abrahams entails."[63] In other words, these narratives serve as a bridge to connect Jesus (New Testament) and Abraham (Old Testament).

Paul's writing in the New Testament also provides many examples of universality. For instance, Romans 1:5 says, "[T]hrough him [Jesus Christ our Lord] and for his name's sake, we received grace and apostleship to call people from among all the Gentiles to the obedience that comes from

---

62. Wright, *The Mission of God*, 243.
63. Wright, *The Mission of God*, 245.

faith."[64] In fact, the expression "all the Gentiles (*panta ta ethne*)" can be translated to mean "all the nations," thus proving God's universal salvation is for all nations.[65] Not only is this expression directly related to the Great Commission in Matthew, but there are many other passages in the Pauline epistles that further draw us to universality. For this reason, it is important to have a proper understanding of Paul's message regarding God's universality. Wright says,

> It is clear from the whole body of Paul's writing that he preached and taught a message with universal claims: one universal God, one universal Savior, one universal climax to history for the entire creation. Yet it is equally clear that this never evaporated into an abstract or philosophical universality. It was always rooted in the story of Israel and especially in the promise to Abraham.[66]

Universality is not a new revelation, and although it is clearest in Paul's writing, it can be found in the accounts of Israel and the Abrahamic covenant.

If we agree that universality (God's love for all nations) is a dominant theme throughout the Bible, why did God use the problematic tool of election? What is the meaning and purpose of particularity in election? Biblical truth proposes that election is for service and not for the privilege of the elect. Bosch says, "God as revealed in history is . . . the One who has elected Israel. The purpose of the election is service, and when this [service] is withheld, election loses its meaning."[67] This service is especially for God's universal purpose of salvation.

God is interpersonally related to human beings through the Trinity. For this reason, God invites us to mutual and collective responsibility in his salvific work in order to save all. In this regard, Newbigin says,

> [I]f the truly human is the shared reality of mutual and collective responsibility that the Bible envisages, then salvation must be an action that binds us together and restores for us the true mutual relation to each other and the true shared relation to the world of nature. This means that the gift of salvation would be bound up with our openness to one another. It would not come to each, direct from above, like a shaft of light through the roof.[68]

---

64. Wright, *The Mission of God*, 247.
65. Wright, *The Mission of God*, 247.
66. Wright, *The Mission of God*, 248–249.
67. Bosch, *Transforming Mission*, 18.
68. Newbigin, *The Open Secret*, 70–71.

Participation in God's salvific work is not a onetime event that belonged solely to Israel; rather this is God's ceaseless calling, which needs to be carried out by each Christian and by the church until our mission is accomplished. Having an understanding of universality brings an awareness of the immeasurable responsibility in particularity. In *The Missionary Nature of the Church*, Dutch theologian Johannes Blauw emphasizes, "If the responsibility is refused, election can even become the motive for divine punishment: 'You only have I known of all the families of the earth, therefore I will punish you for all your iniquities' (Amos 3:2)."[69]

While many scholars view particularity and universality as motivational foundations of mission and evangelism, Chuck Van Engen insists that the unique characteristic of the relationship between universality and particularity is a primary reason why churches in North America must pursue multiculturalism. Van Engen, professor of Biblical Theology of Mission at Fuller Theological Seminary, proposes that "because God's mission seeks careful and balanced complementarity between universality and particularity, churches in North America should strive to be as multi-ethnic as their surrounding contexts."[70] In the pursuit of multicultural churches, for Van Engen, two extremes should be avoided:

> Too strong an emphasis on universality will drive us toward uniformity and blind us to cultural distinctives. Too strong an emphasis on particularity will push us toward either exclusivist homogeneity or fragmented ethnocentrism, and create serious questions about our oneness in Jesus Christ.[71]

In other words, we must keep both cultural distinctiveness and oneness in our practice of particularity and universality. In Genesis 11, God affirms cultural distinctiveness by diversifying languages at Babel instead of destroying them. Cultural distinctiveness, therefore, should not diminish our intimate relationship with God. Woodberry says,

> Yet these distinctive features of multiple cultures are not allowed to divide humanity's relation to YHWH, nor to support the concept of a national or ethnic plurality of gods. There is one God, creator and sustainer of *all peoples*. Oneness in plurality, plurality in oneness. Particular universality, universal particularity.[72]

---

69. Blauw, *Missionary Nature of the Church*, 23.
70. Van Engen, "Is the Church for Everyone?," 1.
71. Van Engen, "Is the Church for Everyone?," 4.
72. Woodberry, *Reaching the Resistant*, 42.

Van Engen insists, "This theology of humanity should be normative for us as we consider the missiological implications of planting multi-ethnic churches in North America. It is the bottom-line biblical motivation for such activity."[73] According to Van Engen, if we recognize the sociological reality of the twenty-first-century multicultural United States and the complementarity between universality and particularity, this recognition will help us to rethink the significance of multicultural churches. This is possible if responsible Christians keep in mind the importance of service. Although Newbigin did not specifically address multicultural churches, we can sense the seriousness of the responsibility for the church to embrace diverse people of all cultures in his statement:

> Through the repeated hammer blows of defeat, destruction, and deportation, interpreted by the faithful prophets, Israel has to learn that election is not for comfort and security but for suffering and humiliation . . . Israel's election means that it is called to be servant and witness of the Lord for all the nations, not to be ruler of the nations. To be the elect is a fearful responsibility.[74]

God is gracious, but He is also strict and to be feared when it comes to His purpose of salvation. Christians who pursue the multicultural church, whether as a member or as a part of their vocational ministry, must step out of their comfort zones. In this process, some Christians who seek the success of multicultural churches may even face humiliation or suffering through their sacrificial giving, but such sacrifice is consistent with the biblical message. As Christians (particular chosen people), we are drawn by universality to serve others who are different from us culturally, ethnically/racially. The recognition of the responsibility given to chosen people compels us to take bold steps to go beyond our comfort zones and to sacrifice ourselves in order to embrace others who have different ethnic/racial backgrounds, especially within a multicultural society. This is what multicultural churches are pursuing. Therefore, a biblical understanding of the complementarity between particularity and universality compels us theologically to participate in the multicultural church movement.

Missional Church Movement

In 1998, the publication of the landmark book, *Missional Church: A Vision for the Sending of the Church in North America*, ignited the missional

---

73. Van Engen, "Is the Church for Everyone?," 4.
74. Newbigin, *The Open Secret*, 73.

church movement. This book, edited by Darrel Guder, brought together the contributions of theologians, missiologists, and ministry practitioners to address the nature and calling of the church in North America. As a result of its publication, the understanding of the "missional church" and the "missional" concept which the book advocated has greatly influenced both the ecclesiology and the activities of the North American church.[75] Along with its own focus on North American ecclesiology more broadly, the missional church movement also provides a sound theological foundation for the multicultural church movement by revealing and highlighting the importance of multicultural ecclesiology.

The Trinitarian concept of "missional" was first introduced by Johannes Dürr in an article published only months prior to the International Missionary Council (IMC) conference held in 1952 at Willingen, Germany.[76] In "Die Reinigung der Missionsmotive," Dürr stated that "the original meaning of the word 'missio' developed in the doctrine of the Trinity and meant the sending of the Son from the bosom of the Father. It was thus a theological, redemptive-historical term."[77] Such a Trinitarian understanding of mission began to gain broader attention at the Willingen Conference which followed. According to Bosch, the conference understood mission to be "[t]he classical doctrine on the *missio Dei* as God the Father sending the Son, and God the Father and Son sending the Spirit was expanded to include yet another 'movement': Father, Son, and Holy Spirit sending the church into the world."[78] In 1958, German missiologist Georg Vicedom deepened the concept with the publication of his book *Missio Dei*, which was translated into English in 1975.[79] In the meantime, retired missionary Lesslie Newbigin came to the realization that Western society was also a mission field. Newbigin began to pose a question: "What is involved in a missionary encounter between the gospel and a modern Western culture?"[80] As a result, missiologists who were concerned with this issue organized the Gospel and Our Culture Network (GOCN) in the

---

75. Missional church began with the recognition of *missio Dei* that "God's mission is calling and sending us, the church of Jesus Christ, to be a missionary in our own societies, in the cultures in which we find ourselves." Through this understanding, missional church movement advocates insist that "our challenge is to move from church with mission to missional church." Guder, *Missional Church*, 5–6.

76. Flett, *The Witness of God*, 14.

77. Flett, *The Witness of God*, 14, quoted from Durr, "Die Reinigung der Missionsmotive."

78. Bosch, *Transforming Mission*, 390.

79. Lee, "From Traditional to Missional Church," 69.

80. Lee, "From Traditional to Missional Church," 70.

mid-1980s, which began to have its own voice by the mid-1990s. Through this group's work, the missional church movement came into being, accelerated through the publication of a series of books by Eerdmans Publishing, starting with Darrel Guder's *Missional Church*.

How then does the missional church movement impact the multicultural church movement? Among the many emphases and characteristics of the missional church, I believe three are crucial for the multicultural church movement: being sent, being contextual, and being incarnational. Whereas the complementarity between particularity and universality brings us to the realization of the theological motive for the multicultural church movement, three distinctive natures of the church founded in the theological reflection on the missional church—being sent, being contextual, being incarnational—provide a multicultural ecclesiology for the multicultural church movement.

First of all, a fresh understanding of the nature of the church from the missional church movement brings us to the recognition of the church's being *sent* by God to the world. In the mindset of Christendom, before the recognition of church's identity as being sent, the Western church sought to reach out and draw people into the church, which is called the "attractional" model. This attractional model does not fully take into consideration the cultural differences between different people groups within and outside of the church, and instead seeks to attract "like-us people" to the church.[81] Craig Van Gelder defines the missional church, on the other hand, as "a community created by the Spirit that is missionary by nature in being called and sent to participate in God's mission in the world."[82] It reveals a paradigm shift in ecclesiology from "church with mission" to "missional church." In other words, "mission is not just a program of the church. It defines the church as God's sent people."[83] In the missional church, "mission" or "missional" does not refer to the traditional concept of sending and supporting missionaries; instead, the recognition of being sent compels the church to be sent both individually and collectively. In other words, in this understanding no one can "opt out" of his/her participation.

---

81. Alan Hirsch describes the attractional church that "operates from the assumption that to bring people to Jesus we need to first bring them to church. It also describes the type or mode of engagement that was birthed during the Christendom period of history, when the church was perceived as a central institution of society and therefore expected people to "come and hear the gospel" rather than taking a "go-to-them" type of mentality. Not to be confused with being culturally attractive." Hirsch, *The Forgotten Ways*, 275.

82. Gelder, *Missional Church and Denominations*, 43.

83. Guder, *Missional Church*, 6.

The emphasis on the contextual nature of the missional church makes it meaningful in the multicultural context. Guder, for example, states, "A missional ecclesiology is contextual. Every ecclesiology developed within a particular cultural context."[84] Gelder adds that "[t]he gospel is always conveyed through the medium of culture . . . To be faithful to its calling, the church must be contextual, that is, it must be culturally relevant within a specific setting. The church relates constantly and dynamically both to the gospel and to its contextual reality."[85] In fact, "submerged racial and ethnic identities in a stew-pot society"[86] is one of the realities which everyone in North America encounters and by which they are enormously impacted. Specifically, the missional church movement draws attention to "multiple cultures" as one of our main contexts in North America. Gelder states, "Globalization is now leading to multiple ethnic cultures and racial traditions living together in the same neighborhoods. With increased immigration and migration . . . more persons now come into direct contact with cultures, religions, and traditions other than their own."[87] This diversity of ethnicities and cultures within the same neighborhoods solicits the church to provide true unity among diverse people.[88]

In relation to the multicultural church movement, the missional church movement's emphasis on contexts reminds us that the church itself is to be multicultural in order to be a witnessing community. Guder says, "From the outset, the church of Christ was mandated to be multicultural: to witness in the distinctive contexts of Jerusalem, Judea, Samaria, and to the ends of the earth."[89] He again emphasizes that "the biblical definition of the church's mission makes plain that the church is essentially multicultural, because God's people are formed in distinctive ways in each context, interacting with every culture in order to form itself visibly as a community of witness."[90] In fact, the recognition of globalization and multiple cultures reminds us that the more our society becomes multicultural, the more the church, too, needs to be multicultural.

Another relevant characteristic of the missional church is its emphasis on incarnational mission. While the "being sent" nature of the church gives it a direction of mission, an "incarnational" understanding of the church clarifies

84. Guder, *Missional Church*, 11.
85. Guder, *Missional Church*, 18.
86. Guder, *Missional Church*, 20.
87. Guder, *Missional Church*, 42.
88. Guder, *Missional Church*, 45.
89. Guder, *Missional Church*, 231.
90. Guder, *Missional Church*, 233.

the definition of "to the world" as "to our neighbors"; it makes a theological and ecclesiological understanding of the church practical. The missional church movement teaches that our focus is not on an anonymous person or an unspecified world, but rather on our neighbors whom we meet every day and who live next to us. In this regard, Michael Frost believes,

> Incarnational mission means moving into the lives of those to whom we believe we've been sent. Living in one neighborhood, working in another, playing in another, and churching in yet another doesn't model to people that Jesus is willing to move into their neighborhoods. It says that if Jesus' followers don't want to live here, neither would Jesus.[91]

The paraphrase of John 1:14 by Eugene Peterson in *The Message* emphasizes that the incarnational nature of the church comes from Jesus' own life: "The Word became flesh and blood, and *moved into the neighborhood.*"[92] Likewise, the incarnational nature of the church compels us to move into the diverse neighborhoods of today's globalized multicultural society. Christine Sine, a co-founder of Mustard Seed Associates and a writer, makes a striking observation of how important it is for the church to be incarnational in this multicultural society:

> Yesterday as I was driving to a local church to speak, I passed a homeless man standing on the street corner. That was not unusual. The corner he stood at was a popular place for the destitute to beg. His face was hidden by a sign that read *Homeless and Hungry*. That wasn't unusual either. As the impact of the recession continues, more people are being driven onto the streets to live. What was unusual was that the sign was written in seven different languages.

> My first response was to want to reach for my camera which unfortunately I did not have with me. But then I started to think. This man obviously knows the neighbourhood far better than I do. He knows who lives in the area and how to communicate with them. He knows where and when people are likely to be generous. He probably also knows where he can get a meal and shelter for the night. And I am sure he is very aware of who will show a little compassion and who is more likely to respond in anger and hostility.

---

91. Frost, *The Road to Missional*, 123.
92. Frost, *The Road to Missional*, 123.

> The church I was heading for on the other hand seemed to know very little about their neighbourhood. Not only were they unaware of the man on the corner only a few hundred yards from their door, they were also unaware of the rich ethnic diversity that surrounded them and certainly had little desire to reach out and encounter that diversity. Not surprisingly this church was shrinking. And the parishioners were withdrawing in fear and denial, talking about removing the last row of pews so that the seats did not look so empty. We live in a strange world when the homeless are better acquainted with their world and can respond better to changes and transitions than the church does.[93]

This radical contrast between the homeless man and a local church in the same area reveals the reality of most churches in multicultural cities. Based on her observation Sine boldly asserts that the homeless are better that the church in understanding and communicating with their diverse neighbors.[94] In this picture, we can diagnose the church as being sick not because it is shrinking, but because it loses sight of its incarnational nature. In other words, maintaining an incarnational ecclesiology in the church is imperative, and it leads us to move toward being a multicultural church in the multicultural United States.

All in all, though no previous scholars have directly addressed the impact of the missional church movement on the multicultural church movement, it is clear that the missional church movement, by emphasizing the nature of the church as being sent, contextual, and incarnational, gives us room to look at the multicultural church as a form that God wants us to take in order to be faithful to his calling in the twenty-first century.

New Perspectives on the Homogeneous Unit Principle

For some church leaders, one of the biggest challenges in pursuing the multicultural church is a presupposition that the multicultural church is abnormal and in opposition to the homogeneous unit principle (HUP)—both cannot coexist. This dualistic black and white approach leads them to choose one position— either the HUP or the multicultural church—and to exclude the other. In reality, however, there is no church which is either totally homogeneous or which is completely multicultural with no homogeneity. What, then, is a correct and desirable understanding of the HUP in relation to the multicultural church? In this section, I will present 1) a new perspective

93. Sine, "Where Is Jesus in Your Neighbourhood?"
94. Sine, "Where Is Jesus in Your Neighbourhood?"

on the relationship between the HUP and the multicultural church, 2) Andrew Walls's indigenizing and pilgrim principles and their similarity to McGavran's approach with the HUP, and 3) a case study of a growing multicultural church that shows homogeneity in the midst of diversity. My intent to include the discussion of the new perspectives on the HUP in this theological foundation section is not to argue that the HUP is a main or necessary concept to pursue a multicultural church model but to remove an unnecessary but major conceptual obstacle—the common belief that the HUP and the multicultural church cannot coexist. As evidence to counteract this common assumption, I also will demonstrate homogeneous units' coexistence under the umbrella of multicultural churches by presenting two examples in two different leading multicultural churches: Mosaic Church of Central Arkansas and Mosaic Church in Los Angeles.[95] As a result, this section will reveal the applicability of the HUP, and these new perspectives on it, to the missiological foundation of a multicultural ecclesiology.

Introduction of McGavran and the HUP

In 1955, Donald McGavran, who was born in India as a third-generation missionary, proposed the homogeneous unit principle (HUP) in his book *The Bridges of God*, saying, "It [the growth of People Movements] shows that peoples become Christian fastest when least change of race or clan is involved."[96] After more than a decade with much deliberation, McGavran fully developed and meticulously explained what he meant by the HUP in his book *Understanding Church Growth*: "Men like to become Christians without crossing racial, linguistic, or class barriers."[97]

McGavran defines a homogeneous unit as "a section of society in which all members have some characteristics in common."[98] For McGavran these characteristics included linguistics, ethnicity, economic status, and educational level.[99] Even though McGavran pays attention to racial and ethnic barriers, his primary purpose in defining the HUP is not to segregate diverse people according to various demographic categories, but to proclaim the gospel effectively, which is the church's main task. With regard to the

---

95. Readers also can find an example of such co-existence between homogeneous units and a multicultural congregation in one of the case study churches, Covenant Fellowship Church, as described in chapter 5.
96. McGavran, *The Bridges of God*, 23.
97. McGavran, *Understanding Church Growth*, 223.
98. McGavran, "Homogeneous Unit Principle," 2.
99. McGavran, *Understanding Church Growth*, 225.

multicultural church, he uses the term "conglomerate church" and discusses some exceptions to the HUP principle in metropolitan cities where integration was already taking place. This becomes clearer in the revised version of *Understanding Church Growth* in which Peter Wagner states,

> Only in true social melting pots is [the conglomerate church] a significant option. The old segments of society are in fact breaking down. Many mixed marriages are taking place. Children growing up together in school regard each other as essentially one people. There conglomerate congregations are both possible and desirable. There the best opportunity for growth may truly be that of bringing into one congregation converts of the new people being formed.[100]

Becoming a melting pot is what most cities in America are now experiencing. Thus, George Hunter emphasizes that homogeneity and heterogeneity always coexist in churches, whether they are homogeneous or conglomerate. Hunter says, "Many conglomerate churches are . . . more homogeneous than we thought," and "many 'homogeneous churches' are more heterogeneous than we thought."[101] Therefore, we can assume that there are some relationships between the HUP and the multicultural church, even though the precise nature of those relationships is not yet clear.

Mark DeYmaz's View on Donald McGavran and his HUP

In his e-book *HUP: Should Pastors Accept or Reject the Homogeneous Unit Principle?*[102], Mark DeYmaz, author of *Building A Healthy Multi-Ethnic Church* and *Ethnic Blends*, challenges long-believed assumptions concerning the HUP. Since the introduction of the church growth movement, this principle has been considered a pragmatic method to lead successful church growth measured mainly by numbers, especially in North America. In his book, however, DeYmaz helps us better understand what McGavran believed about the HUP, which most of us apparently do not know well.

DeYmaz claims that McGavran's primary intention for the HUP was not the building of large churches, but was initially about "international, cross-cultural, evangelism and discipleship of the nations."[103] DeYmaz provides two supporting factors that indicate that McGavran considered the

---

100. McGavran, *Understanding Church Growth*, 3rd ed., 261.
101. Hunter, "'Homogeneous Unit' Principle, Revisited."
102. DeYmaz, *HUP*.
103. DeYmaz, *HUP*, 11.

HUP an evangelistic missionary principle concerned with cross-cultural contexts. First, the fact that there was a strict, intentional requirement—cross-cultural experience and fluency in a second language—for applicants to the program which McGavran founded at the Fuller School of World Mission shows that McGavran's intention was to accomplish the Great Commission by using the HUP, especially in a cross-cultural environment. DeYmaz says:

> As a career missionary, it was Donald McGavran's primary concern to reach the nations; and soon he wanted to share his insights with others who desired take the gospel to people in foreign lands who had never heard of the Fuller School of World Mission (1966), he deliberately excluded from the program pastors from North America by requiring three years of cross-cultural experience, validated by one's fluency in a second language, just to get in! Such requirements effectively eliminated most church leaders in North America and more importantly, revealed his heart for cross-cultural application of the principles he espoused.[104]

A letter from Donald McGavran to Martin Marty also supports DeYmaz's contention that McGavran intended for the HUP to become an evangelistic missionary principle. In 1978, six years after North American pastors began studying church growth and adopting the HUP in their own churches, Martin Marty, a history professor at the University of Chicago Divinity School, published a critical article about the HUP titled "Is the Homogeneous Unit Principle Christian?" This spurred an exchange of letters between Marty and McGavran between April and May of 1978. In his letter dated April 24, 1978, McGavran responded to Marty's article by presenting the HUP as an evangelistic principle:

> The HU principle arose facing the three billion who have yet to believe. Tremendous numbers of people are not becoming Christian because of unnecessary barriers (of language, culture, wealth, education, sophistication, imperialistic stance) erected by the advocates. The HU principle was first enunciated by a missionary carrying out what our Roman Catholic brethren call 'the apostolate.' . . . Do, I beg of you, think of it primarily as a missionary and an evangelistic principle.[105]

---

104. DeYmaz, *HUP*, 13.

105. DeYmaz, *HUP*, 15. This is the part of McGavran's letter, dated April 24, 1978, to Martin Marty's article.

While maintaining his belief that each local church has to remove unnecessary barriers for unreached people, McGavran emphasizes that the HUP is "a missionary and an evangelistic principle," applicable to the three billion non-Christians at the time.

The second surprising aspect of Donald McGavran is that he not only advocated unity between brothers and sisters with different racial backgrounds, but he also pursued and practiced fully inter-racial brotherhood and unity, which are the norm in today's multicultural churches, in his own church life. In his letter to Marty, McGavran defended his intent on the use of the HUP, which did not oppose the concept of multicultural/multiethnic churches, by sharing his church life. McGavran wrote:

> Remember also, that those who advocate [the HUP] also advocate full brotherhood. In fact, while I was formulating the HU principle, Mrs. McGavran and I were the only white members of the All Black Second Christian Church of Indianapolis. We have spent more than thirty years living among dark skinned people in India, eating with them, working with them, regarding them in every way as brothers and sisters . . . There is danger, of course, that congregations (whether established according to the HU principle or not) become exclusive, arrogant, and racist. That danger must be resolute . . . So be assured that [Peter] Wagner and I and others using the Homogeneous Unit Principle are with you a hundred percent in your conviction that brotherhood and unity are of the essence. We hope you will be with us a hundred percent in our conviction that unnecessary obstructions to accepting the Christian Faith be recognized and done away with.[106]

Somewhat surprisingly, McGavran and his wife were the sole white members of an African-American church in Indianapolis, because he believed that full brotherhood was as important as church growth. Furthermore, McGavran warns that local churches can become exclusive and racist regardless of the HUP.

This kind of two-stage approach on the HUP introduced by McGavran above is more clearly represented in "LOP 1: The Pasadena Consultation - Homogeneous Unit Principle." The two-stage approach means even though people accept the gospel within their own cultural boundaries (the HUP), as the new Christians mature they are drawn to a broader vision, which means unity in diversity. In this regard, McGavran and the HUP advocates state,

---

106. DeYmaz, *HUP*, 15. This is the part of McGavran's letter, dated April 24, 1978, to Martin Marty's article.

> The Christian attitude to HUs is often called the "realist attitude," because it realistically accepts that HUs exist and will always exist. We would prefer, however, to call this an attitude of "dynamic realism" because we wish also to affirm that HUs can change and must always change. For Christ the Lord gives to his people new standards. They also receive a new homogeneity, which transcends all others, for now they find their essential unity in Christ, rather than in culture.[107]

Furthermore, McGavran asserts, "Not that change can be taken for granted, for it does not always happen automatically. It needs to be actively sought."[108] In this pursuit of such change, McGavran offers some possible models of multicultural congregations.[109] For instance, "Another model a multicultural Sunday congregation which divides into mid-week HU house churches, while a third and more radical way is to work towards integration, although without cultural assimilation."[110]

Based on his understanding of McGavran's primary intention for the HUP and his own ministry experience at Mosaic Church of Central Arkansas, DeYmaz proposes a model called "graduated inclusion," which attempts to harmonize the HUP and multi-ethnicity. Through this model, he insists on the importance and effectiveness of HUP-driven cross-cultural ministry. Mosaic provides ministries and meetings based on language preference: Korean-speaking, English-speaking, Spanish-speaking, and Yoruba-speaking (Nigeria). DeYmaz identifies two reasons why the Mosaic Church provides HUP-driven cross-cultural ministry. First, providing cross-cultural ministry is for the purpose of building relationships and evangelism to first-generation immigrants. Second, cross-cultural ministry provides comfort for internationals who come to Christ but are not yet fluent in English nor familiar with American culture.[111] Alongside of this HUP-driven emphasis, however, Mosaic Church encourages all members' active involvement in the church as a whole regardless of ethnic and language backgrounds.

All in all, Mark DeYmaz not only discovered the primary intention of the HUP (evangelism) but also proved the possibility of its coexistence with diversity. DeYmaz's understanding brings us to a new world where the HUP

---

107. Lausanne Committee, "LOP 1: The Pasadena Consultation," 5.

108. Lausanne Committee, "LOP 1: The Pasadena Consultation," 5.

109. For example, a large city church (or congregation) can have several HU subchurches (or subcongregations) that normally worship separately but sometimes together.

110. Lausanne Committee, "LOP 1: The Pasadena Consultation," 4.

111. DeYmaz, *HUP*, 26.

and multi-ethnicity work together for the fulfillment of the Great Commission in a multicultural church.

Andrew Walls's Indigenizing Principle and Pilgrim Principle

Interestingly, Andrew Walls's concepts of the "indigenizing principle" and the "pilgrim principle," which he describes as "the essence of the Gospel" in *The Missionary Movement in Christian History* are quite similar to McGavran's two-stage approach to the HUP.[112] Walls argues that the indigenizing principle, which states that God accepts people as they are in their own cultures, is biblical as well as historical:

> On the one hand it is of the essence of the Gospel that God accepts us as we are, on the ground of Christ's work alone, not on the ground of what we have become or are trying to become. But, if He accepts us "as we are" that implies He does not take us as isolated, self-governing units, because we are not. We are conditioned by a particular time and place, by our family and group and society, by "culture" in fact. In Christ God accepts us together with our group relations; with that cultural conditioning that makes us feel at home in one part of human society and less at home in another . . .
>
> The impossibility of separating an individual from his social relationships and thus from his society leads to one unvarying feature in Christian history: the desire to "indigenize," to live as a Christian and yet as a member of one's own society, to make the Church . . . *A Place to Feel at Home*.[113]

Walls makes a case for the legitimacy of the indigenizing principle, arguing that a non-believer becomes a Christian in his/her own culture and society, in which he/she feels at home. This, he says, is the essence of the Gospel. Walls' understanding reminds us of McGavran's words in *Understanding Church Growth*: "Men like to become Christians without crossing racial, linguistic, or class barriers."[114]

Walls insists that the indigenizing principle alone is but one side of the essence of the Gospel and requires another side, which he calls the "pilgrim principle". Regarding the pilgrim principle, Walls states,

---

112. Walls, *The Missionary Movement*, 7–9.
113. Walls, *The Missionary Movement*, 7.
114. McGavran, *Understanding Church Growth*, 223.

> Not only does God in Christ take people as they are: He takes them in order to transform them into what He wants to be. Along with the indigenizing principle which makes his faith a place to feel at home, the Christian inherits the pilgrim principle, which whispers to him that he has no abiding city and warns him that to be faithful to Christ will put him out of step with his society; for that society never existed, in East or West, ancient time or modern.[115]

Though non-believers become Christians through the indigenizing principle, that is not the end of their spiritual journey; rather, Christ leads them to the society to which they are not accustomed. Therefore, Walls says, "Every Christian has dual nationality, and has a loyalty to the faith family which links him to those in interest groups opposed to that to which he belongs by nature."[116] This is what God teaches us through the Bible. Peter and Paul clarify Christians' dual identities as simultaneously "temporary residents and foreigners"[117] in the world and "citizens of heaven."[118]

This dual identity as pilgrims makes it possible for us to have a new set of relationships with others in faith. Accordingly, in faith, all Christians are connected to Israel as well as Abraham.[119] This is significant because "[t]he adoption into Israel becomes a 'universalizing' factor, bringing Christians of all cultures and ages together through a common inheritance, lest any of us make the Christian faith such a place to feel at home that no one else can live there; and bringing into everyone's society some sort of outside reference."[120] Thus, the pilgrim principle, as the other side of the indigenizing principle, leads us to willingly embrace others beyond our natural preferences. In other words, Walls demonstrates two different concepts of the gospel—the indigenizing principle and the pilgrim principle—coexisting in harmony and working complementarily.

Consequently, Walls's understanding of the relationship between the indigenizing principle and the pilgrim principle, which reminds us of the two-stage approach to the HUP, also leads us to a new perspective that the HUP, as a way of pursuing and advocating a broader vision of full brotherhood, can coexist within the multicultural church in order to be faithful in our mission, the Great Commission.

---

115. Walls, *The Missionary Movement*, 8.
116. Walls, *The Missionary Movement*, 9.
117. See 1 Peter 2:11 (NLT).
118. See Philippians 3:20 (NLT).
119. Walls, *The Missionary Movement*, 9.
120. Walls, *The Missionary Movement*, 9.

Mosaic Church's Homogeneous Units in a Multicultural Setting

Gerardo Marti's *A Mosaic of Believers: Diversity and Innovation in a Multi-ethnic Church* is another important source that provides a strong example of how the HUP can coexist with diversity in a multicultural church. Marti, a sociologist and pastor, studied another "Mosaic Church"[121] located in Los Angeles. Mosaic Church, one of the most culturally diverse groups in the country, is a multiethnic church which consisted of 32.8 percent Caucasian, 30.3 percent Hispanic, 27.8 percent Asian, and 9.1 percent "others" in 2000.[122] Mosaic is not a multi-congregational church in which multiple congregations worship separately. A multi-congregational church might, for example, have three distinct congregations: one Korean-speaking, one English-speaking, and one Spanish-speaking. Marti's analysis provides interesting and valuable conclusions regarding the multiracial church. According to Marti, even though the Mosaic Church is multiethnic[123] [multiracial], the church is not defined by multiethnic and multiracial characteristics. He says, "Mosaic is attracting an ethnically diverse group of primarily young adult urbanites who are open to artistry, creativity, and change, and who ultimately act on a mission-driven theological framework."[124] In other words, Mosaic has five homogeneous units under the umbrella of one multicultural church. Mosaic became multicultural not through a focus on anti-racism or racial reconciliation, but mainly through the congregation's evangelism-centered commitment to embrace diverse people in the community.

As a result of its evangelistic efforts, Mosaic has become one of the largest multiracial churches in America with five key distinctives—theological, artistic, innovative, age-related, and ethnic dimensions. Marti calls these distinctives "havens," because they show "what they are escaping from and what they are finding shelter in."[125] First of all, the "theological haven" refers to the fact that the Mosaic church declares orthodox Christian beliefs in a culturally relevant manner. Mosaic provides a place for people escaping traditional churches that they consider "boring, irrelevant, closed communities that remain isolated from the world around them."[126] The distinctive

---

121. See http://mosaic.org/
122. Marti, *A Mosaic of Believers*, 29–30.
123. In *A Mosaic of Believers*, Marti did not distinguish the terms between multiethnic church and multiracial church, but later he used "multiracial" for Mosaic Church.
124. Marti, *A Mosaic of Believers*, 3.
125. Marti, *A Mosaic of Believers*, 6.
126. Marti, *A Mosaic of Believers*, 60.

theological haven of Mosaic church plays a crucial role in providing a foundation for overcoming racial and ethnic differences.[127]

Mosaic Church is also characterized by artistic creativity in its worship and events, which Marti calls the "artistic haven." Mosaic's proximity to Hollywood and its high ratio of artistic members allow Mosaic to be a haven for artists. Both the *Los Angeles Times* and knowledgeable people at Mosaic estimate that more than thirty percent of the attendees of Mosaic services are involved in the entertainment industry. Furthermore, the artistic haven of Mosaic creates a space not only for those working in the film industry, but also for those who have a passion for art, including visual and graphic arts, dance, drama, and music. Art draws different people together into Mosaic, committed Christians and non-Christians alike. Mosaic intentionally creates "a forum for dancers, for writers, for actors, for painters."[128] According to Marti, artistic activity is more prevalent than either social services or political activity in the church.[129]

Pastor Erwin McManus describes one of the common characteristics of people at Mosaic: they are innovators who like an adventure. Through what Marti calls the "innovator haven," Mosaic provides "a refuge for people who in other churches have been called mavericks, rebels, or freaks. These are catalysts, change-friendly and change-initiating individuals."[130] In this regard, McManus says:

> They're on the far left of the adapter categorization. Our target group is people on the left side, the innovators and early adaptors. That's our people. We tend to capture a certain dynamic in the way people address change, innovation, and risk, and draw people who are highly intuitive . . . We have people who lean toward innovation, toward change, toward invention, toward risk, toward adventure. We tend to filter out into other churches people who would like stability, security, and predictability. Our clear target group is the former on that scale. [. . .] I think that's our secret.[131]

Through interviews, Marti found that many respondents expressed their preference for change and high expectation of unknown adventures in Mosaic. For instance, someone says, "What I love about [Mosaic] is that it

---

127. Marti, *A Mosaic of Believers*, 59.
128. Marti, *A Mosaic of Believers*, 90.
129. Marti, *A Mosaic of Believers*, 89–91.
130. Marti, *A Mosaic of Believers*, 9.
131. Marti, *A Mosaic of Believers*, 120.

does change. And that's Mosaic, it changes a lot. If it doesn't work, you just try something else."[132]

The fourth haven of Mosaic is the "age haven." Mosaic provides room for those who are mostly single twenties and early thirties in order for them to cultivate leadership, creativity, and meaningful responsibility by escaping churches run by older people.[133] According to Mosaic, the average age of visitors between February 2002 to February 2003 was twenty-six, and approximately ninety percent of them were single. The other 10 percent were mostly married couples who were on average thirty-eight years old. All in all, the "average age of Mosaic's members is thirty-five years."[134]

The fifth and final haven of Mosaic is the "ethnic haven," which means that Mosaic is a community where members constantly emphasize a new, shared religious identity over differing ethnic identities. Mosaic provides a haven for the second- and third-generation young ethnic minorities escaping from home churches that function as ethnic enclaves for their parents and grandparents. For the whites, Mosaic is "a place to experience diversity within a culturally familiar setting."[135] In this regard, one of the pastors at Mosaic, Eric, says, "Our church is not multicultural; it's multiethnic. We have many ethnicities but only one culture. We are all dedicated followers of Jesus Christ."[136] While emphasizing a shared religious identity as a follower of Jesus Christ, minorities and whites experience the fulfillment of their desire to experience ethnic diversity or to escape ethnic enclaves.

In accordance with McGavran's line of thinking, these five distinctive havens of Mosaic represent different kinds of homogeneity in theological belief, age, preference in change and risk-taking, vocation and talent in art, and primary concern with religious identity. Even though members of Mosaic do not share the same ethnic or racial backgrounds, they are homogeneous in these other five categories. Through this case study at Mosaic church in Los Angeles, Marti proves that the HUP can exist under the umbrella of the multicultural church, which most have considered impossible in the past.

---

132. Marti, *A Mosaic of Believers*, 121–122.
133. Marti, *A Mosaic of Believers*, 10.
134. Marti, *A Mosaic of Believers*, 55–56.
135. Marti, *A Mosaic of Believers*, 157.
136. Marti, *A Mosaic of Believers*, 156.

The Development of the Multicultural Church Movement

Even though the history of the multicultural church movement is not long, it would be beneficial to trace the historical changes and events which have shaped it in order to understand and foresee future direction. In this section, I will show where we are based on Mark DeYmaz and Harry Li's stage model.

Mark DeYmaz & Harry Li's Stage Model

In their book *Ethnic Blends: Mixing Diversity into Your Local Church*, Mark DeYmaz and Harry Li provide a map for helping readers understand the historical development of the multiethnic church movement over the last several decades. According to DeYmaz and Li, the growth of the multiethnic church movement can be divided into four stages: 1) the Forerunner Stage, 2) Pioneer Stage, 3) Early Adopter Stage, and 4) Multi-ethnic Mainstream Stage. In fact, the third and fourth stages are the expectations of the future.

First, the Forerunner Stage was marked by three events: 1) the emergence of multiracial churches, 2) the Promise Keepers movement, and 3) the publication of *Divided By Faith* in 2000. Curtiss Paul DeYoung, Michael O. Emerson, George Yancey, and Karen Chai Kim, in their book *United By Faith*, provide a brief overview of how multiracial congregations emerged in the second half of the twentieth century. They present several examples, such as Glide Memorial United Methodist Church (Cecil Williams) in San Francisco, California, Brooklyn Tabernacle (Jim Cymbala) in New York City, and Harvest Rock Church (Che Ahn) in Pasadena, California. Another characteristic of this stage is the birth of a new movement called Promise Keepers. Though the primary concern of this movement was men's spirituality rather than racial reconciliation or multiethnic/multicultural church, Promise Keepers exhibited a break in segregation between different ethnicities and races. DeYmaz and Li describe how "black and white men stood side by side with Latinos and Asians, filling entire stadiums, to sing, study, pray, and even weep together, united by a common faith and their love for Jesus Christ."[137] In addition, speakers within the movement sometimes emphasized unity beyond ethnic and racial differences. Michael O. Emerson and Christian Smith give us a glimpse of the event:

> "Gentlemen," the Promise Keeper speaker bellowed from the podium to a crowd of 60,000 largely evangelical men, "we have grieved our brothers and sisters of color. We have ignored their

---

137. DeYmaz and Li, *Ethnic Blends*, 22–23.

pain and isolation. We have allowed false divisions to separate us. We must reconcile our differences, and come together in the name of the Almighty God! Turn now to a brother of a different race, confess your sins and the sins of your fathers, and pledge to unite!" . . . "What we have witnessed here, men," . . . "is the power of God's unity. You have tasted it. Now pursue it with a passion! Commit to forming a friendship with a brother of a different race. Be yokefellows, carry each other's burdens, and demonstrate true reconciliation!"[138]

The other notable feature of this stage was in publishing. In the beginning of the twenty-first century, *Divided by Faith*, a landmark book by Emerson and Smith, was published by Oxford University Press. In DeYmaz's analysis, this book ended the Forerunner stage and introduced the next stage, which he named the Pioneer stage, of the multi-ethnic church movement. The book is groundbreaking because in it Emerson and Smith use statistical data to reveal the reality of systematic racial segregation in American local churches. Studying both Catholic and Protestant churches, Emerson and Smith showed that only 7.5 percent of American churches are multiracial and the remaining 92.5 are monoracial. Furthermore, local churches and their members play a role in solidifying institutional racism. For example, evangelicals spend over 70 percent of their social time with people from their own congregations.[139] With this finding, Emerson and Smith "propose that one of the best ways to address this systematic problem is to establish multiracial, multi-ethnic churches in which all people are welcome, loved, and cross-culturally engaged."[140] This period was called the Forerunner stage because in it the Homogeneous Unit Principle of church growth prevailed in the local church in the United States.

The second period, according to DeYmaz, was the Pioneer Stage, in which people recognized the "intrinsic value and significance" of the multicultural/multiethnic church and took a risk by pursuing that dream. This stage occupied the first decade of the twenty-first century and was made apparent through several factors. An initial sign of the Pioneer stage was that a great number of books were published with regard to the multicultural/multiethnic church. Also, multicultural churches became a popular subject in periodicals and on the internet. For example, online blogs and newsletters such as *The New Culture*[141] catalyzed the movement, and there is now an

138. Emerson and Smith, *Divided By Faith*, 51.
139. DeYmaz and Li, *Ethnic Blends*, 24.
140. DeYmaz and Li, *Ethnic Blends*, 25.
141. Visit http://renewpartnerships.org/.

increasing number of churches introducing themselves as a multicultural, multiethnic, or multiracial church on their websites.

Further evidence of the Pioneer Stage is found in the emergence of large and well-known conferences on multicultural and multiethnic churches. For instance, Exponential (previously known as the National New Church Conference) in Orlando, Florida hosted pre- and main conference tracks on multicultural/multiethnic churches. In addition, the Ethnic America Network has had similar national conferences. Dave Gibbons, lead pastor of Newsong, a multi-site and multicultural church based in Irvine, California was a main speaker in the 2008 Purpose Driven Network Summit. In the same year, two leaders of the multicultural/multi-ethnic church movement were featured in two different conferences: Efrem Smith was invited to Willow Creek's Leadership Summit, and David Anderson was in the National Outreach Convention.

An additional mark of the present Pioneer Stage was evidenced in some denominational changes, such as in the Evangelical Covenant Church, the Evangelical Free Church of America, and the Reformed Church in America. These denominations are now pursuing the same vision through staffing and creating new departments focused on establishing multicultural churches and pastoral teams. Also, from the two different Mosaic Churches (in Los Angeles and in Central Arkansas), Erwin McManus and Mark DeYmaz relaunched Mosaix, a network that connects multicultural workers, such as church planters, pastors, reformers, and educators, across various denominations. Through this network, they want to catalyze the multi-ethnic church movement by casting vision, networking likeminded church leaders, coaching, and conferencing.[142]

Next, according to DeYmaz, the third step will be the Early Adopter Stage, wherein twenty percent of churches in the United States will have at least twenty percent diversity. In this stage, multicultural/multi-ethnic churches will be more common and gain momentum to move forward. Though no one knows when this will happen, DeYmaz and his colleagues in this movement pray that it will become a reality by 2020.[143]

The fourth and final stage will be the Multi-ethnic Mainstream Stage. DeYmaz hopes, following the success of the Early Adopter Stage, that the multi-ethnic church will become the dominant form of the American church. In other words, DeYmaz expects fifty percent of churches to accomplish fifty percent diversity in the church by the year 2050.[144]

142. DeYmaz and Li, *Ethnic Blends*, 26–27.
143. DeYmaz and Li, *Ethnic Blends*, 28.
144. DeYmaz and Li, *Ethnic Blends*, 28.

Multi-Leadership Stage

Mark DeYmaz and Harry Li's understanding of the multiethnic church movement, described in *Ethnic Blends: Mixing Diversity into Your Local Church* (2010), helps us grasp the different stages of the movement and its distinctions, as well as its leading figures and organizations. Specifically, his descriptions of the two stages which have already occurred (the Forerunner and the Pioneer stages) are accurate and proper. The stages to come (the early adopter stage and the multi-ethnic mainstream stage), however, are an expectation rather than a reality. Though I do hope to see multicultural churches become a major form of churches in the United States, I think we need to pay attention to emerging minority leaders and their multicultural churches. These new figures, non-Caucasian church leaders, such as Korean-American church leaders, and their churches are more than significant because they make it possible for the multicultural church movement to leap to the next stage. I would call this the multi-leadership stage. I observe two characteristics of the multi-leadership stage: 1) the addition of minority leaders to the multicultural church movement, and 2) the moving emphasis of the multicultural church from racial reconciliation to evangelism.

In 2010, Sharon Kim published a book entitled *A Faith of Our Own: Second-Generation Spirituality in Korean American Churches*. In her book, Kim investigates the development and growth of second-generation Korean-American Christians and their churches over ten years (from 1996 to 2006) through various research methods such as participant observation, interviews, surveys, and literature reviews. In this study, Kim reveals that among twenty-two Korean-American case study churches in the Los Angeles area, sixteen (73 percent) have pan-Asian composition and are thus multiethnic and multicultural. Ten pastors out of the sixteen churches identify their churches as in a transitional stage moving into being a multiracial church. According to the Korean American Ministry Resource, there were 56 second-generation Korean-American churches in the Los Angeles area in 2007.[145] Thus, even though the area of this study is limited to the Los Angeles area, we can assume that the data presented by Kim reveals the reality that majority of second-generation Korean-American churches are already multicultural or moving in that direction. For example, pastor Choi of Fruitful Church says, "When we first planted this church ten years ago, we were hoping to develop an Asian American church. Now that we are fully Asian American, I realize that this should not be our final destination. We need to stretch our boundaries even further and become fully multiracial."[146] In fact, in the study

---

145. Kim, *A Faith Of Our Own*, 15.
146. Kim, *A Faith Of Our Own*, 146.

many second-generation Korean-American pastors argue that monoethnic churches are essentially problematic and pursue multiracial churches instead. Furthermore, in her follow-up studies conducted in 2008, Kim found that four of the churches had more than 20 percent non-Asians.

All in all, most second-generation Korean-American churches are either already multicultural churches or are moving in that direction. Though this trend has not been widely observed, the diversity exhibited in the leadership of the multicultural church movement is helping it to become truly multicultural, not only in terms of direction but also in terms of those spearheading it.

Conclusion

The multicultural church is not a new Christian invention of the twentieth century; the church was multicultural from its beginning. Nevertheless, Christians in general have sometimes misunderstood the Bible and have therefore, within the American historical context, supported the racist ideology of white superiority and black inferiority, based on the "curse of Ham." White American Christians in the nineteenth and twentieth centuries also used anthropology and psychology, measuring human skull sizes and employing eugenics and IQ tests, as scientific instruments for proving white superiority and black inferiority. Furthermore, white Christian leaders, particularly in the southern United States, influenced American society to legislate this distorted belief (e.g. Jim Crow laws) in order to systematically deepen the advantage of white superiority. On the other hand, another group of people came to the realization of their sin through the biblical understanding of race relations, which espoused equality and tried to remedy the problem of racial discrimination. The Civil War and the Civil Rights Movement were crucial historical events in this regard. In addition, the Immigration Act of 1965 dramatically transformed American society into being multicultural.

In addition to sociopolitical changes and the realization of equality in race relations, some theological recognitions also paved a new way for the multicultural church movement. The biblical understanding of particularity and universality turned the Christian mindset upside down. Through this new interpretation, particularity is now seen as both a blessing and a responsibility for the salvation of all nations. Even though proponents of the missional church movement did not necessarily intend to promote the multicultural church movement, the missional church movement made it possible for the church in North America to embrace its multicultural neighbors. Specifically, the recognition of the nature of the church—being sent, being contextual, and being incarnational—provides a sound theological foundation for the multicultural church, one which I call multicultural ecclesiology. Also, some scholars/practitioners discovered that the homogeneous unit principle and the concept of the multicultural church, which were traditionally understood as opposites, could coexist in a multicultural church. This new understanding both helps us to remove and overcome a conceptual obstacle that the HUP cannot exist in the multicultural church and also even demonstrates the applicability of the HUP for actually enhancing the multicultural character of a multicultural church.

Along with the investigation of historical and theological changes, periodization of the multicultural church movement, based on DeYmaz and Li's stage model, gives us a map for understanding its development. Drawing from their model, we can describe the multicultural church movement as having three stages: Forerunner, Pioneer, and Multi-leadership. The third period has just been revealed, and I call it the Multi-leadership stage because of the emergence of minority Christian leaders within the movement. Although this cannot be easily recognized, multiethnic and multicultural leadership distribution will make a significant difference to the movement. The increasing number of minority leaders in the multicultural church movement will make it more multicultural. Among Koreans, the second-generation Korean-American pastors and their churches represent the group with the most potential in this stage.

4

Study of Four Multicultural Churches

IN THIS CHAPTER, I will analyze my field research conducted in three Korean-initiated multicultural churches and one Dutch-initiated multicultural church. First, I will introduce the churches by describing their histories, their senior/lead pastors, their goals, and what makes each church unique. Then I will discuss the transition process from monoethnic/monocultural church to multicultural one (T-process hereafter) of each church that I found in the research. I also will address the characteristics of the four multicultural churches that can be helpful or applicable for churches that want to become multicultural. Lastly, I will discuss the factors which contribute to why people visit and stay at these multicultural churches and whether or not the multicultural distinctions of the churches are influential in evangelism.

T-processes of Four Multicultural Churches

The field research took place in January and October 2012. Initially, I had selected eight Korean-initiated multicultural churches as candidates for this research, drawing from information acquired through pastors, friends, missionaries, and their church websites. Then, based on those church leaders' willingness to participate in my study and their availabilities, I chose three Korean-initiated multicultural churches and added one Dutch-initiated multicultural church for comparison. The selected churches were Covenant Fellowship Church (Urbana Champaign, Illinois), Lakeview Church (Chicago, Illinois), Renewal Presbyterian Church (Philadelphia, Pennsylvania), and Madison Square Church (Grand Rapids, Michigan). Basic information regarding these case study churches is in presented in Table 1.

Table 1. Basic Information of Four Case Study Multicultural Churches

Church Name	Covenant Fellowship Church	Lakeview Church	Renewal Presbyterian Church	Madison Square Church
Senior/Lead Pastor	Min Joshua Chung	Joshua Kang	Dwight Yoo	David Beelen
Denomination	Non-denominational	Evangelical Covenant Church	Presbyterian Church in America	Christian Reformed Church
Location	Urbana-Champaign, IL	Chicago, IL	Philadelphia, PA	Grand Rapids, MI
Established	1990	1990/ 2004*	1990/ 2006*	1914/ 1970*
Visitation	Jan. 13–15, 2012	Jan. 16–18, 2012 Oct. 20–21, 2012	Jan. 19–22, 2012	Jan. 25–29, 2012
Number of Congregations	1 Congregation (in 5 locations)	3 Congregations (including 1 Korean)	2 Congregations **	2 Congregations
Homepage	http://cfchome.org/	http://www.elakeview.org/	http://www.renewalchurch.org/	http://madisonsquarechurch.org/

* This mark indicates the year being independent.

** Two campuses of Renewal Presbyterian church (West Philly & Devon) became two independent churches after my field research (March 2012).

To examine the four multicultural churches, I will present an overview of each case study church first, and then analyze its T-process based on its history. After the examination of each church's T-process, I will then discuss the unique steps in its T-process that are applicable as well as significant for other churches that want to become multicultural.

Overview of Covenant Fellowship Church

Rev. Min Joshua Chung, founding and senior pastor of Covenant Fellowship Church (CFC), started a campus church targeting Korean-American students at the University of Illinois at Urbana-Champaign (UIUC) in August 1990. He was a student at UIUC before going to Biblical Theological Seminary in Hatfield, Pennsylvania. While a student at UIUC, he was involved in a student ministry at the school and had gone on evangelistic tours with a praise band named "Alpha and Omega," with the goal of sharing the gospel with the Korean-American young generation. Through this ministry, Chung became well-known as an evangelist among teenage and college-aged Korean-American youth.[1] God inspired Chung to invest his life in college ministry, with a conviction of its importance because college students face critical choices and life decisions about what they want to be and how they want to live for the rest of their lives. What they decide when they leave college often determines the course of their lives, whether they will live for God or live for the world.

Thus, Rev. Chung came to UIUC and started a campus church with some students he already had relationships with. CFC was originally named Korean Christian Fellowship; however, as a number of non-Korean participants began coming, "Korean" was soon removed from the church's name, which then became Covenant Fellowship Church. This occurred about six months after the new planting. There is no clear data regarding when CFC became a multicultural church with over twenty percent of non-Korean members.

In terms of the number of participants/worshippers, CFC started with a few Korean-American students and finished its first year (1990) with about 145 people. By 1999, the number had grown to 715. By 2011, according to the CFC 2011 Annual Report, small group members totaled over 1,200 people in 66 groups with 175 leaders. This number includes CFC's ethnicity-focused ministries, with 241 participants, including 34 leaders in 11 groups. CFC has several ethnic/linguistic small groups including Indian, Japanese, Filipino, Korean, Taiwanese, and international student groups.[2] As of 2012, CFC has approximately 800 Sunday regular worshippers except for during school break periods.

In terms of race and ethnicity, in 2011 the number of Koreans was 45 percent (461) and Chinese/Taiwanese 34 percent (354) of the worshippers. Other racial and ethnic groups accounted for 21 percent (220), which included Indian, Caucasian, Hispanic, African-American, and others.[3] In

---

1. When I visited CFC, I met a Korean-American leader in his mid 40s who joined this church 6 or 7 years ago because of the impact of Chung's evangelistic ministry thirty years prior. He remembered that Chung and his band was quite famous among Korean-American churches at the time that had no such evangelistic praise bands.

2. According to "2012–13 CFC Census," 84 percent of survey participants indicate that English is their primary language followed by Korean (8 percent), Mandarin/Cantonese (6 percent) and others such as Indonesian, Japanese, Spanish, Thai, Taiwanese, and Burmese.

3. Others include Indian, Filipino, Japanese, Indonesian, Vietnamese, Burmese, Malaysian, Singaporean, Pakistani, Mexican, Thai, Turkish, Mongolian, African, and Multi-Racial.

1999, the Korean population was 67 percent and the Chinese 22 percent. Comparison of these two sets of data shows deeper diversification in ethnic/race distribution with a growing number of the Chinese/Taiwanese population. In terms of primary language, English is the most dominant, since it is used by 73 percent of CFC members; other languages used within the church are Chinese (9.4 percent), Korean (9.1 percent), Japanese (2.7 percent), Hindi (1.8 percent), and others (3.9 percent).

One of the most interesting things about CFC is that it has been successful in reaching out to unchurched people. According to a recent CFC census, about 15 percent of its members had no Christian backgrounds before coming to CFC and became Christians through its ministries.[4] Furthermore, there are approximately 150 additional non-Christian small group participants who do not attend Sunday worship services. These people are not yet Christians but are tasting Christian fellowship in a small group setting and are slowly moving toward Christian faith through it. An encouraging aspect of these two groups of people is the fact that many of them are non-Koreans, especially international students. Every year, for instance, CFC reaches out to about 150 students through its international student ministry. In other words, CFC is effectively reaching out to non-believers of different ethnic/racial backgrounds and helping them become Christians and eventually kingdom workers.

With regard to the neighborhood, as a campus church, CFC sees UIUC's students as both their neighbors as well as their target population. Thus, the demographic of UIUC is important. According to UIUC's record on its 2011 Fall Semester enrollment, the school had about 8,000 international students out of approximately 42,000 total students.[5] In fact, UIUC is known for having the second highest number of international students among colleges in the United States.[6] In addition, there are about 9,000 non-white Americans (Asian, Hispanic, African-American, and others) as well. In other words, CFC has an extremely diverse, young neighborhood. CFC considers this reality as a great opportunity for outreach.

As of January 2012, there were 5 full time pastors and two intern pastors on staff at CFC. One intern pastor was Indian-American, and the rest of them were Korean-Americans. However, there were many non-Korean small group leaders.

---

4. Covenant Fellowship Church, "2012–13 CFC Census," 40.

5. University of Illinois at Urbana-Champaign, "On-Campus Fall 2011 Statistical Abstract."

6. O'Shaughnessy, "10 Most Popular Universities"; International Students & Scholar Services, *Fall 2012 International Statistics*.

CFC has several characteristics that distinguish it from other churches. It is a kind of "nomad church" because they move around for Sunday worship. Even though CFC has about 800 Sunday worshipers, it does not own a church building. Therefore, CFC rents five places, including non-church buildings, and it has two regular worship times: 9:30 a.m. and 12:30 p.m.. Meeting and worship locations change often and are updated regularly through its homepage, depending on the situation. For instance, when I visited CFC in January 2012, CFC had worship in one location with about 400 attendants because it was at the end of winter vacation. Rev. Chung said that he often jokes that students who are not smart cannot be a member of CFC because they are moving around all the time.

CFC also can be called *homecoming church*, because a good number of former members visit the church after leaving. Since CFC is located on the campus of U of I at Urbana-Champaign, it is natural that whenever college or graduate students finish their studies, many of them leave CFC as they pursue new jobs elsewhere. However, one thing outstanding to me was that CFC's alumni (old church members) visit the church and maintain a close relationship with CFC and Rev. Chung long after their graduations. When I went to a CFC family retreat, I had a chance to interview a young couple who introduced themselves as regular attendees of this retreat every year. They said that there are many other old members who keep in touch with and visit CFC regularly because they consider CFC as a spiritual home. In fact, on another occasion I found by accident an old member's reply to Rev. Chung's Facebook account: "My sister booked a flight back for the retreat where you do old school praise. She is super excited."

Another important strength, demonstrated specifically in CFC, is a dedication to helping church members develop a prayer life that can assist them in growing spiritually. Donald McGavran asserts that "prayer for spiritual infilling has again and again played an important part in the growth of the Church."[7] Based on my observation, I can easily see how much CFC's strength in prayer has led the church to grow. Many scholars recognize that Christianity in Korea grew rapidly because of its emphasis on prayer through their traditions of Early-Morning Prayer and Friday All Night Long Prayer Meetings. Drawing on its Korean heritage in this area, CFC as a church helps its members to engage in prayer by holding many prayer meetings, such as Early Morning Prayer at 6:30 am on Monday through Friday, Wednesday Prayer Meeting from 10:00 pm to 3:00 am, Thursday Prayer Meeting at 7:00 pm, and Missions Prayer Meeting on Sunday at 7:00 pm.

---

7. McGavran, *How Churches Grow*, 57.

The frequency and the length of these prayer times at CFC are even greater than what is found in most Korean churches, both in America and in Korea. In fact, one Caucasian female member of CFC told me how the church has influenced her husband in his spiritual growth through this emphasis on prayer. She said, "I could see my husband's growth through this church; his dedication to prayer . . . Rather than just saying he will pray about something, he actually carves out chunks of time in his schedule to pray, both corporately and personally. This is a priority." Whereas many Christian leaders emphasize the importance of prayer, it is hard to find churches which really commit to prayer to the extent that CFC does.

The T-process of Covenant Fellowship Church

Korean-Am Campus Ministry ↓	Rev. Min Chung planted a Korean-American campus church in UIUC in 1990. He named it "Korean Christian Fellowship."
Influx of Non-Koreans ↓	About six months after the new church planting, non-Korean students started to come. Until this time, Rev. Chung had no intention for the church to be multicultural.
Change Church Name ↓	As non-Koreans came, Rev. Chung changed the church's name into the non-ethnic "Covenant Fellowship Church" by removing the word "Korean," so that non-Koreans could come without the hurdle of an ethnic distinction.
Train People ↓	Rev. Chung started to train people, small group leaders and others, in order to provide a welcoming environment for non-Koreans. Through this training, Rev. Chung aimed to remove cultural hindrances like speaking Korean, and to welcome non-Koreans. He trained small group leaders not only to welcome non-Koreans but also to be able to minister to them in the small group setting with cultural sensitivity.
Adopt Strategic Inequalities ↓	For the sake of the kingdom of God, CFC intentionally appointed less qualified non-Korean members as small group leaders to be trained and equipped in order for them to be able to help and strengthen weak ethnic churches in the future.

Diversify Front Faces ↓	Also, for the sake of getting more diverse people into the church and for maximum impact for the kingdom of God, CFC gave chances, as many as it could, for non-Koreans to be up front as presiders, praise leaders, and worship band members, so that non-Koreans would not feel isolated or intimated; rather, they would know they were a crucial part of CFC.
Provide Ethnic Ministries/ESL ↓	As the number of non-Korean ethnic people increased, CFC decided to provide small groups for the church's ethnic minorities such as Japanese, Chinese/Taiwanese, Filipino, and Indian, as well as other international small groups. In addition, CFC provided ESL classes for those who did not use English as their first language.
Hire Indian-Am Intern Pastor	CFC hired an Indian-American intern pastor.

Characteristics of the CFC's T-process

CFC has several unique distinctions that promote its T-process: one clear target group, emphasis on inclusive personal evangelism, ethnic ministries, and training people. Even though these characteristics were not implemented for the purpose of moving toward becoming a multicultural church, they have helped CFC's transition from being monoethnic to becoming multicultural.

One Clear Target Group

Even though the degree of diversity in terms of the number of non-Koreans is highest in CFC (55 percent non-Koreans) among the four case study churches, CFC has the clearest target group, college/graduate students, within the context of UIUC. It is characterized by homogeneity in age and economic status among a church population which is ethnically and racially diverse.

Emphasis on Inclusive Personal Evangelism

One of the unique characteristics in CFC's T-process is in emphasis on inclusive personal evangelism. While meeting Rev. Chung for an interview and conversation, he repeatedly emphasized how he encourages CFC's members by saying "Whoever you meet in your neighborhood, in class, in the office, or elsewhere, love them, pray for them, share with them the gospel." Since CFC started as a campus church, the usual focus for evangelism is classmates or roommates, people who have different ethnic/racial backgrounds in many cases. Active daily evangelism without racial/ethnic distinctions has made it possible for CFC to have extensive ethnic diversity in the church.

Ethnic Ministries

Ethnic ministries such as Indian, Taiwanese, Filipino, Japanese, Korean, and international student small groups have accelerated the multicultural character of CFC. According to the Institute of International Education's annual survey, UIUC has the second largest number of international students among colleges and universities in the United States, 8,683 students in 2012.[8] In this given situation, ethnic ministries play a crucial role in attracting and transforming the ethnically/racially diverse (international) students at CFC. According to CFC's 2011 Annual Report, English is the primary language for 73 percent of its members; in other words, at least 27 percent of CFC members are more comfortable in using their own language instead of English. As a result, 241 people (over 20 percent) including leaders belong to ethnic ministries. In this regard, Tony Thomas, an Indian-American intern pastor, says, "The church always emphasized learning to pray for your own people group and have a heart for them. Also, the church supported various ethnicities to develop ministries within the church to reach their own people."

Unlike the assumption that ethnic small groups and ethnic ministries hinder the unity of the multicultural church and cause segregation among different ethnic groups, we can find that some multicultural churches, like CFC, effectively employ ethnic ministries based on the primary languages of each ethnic group. For example, Mark DeYmaz and Harry Li insist on the usefulness of ethnic ministries in their book *Ethnic Blends*. According to DeYmaz and Li, Mosaic Church of Central Arkansas "began to make room for language-specific small groups that could meet at the church" in 2006.[9] Mosaic has four different language groups—Korean, Yoruba, Spanish, and English. Through each ethnic/linguistic fellowship, which they call "graduated inclusion," Mosaic could have "a both/and approach to

---

8. O'Shaughnessy, "10 most popular universities"; International Students & Scholar Services, *Fall 2012 International Statistics*, 4.

9. DeYmaz and Li, *Ethnic Blends*, 107–111; Mark DeYmaz, *HUP*, 26–27.

evangelism, discipleship, and leadership development, involving the entire congregation."[10] The purpose of the Homogeneous Unit Principle (HUP)-driven approach, providing ethnic ministries, is mainly for two reasons: "First, for the purpose of evangelism—to preach and share the gospel in a way that is most accessible to the 1.0s [first-generation immigrants] we are trying to reach. Second, to establish an initial level of comfort for internationals coming into the church who are not yet fluent in the language or culture of the United States."[11] In *Building a Healthy Multi-Ethnic Church*, we can find the same approach in Village Baptist Church at Beaverton, Oregon. As people from different cultures and ethnic groups have come to Village, the church has developed several ethnic/linguistic fellowships such as Indian, Hispanic, Korean, and Chinese in order to become a healthy multi-ethnic church.[12]

Training People

The T-process of CFC teaches us the importance of training. As we see in Chart 1, it seems the T-process of CFC is much simpler than the other three case study churches, although the percentage of non-Koreans (or non-Caucasians) is the highest. When I asked a question about what kind of transition methods CFC adopted to become a multicultural church, Rev. Chung's first and foremost emphasis was on "training people." For him, training people has two layers. First, CFC has trained people not to be a hindrance but to welcome non-Koreans into the small group. Second, CFC has trained small group leaders not only to welcome non-Koreans but also to be able to make them into disciples. Most pastors of multicultural churches would agree on the importance of training people in order for congregations to welcome different ethnic/racial people. What makes CFC unique and effective in terms of training can be found in two things: the training tool and its goal. Many pastors who pursue the goal of becoming a multicultural church try to change members into having proper minds and attitudes toward different ethnic people through vision sharing, preaching, and teaching; the effect is not easy to measure. In the case of CFC, Rev. Chung considers the small group to be the crucial tool for training both members and small group leaders. Furthermore, the goal of training people in the small group is not merely to be hospitable to non-Koreans, but to disciple them as well. In other words,

---

10. DeYmaz and Li, *Ethnic Blends*, 108–109.
11. DeYmaz and Li, *Ethnic Blends*, 109.
12. DeYmaz, *Healthy Multi-ethnic Church*, 166–167.

if non-Koreans stay at CFC, they will likely become future disciplers/leaders through their small group participation.

Tony Thomas, an intern pastor, describes the process of how CFC elects and trains leaders as such:

> 1. **Plug into church:** Have people who are part of the church (freshmen or newcomers in general) be part of a small group and, attend weekly meetings, and get acclimated to the church in general
>
> 2. **Helpers Program:** By their second or third year, we learn from small group leaders a person's spiritual maturity, faithfulness, character, etc. and select them to be part of the "Helpers Program," which is a series of lectures on basic of spiritual growth and leadership as a way to train them to be helpers in the small groups (not an official leadership position).
>
> 3. **Co-Servant:** After successful completion of Helpers Program—we again see if leaders would recommend them to become leaders of a small group. Through the evaluations and pastor and other church leaders' discernment we then ask if people will choose to serve as small group leaders.
>
> 4. **Servant:** Within small groups we have co-servants and then servants. Servants are the main small group and bible study leader. Co-servants support the servant and are being trained and do different administrative tasks as needed. People are usually co-servants for 1–2 years before they can become servants (again, they must be recommended before becoming servants—same as prior process).
>
> 5. **Other Ministry Leadership:** Beyond the small group system, there are various other means of serving—through different ministries, being a coach for small group leaders, being a church officer, etc. It is a mix of appointment and volunteer system for those different types of roles.
>
> **Note:** Usually ethnic bible study leaders have gone through the regular small group system before leading in ethnic ministries.[13]

This uncommon but extensive training in relation to small groups makes CFC members and regular attendees have a strong commitment to various ministries. Young people have lots of energy, and they are looking for something valuable to invest themselves in. CFC challenges the congregation

13. Tony Thomas, e-mail message to author, December 20, 2012.

to be strongly committed and brings them a high standard of Christian living through small groups, leaders' training, prayer meetings, etc. CFC's Servant Meeting Commitment Sheet shows how much this training and emphasis on commitment can affect a Christian's life. It provides the following summary of a leader's requirement in terms of attendance: Saturday Servants (Leaders) Meeting (8:00 a.m.–12:30 p.m.), Sunday Service, Small Group (M,T, or W), Friday Large Group, Small Group Leaders Preparation and Prayer (do independently), and Small Group Leaders Evaluation and Prayer (do independently) and Servants' Retreat (once a year).[14] In this commitment, CFC also requires a minimum GPA and a good attitude toward CFC, encouraging leaders to be good examples for others. This is the secret of how CFC has become successful in making the church multicultural, through its emphasis on "producing Kingdom workers."

Overview of Lakeview Church

Lakeview Church originally started as the English ministry (EM) of the Lakeview Korean Presbyterian Church (LKPC), located in Niles, Illinois, in 1990. LKPC was planted in 1977 by Rev. Jong-Min Lee with an emphasis on the education of the next-generation of Korean-Americans. Nevertheless, like other Korean churches in America, LKPC found that conducting an English ministry was not easy, and this area did not grow until Rev. Joshua Kang came to LKPC in 1996. When Rev. Kang came to LKPC as the EM pastor, there were only 25 EM members. Before coming to LKPC, Rev. Kang was the EM pastor of Youngnak Presbyterian Church of Los Angeles, one of the largest Korean churches in the United States. As the EM ministry grew to about 300 members under his leadership, it found that the limited facilities of LKPC could not accommodate both congregations (Korean speaking congregation and EM) together any more. As a result, with the blessings of the first-generation Korean congregation, EM of LKPC became an independent Lakeview Church (Lakeview hereafter) and moved to Northbrook, Illinois in 2004. Soon after Lakeview became independent, it intentionally pursued the goal of becoming multi-ethnic; that is the reason they removed "Korean Presbyterian" from their name. In 2006, Lakeview also launched its second campus at Palatine, Illinois and became a multisite church. In 2010, the Palatine Campus moved to a new Vernon Hills Campus, hiring an Anglo teaching pastor in order to reach more diverse people. Hiring an Anglo pastor helped Lakeview to be more diverse because his presence increased

---

14. Covenant Fellowship Church, "CFC SERVANTS MEETING COMMITMENT SHEET."

the racial diversity among the leadership of Lakeview. While pursuing being a multi-ethnic church in both campuses, in 2011 Lakeview also merged with a small Korean immigrant church that had ownership of the church building that Northbrook rented. Lakeview became a multicultural, multi-site church with three congregations (two English-speaking congregations and one Korean-speaking congregation) in two locations. Among the three, two congregations are multicultural (Northbrook and Vernon Hills), and the Korean congregation is mono-ethnic (Northbrook Korean[15]).

In terms of the number of worshippers, Lakeview has an average of about 470 Sunday worshippers including children in three congregations. According to Jana Holiday, a full-time female Anglo staff, the Northbrook congregation has about 200 adults and 50 children, the Vernon Hills campus has about 70 adults and 30 children, and the Northbrook Korean campus has about 100 adults and 20 children. In terms of ethnic and racial backgrounds, Northbrook is probably 70 percent Korean, 20 percent pan-Asian such as Chinese and Japanese, and 10 percent Caucasian and Hispanic; Vernon Hills consists of 50 percent Korean, 35 percent Caucasian, and 15 percent pan-Asian; the members of the Northbrook Korean campus are all Korean.

In terms of neighborhood, the Northbrook campus is located in a Chicago suburb where mostly Anglo-Americans and many Jewish Americans live and not many members or attendees come from this neighborhood.[16] On the other hand, the Vernon Hills campus has many members from the neighborhood. According to the 2010 census, this neighborhood is composed of 65 percent white, 19 percent Asian, and 11 percent Latinos. The Vernon Hills campus is located in a different suburb of Chicago, and it appeals much better to the neighborhood, not because of location, but because of its Caucasian teaching pastor and from its having about 50 percent white members from its beginning.

---

15. Since the Korean congregation (Northbrook Korean Campus) was only recently added into Lakeview, in this paper I will mainly discuss two multicultural English speaking campuses (Northbrook and Vernon Hills).

16. According to 2010 US Census, the demographics of Northbrook, Illinois composed of 84.1 percent non-Hispanic White, 11.7percent Asian, and few others.

The T-process of Lakeview Church

EM in a Korean Church	Lakeview began as the EM of Lakeview Korean Presbyterian Church (LKPC) in 1990.
Hire Rev. Joshua Kang	In 1996, Rev. Joshua Kang came to LKPC as the EM pastor. There were only 25 congregants in the EM. Under the outstanding leadership of Rev. Kang, the EM congregation grew continually.
Influx of Some Non-Koreans	As the EM congregation grew, some non-Koreans started to come and join, such as Filipinos, Japanese, and Chinese.
Have Autonomy	The first-generation Korean leaders, the senior pastor, and the session allowed the EM to become autonomous in finances and governance. The EM appointed deacons and elders and used their finances by their own will without paying any money to the Korean side. As a result, before becoming independent, the EM saved several hundred thousand dollars.
Become Independent	As Lakeview's EM grew and reached about 300 Sunday worshippers, Lakeview Korean Presbyterian Church's building could not accommodate both congregations. To grow continually, the EM and KM harmoniously came to the conclusion that the EM should become independent.
Relocation & New Name	To be independent, the Lakeview EM moved out, rented a different church building, and chose a new name—Lakeview Presbyterian Church. Lakeview simply removed the word "Korean" from its name, but kept the rest of it, because of its good relationship with the mother church.
Vision Casting	As soon as Lakeview became independent, Rev. Kang took a month off to seek God's will as to what kind of church Lakeview should be. He searched Scripture and had conversations with church leaders. As a result, Lakeview had a three-word vision: seek, transform, and multiply. To foster this multiplication, Lakeview decided to become multiethnic so that they can multiply beyond the Korean ethnic barrier.

Hire Non-Asian Staff ↓	Since Rev. Kang is a 1.5-generation Korean American, he felt he had a limitation for pursuing a multicultural church. Therefore, Lakeview hired several non-Asian staff members to move forward into becoming a multiethnic church.
Grand Opening Event ↓	Lakeview sent out 40,000 invitation cards 4 or 5 times continually before their grand opening in order to reach out to non-Asians. The strategy aimed to have many Caucasians all at once so that they would not be intimidated by all the Asians. At the grand opening in 2004, about 100 Caucasians came, and approximately 20 of them stayed. They became the nucleus for multicultural ministry.
Vision for Multi-site ↓	Even though non-Asians were continually coming, the worship space was already full. Thus, Lakeview prayerfully decided to adopt a multi-site church strategy.
Have a Vision Night ↓	One day Lakeview had a "Vision Night" to start a new campus, with a desire to have 50 founding members. That night, 25 Asians and 25 Caucasians responded to the call and became founding members of the second campus.
Fundraising ↓	Lakeview raised the money for launching the new campus within six months from the vision night.
Launch a Multiethnic Campus ↓	Six months later, Lakeview launched the Vernon Hills campus with a Caucasian campus teaching pastor and 50 initial members.
Send out Mailers	Since then, once or twice a year, Vernon Hills campus has continually sent out mailers in order to reach out to diverse people, especially non-Asians.

Characteristics of Lakeview Church's T-process

Some unique characteristics can be found in Lakeview's T-process: adoption of church planting strategy and multicultural staffing.

Adoption of Church Planting Strategy

One thing special in the Lakeview Church's T-process is its adoption of a modern church planting strategy, which included a "grand opening event" and "sending out mailers." In this process, Rev. Jon Ro, executive pastor, played a crucial role, drawing on his experience as an associate pastor at Community Christian Church in Naperville, a large multi-site model church, where he had experienced a similar church planting strategy. After Lakeview Church moved to a new location as a tenant, the church prepared two things before its "grand opening event" in order to reach out and welcome new people. First, Lakeview remodeled the old church building so that visitors could have a good first impression. Second, Lakeview tried to improve the quality of worship and other ministries, such as its children's Sunday school and youth ministry. Ro says, "We first had to come here and launch a healthy church plant . . . And then from here, we developed this space here into very contemporary style . . . We had . . . to hire the staff and make sure that we had a quality ministry." Then Lakeview planed a "grand opening" to invite its neighbors, especially the Caucasian population, which makes up the majority of the neighborhood in its new location. After setting the date for the event, Lakeview Church sent out 40,000 mailers in the five-mile radius centered on the church building. It sent the mailers out continually during the four weeks before Easter so that neighbors, specifically the Caucasians, would come at one time and feel comfortable with each other. Lakeview also advertised on the radio through a Christian radio station. Finally, Lakeview had two worship services on Easter Sunday to provide more room for guests. As a result, about 100 Caucasians came, and eventually approximately 20 of them stayed at Lakeview Church. Lakeview's is a useful and applicable strategy for a church who wants to become multicultural, but whose church members are mostly of a different race from that of the target population.

As Lakeview Church grew continually after the grand opening event, it decided to launch a multiethnic second campus to grow and reach out to more people that are diverse. In this regard, David T. Olson offers church planting as an effective way of establishing multiethnic/multicultural congregations in dealing with the crisis in the American Church.[17] For the planting of the new campus, Lakeview Church did two things. First, it hired a Caucasian campus teaching pastor who is of the same race of its target population. Second, Lakeview Church had a "Vision Night" in order to share the vision of having a new campus, to gather voluntary founding members, and to raise money for the preparation and launch. As a result, Lakeview Church had

---

17. Olson, *American Church in Crisis*, 156.

50 volunteers who wanted to be founding members of the new campus—25 Asians and 25 Caucasians and Hispanics. Lakeview Church as a community felt that God was pleased with what the church wanted to do through the equal and balanced number of volunteers and the $90,000 commitment (out of a $150,000 target fund) on that day.

Multicultural Staffing

Among the three KIM churches in my field research, Lakeview is the most aggressive church in hiring multicultural staff, as compared to Renewal and CFC. Lakeview has a total of 11 staff members (pastors and directors). There are five Korean-Americans (lead pastor, youth, worship, college, and Korean campus worship director), three Anglo-Americans (campus pastor, children's Sunday school, and community life), one Latina (children's Sunday school), and one half-Chinese half-Korean (executive mission pastor). It is quite diverse staff because of its intentional effort in this area. In fact, most scholars and church leaders in the multicultural church movement (including multiracial and multiethnic) insist that diverse leadership is one of the most crucial elements for developing a multicultural church.[18] Staffing with multicultural leaders is important because it helps facilitate the maintenance of multicultural congregations. Also, diverse leaders can give the impression that different ethnic/racial groups are accepted and represented in the church.[19] In most cases, this kind of diverse multicultural/multiracial leadership comes by the intentional effort of the church leaders, especially the senior pastor. Like the recommendation of many scholars, Lakeview has tried to have racially diverse leaders in both English-speaking campuses. This strategy was powerful when the second campus (Vernon Hills) hired a Caucasian teaching pastor. However, the Lakeview Northbrook (main) campus did not have much development multiculturally even though it has quite diverse leaders from different racial groups. Apparently, the ratio of multicultural staff is outstanding compared to two other KIM churches in my field research, but the effect is not desirable in the main Northbrook campus. What are the reasons? In my observation, if a church wants to maximize the benefit of multicultural leaders, sharing the pulpit is important—that I will discuss more in the next chapter.

---

18. DeYmaz, *Healthy Multi-ethnic Church*, 70–80; DeYmaz and Li, *Ethnic Blends*, 46–47; Yancey, *One Body*, 86–97; Woo, *The Color of Church*, 201–225; Anderson, *Multicultural Ministry*, 103–108; DeYoung et al., *United by Faith*, 177.

19. Yancey, *One Body*, 87; DeYoung et al., *United by Faith*, 177.

Overview of Renewal Presbyterian Church

Renewal Presbyterian Church (Renewal hereafter) was originally the EM of Emmanuel Church of Philadelphia (ECP), a Korean immigrant church planted in 1968. Rev. Henry In-Ho Koh, a 1.5-generation Korean immigrant, was called to be the second senior pastor of ECP in 1972, and his ministry lasted until 1998, when he retired. Since Rev. Koh got saved at a college in the United States, he had a vision for the second-generation of Korean-Americans. Due to this vision, ECP started an English-speaking college ministry in the early 1980s. As the ministry grew, it became an EM primarily for Korean college students, young adults and families in 1990.

In 1993, a Korean deacon was shot and killed in the church parking lot by two African-American teenagers. Even though many members of ECP wanted to relocate the church because of the dangers that came with its lower-income African-Americans dominant urban neighborhood setting, some felt convicted and viewed the shooting as a wakeup call from God. ECP repented because they realized they had not done anything for the neighbors. So, ECP decided to stay there, and then started ministries for the poor in the community, such as tutoring, vacation Bible study, summer camps, etc. ECP also started to give scholarships to a local high school. Because of the incident, ECP, including the EM congregation, saw the needs of the community and started to serve them

With even further growth, ECP's session, the official governing body of the church made up of pastors and elders, encouraged the EM to elect its own elders and to have its own session, and it eventually became independent in 2006. At the time, the new independent church adopted a new church name, Renewal Presbyterian Church. Even after becoming independent, however, Renewal did not move out from ECP, but stayed at the same building for over two years. In early 2009, Renewal purchased an old church building in West Philly and moved into the new meeting place. Renewal moved not because of a bad relationship or conflicts with the first-generation Koreans at ECP, but mainly because of two reasons. First, the facilities of ECP could no longer accommodate both churches because of the growth experienced by both congregations (Korean speaking and EM).[20] Second, since Renewal had a vision to diversify, staying in the Korean church itself became a hindrance.

In April 2009, through a church vote, Renewal decided to become a multi-site church with a vision to spread the gospel throughout the Philadelphia region through multiple local congregations. As a result, the King of Prussia campus was officially launched in 2010 with the addition of a

---

20. According to church record, the number of the congregation was 282 in 2004 and it reached to 340 in 2009 when Renewal moved out of the Korean church building.

new Anglo teaching pastor. In November 2010, the King of Prussia campus moved to its new location in Devon, Pennsylvania.

According to the church document, in 2004, the EM of ECP had 282 members, including 22 percent non-Korean members. In 2009, Renewal had 340 members, with 25 percent non-Koreans.[21] In 2012, the Renewal West Philly (main) campus had about 400 worshippers with about 25 percent non-Korean population, and the Renewal Devon campus had about 100 worshippers with about 50 percent non-Korean population.

In terms of location, the West Philly campus is close to several colleges, including the University of Pennsylvania; on the other hand, the Devon campus is located in a suburban residential area. Due to these regional characteristics, the members of the West Philly campus are mainly college and graduate students. As a result, about 90 percent of the members at the West Philly campus are under 30 years old. In contrast, the Devon campus has diverse age groups from young children to old couples.

The T-process of Renewal Presbyterian Church

Start College Ministry ↓	Emmanuel Church of Philadelphia started its English-speaking college ministry for second-generation Korean-Americans in the 1980s. It became the cornerstone of its EM.
EM in a Korean Church ↓	The college ministry grew and expanded to an English ministry (EM) for all English-speaking congregants in all age groups in 1990.
Start Community Services ↓	In 1993, a Korean deacon was shot in the church parking lot by two African-American teenagers and passed away. It was considered as a wakeup call from God. Emmanuel repented and decided to stay there, and then started ministries for the poor in the community, such as tutoring, vacation Bible study, summer camps, etc. Through the incident and services the EM congregation saw the needs of the community and started to serve them.
Influx of Some Non-Koreans ↓	As the EM congregation grew, it gained some non-Korean members even before pursuing the goal of becoming a multicultural church.

---

21. Data provided by former senior pastor of Renewal Presbyterian Church, Rev Paul Kim.

Become Independent ↓	The EM elected and ordained its own elders, formed its own session, and became an independent church (Renewal Presbyterian Church). Renewal was completely independent in finances as well. This made it possible for the church to save a substantial amount of money for the future.
Vision for Multiethnic Church ↓	Rev. Paul Kim initially shared the vision to become multiethnic in order to be a place where non-Koreans and non-Asians could come without hindrances. The pastoral staff and session formally discussed it and came to agreement easily. The entire church agreed.
Relocation ↓	Even after independence, Renewal, with two Sunday worship services, stayed in the Korean church building and shared facilities with it. However, at some point, the church building and parking spaces could no longer accommodate both congregations (Emmanuel and Renewal). Therefore, at the end of 2008, Renewal bought an old church building and moved to this new location with the blessing of the first-generation Korean-speaking Emmanuel congregation. It was a big step because meeting in a Korean church building had given the impression that Renewal was for Koreans or Asians but not for non-Asians.
Vision for Multisite Church ↓	To spread the gospel in the broader Philadelphia area, God gave the vision of a multisite church to the pastoral staff and elders of Renewal. Renewal had a congregational vote in support of this vision in April 2009.
Hire a Caucasian Pastor ↓	For the new campus, Renewal hired a Caucasian assistant pastor.
Launch a Multiethnic Campus ↓	With the agreement of the congregation, Renewal launched a new Devon campus with ethnically mixed founding members (50 percent Asian and 50 percent non-Asian).
Diversify Leadership	In 2012, the Devon campus ordained four elders, including two Caucasians.

Characteristics of Renewal Presbyterian Church's T-process

The T-process of Renewal has some unique characteristics that can be beneficial to other churches: relocation and starting community services.

Relocation

For Renewal, "relocation," moving out of the Korean church building and into a new location, was a huge step. Unlike Lakeview, Renewal stayed in its old location for about two years after becoming an independent church. Renewal soon discovered, however, that its meeting in a Korean immigrant church's building was a big hindrance for non-Koreans, especially non-Asians. Along these lines, Gary McIntosh and Alan McMahan also suggest "relocation" as the primary option for churches in transition toward becoming multiethnic/multicultural.[22] For McIntosh and McMahan, one key factor regarding relocation is the willingness of existing members to move apart from the left-behind facilities and their memories there.[23] However, in Lakeview's case, it was not a big matter because there was simply no better option. Instead, relocation was seen as the only option for Renewal Church to become a multicultural church. In this regard, Rev. Paul Kim, the senior pastor of Renewal at the time, said:

> I think as long as we were in the Korean church building, no matter what we said on the inside, from the outside it just said, "Oh, the Korean church over there." Because it was. It was a Korean church. Even after we became independent, the person outside wouldn't have known or understood what that meant. I think moving out of our building was a big step, moving out of the Korean church building and getting our own building was a big step.[24]

Rev. Dwight Yoo, former assistant pastor and current senior pastor, said the same thing:

> We realized being in Emmanuel (Korean) Church was limiting, because when people walk by this Emmanuel *kyohoi* [church] they see Korean flags, so they just assume this is for Korean people only. So they kept walking. And if they visited and they walk in and it smells like *jjigae* [a Korean dish with a strong

---

22. McIntosh and McMahan, *Being the Church*, 169.
23. McIntosh and McMahan, *Being the Church*, 169.
24. Paul Kim, interview by author, February 2, 2012.

smell] for some people that's just too much, it's strange, it makes them think maybe this is not for me.[25]

Therefore, for a Korean church that is wanting to become a multicultural church, moving out of the first-generation Korean church's building is a strategically important and huge step to move forward. This process should go together with being independent, or even before it. It would be different in the case of the Anglo-American church or the African-American church. Since they are not considered as foreigners, visitors would not be bothered as much as non-Koreans/non-Asians coming into Emmanuel Church.

Starting Community Services

Starting community services for its neighbors is another extraordinary thing that we find in the T-process of Renewal, because it began after a cruel gunshot incident and the consequent death of a church member. When ECP started to serve the neighborhood after this event, several community services not only changed the relationship between the church and the neighborhood, but also cultivated the congregation's heart to be open towards and love its low-income neighbors, who were mainly African-Americans. According to sociologist Rodney Stark, early Christians' love and charity towards their neighbors had been similarly influential in the Roman Empire, especially when several historical epidemics swept through it, even though Christians were in the minority.[26] When Roman pagans ignored the needs of their sick people and chose to cut their relationships with others to survive, Christians rather demonstrated love in action. This is seen in an excerpt from the Easter letter of Bishop Dionysius from around 260: "Most of our brother Christians showed unbounded love and loyalty, never sparing themselves and thinking only of one another. Heedless of danger, they took charge of the sick, attending to their every need and ministering to them in Christ . . . Many, in nursing and curing others, transferred their death to themselves and died in their stead."[27] The story of how ECP started community services is similar to the story of the early Christians in the Roman Empire.

In 1993, a deacon from the Korean-speaking congregation was killed in a car-jacking by two youths from the neighborhood while waiting in the car for his wife, who was at choir practice. As the teenagers told him to get out, he asked, "Please let me get the baby." But they refused and shot him as he hesitated. He passed away, and they stole the car. Later they dropped the baby off a couple of blocks down. Due to the incident, church

25. Dwight Yoo, interview by author, January 26, 2012.
26. Stark, *The Rise of Christianity*, 73–94.
27. Stark, *The Rise of Christianity*, 82.

members were shocked, and many insisted that they must leave the place saying, "Let's get out of this neighborhood, we don't even belong here, it's dangerous." In the meantime, a local African-American street evangelist came to ECP to ask for forgiveness on behalf of the two youths from the neighborhood. Despite the calls to leave the area, senior pastor Rev. Koh and elders felt convicted that God allowed this to happen because "we have all this money and we drive BMW, Mercedes, we come here every week and we don't do anything for this poor community." So they felt God was rebuking them for their indifference toward their neighbors. They repented and told the church that "this is a wakeup call and we're going to love our neighbors." So the church forgave them, and, rather than leave, started to serve its neighbors in many ways such as starting a scholarship for local high school students, a tutoring ministry, a vacation Bible school, trips to summer camp, a community festival, and so on. It was a turning point for ECP, especially second-generation EM members who were able to help them without a language barrier—to see the needs of their neighbors and to start serving and building a relationship with them.

Even after moving out of the Korean church building, it affected Renewal a lot to pursue reaching out to the neighborhood. Dwight Yoo said, "We still have strong convictions because of that incident—seen the needs in the city, and we have strong convictions to do the best that we can do to serve our neighbors." Renewal provides various serving opportunities for the neighbors and the city of Philadelphia including Lea Elementary School Painting Days, ACTS homeless ministry, Medical Campus Outreach, Bethesda Project (homeless ministry), and Christian Legal Clinics of Philadelphia. A changed heart and love for neighbors do not necessarily lead African-American low-income neighbors to become part of Renewal, but it definitely has led members to open their arms widely to reach out to everyone.

Overview of Madison Square Church

Madison Square Church (Madison hereafter) began in 1914 as a storefront mission called Madison Square Chapel which was an outreach ministry of the Oakdale Park Christian Reformed Church (OPCRC: Dutch speaking congregation in Grand Rapids, Michigan). The Christian Reformed Church (CRC) broke away from the Reformed Church in America (RCA) in the latter part of the nineteenth century, with both denominations initially serving the Dutch Christians in the United States. Rev. Van Wijk, the pastor of the OPCRC, wanted to reach out to non-Dutch people in the Madison Square area, where the upper-middle class and lower working-class white populations lived on two different sides.[28] The lower working class whites were the

---

28. Griffioen, "Madison History," 2.

chosen target group of the Madison Square Chapel, but Madison struggled to reach those who did not speak Dutch. During and after World War II, the population of Madison Square area began to change, and by the 1960s, the majority of the population in the Madison Square area had changed from Caucasians to African-Americans.[29]

Mr. William Navis, a full-time staff member of Madison from 1962 to 1967, made every effort to minister to its multi-ethnic neighbors, particularly its African-Americans, in those days. Nevertheless, the majority of the OPCRC membership pressed Madison to serve only whites. Because of this strong pressure, "he [Navis] decided momentarily that it was 'better that we not contact them, than take them into a hostile environment.'"[30] However, by 1964 and 1965, as white people in the Madison area began moving out to the suburbs, he felt that interracial ministry must take place. Through Navis's efforts, Mr. and Mrs. Toliver became the first black members of Madison on November 5, 1967.[31] In January of 1970, the unorganized Madison Square Chapel became the Madison Square Christian Reformed Church, an independent church in finances and administration.

In the process of Madison moving toward becoming a multicultural church, symbolic decisions were made in choosing pastoral leadership. In 1974, Madison for the first time chose their own pastor, Rev. Virgil Patterson, the third black-ordained pastor in the CRC and the first black CRC pastor in the Grand Rapids area.[32] One year later, in 1975, Madison hired a second black staff member, Mr. Tom Rayser. Having two black staff members soon bore fruit, as "in July of 1975, four black families were baptized into the church. A very positive move [made] toward a well-integrated fellowship."[33]

Despite the progress made in Madison, in 1977 Rev. Patterson resigned due to the racism he encountered in the upper leadership of the CRC denomination. In November of 1977, Rev. David Sieplinga, a white pastor, replaced him. When Tom Raysor also resigned in 1978, Madison called Dante Venegas, a black Puerto Rican from New York City, as its "Minister of Evangelism." After this struggle with racism, the new combination of white (Sieplinga) and black (Venegas) pastors in its new leadership team facilitated a needed racial reconciliation and led to considerable growth during the next few years. In this period, Madison grew from 86 members (27 families) in 1977 to 225 members (50 families) in 1981. In 1982 Rev. Sieplinga moved to Chicago, and Rev. David Beelen, a white pastor, became a co-pastor with

29. Griffioen, "Madison History," 3.
30. Vander Schaaf, "'Square Roots,'" 6.
31. Vander Schaaf, "'Square Roots,'" 9.
32. Vander Schaaf, "'Square Roots,'" 14.
33. Vander Schaaf, "'Square Roots,'" 15. Interview with Virgil Patterson by Douglas Vander Schaaf on 15 November 1978.

Rev. Venegas. The co-pastor system, which shares responsibility equally between black and white pastors, accelerated the growth and multicultural character at Madison. In 1993, the Sunday morning attendance was approaching about 800 people. In 1996, Rev. Venegas moved to a new position, after 15 years of partnership with Rev. Beelen. In 1997, Rev. Samuel Reeves, a black pastor and a PhD graduate of Princeton Theological Seminary, came from Liberia, accepted the call of Madison, and became a co-pastor. When Rev. Reeves returned to Liberia in 2005, Madison decided to use its preaching team—Joy Bonnema (female Caucasian), Cisco Gonzalez (male Hispanic), and Alton Hardy (male African-American)—instead of calling a new co-pastor; they were later ordained as lay pastors.

Due to continuous growth and a desire to reach more diverse people, Madison launched a second campus at Gerald Ford Middle School, about a half mile north of Madison, in 2008. The long-lasting vision of Madison is "to build a community of diverse people who are being transformed by Christ"[34] with an emphasis on anti-racism.

The T-process of Madison Square Church

Outreach of a Dutch church ↓	Madison Square Chapel began in 1914 as a storefront gospel mission of Oakdale Park Christian Reformed Church, a Dutch-speaking congregation. Its target people were the lower working-class Caucasian people in the Madison area.
Changing Neighborhood ↓	After World War II, the population of the Madison area changed from mostly Caucasians to African-Americans.
Decide to Stay ↓	Since Caucasians were the initial target, there was pressure to not minister to African-Americans, and some insisted on moving to another location. However, Madison decided to stay there and minister to the changed population—the poor (black and white)— regardless of racial differences.
Influx of African-Americans ↓	In the 1960s, a few African-Americans joined Madison even before it became an independent church.

---

34. Vision Statement of MSC, see http://www.madisonsquarechurch.org/about_us/our_vision.php.

Become Independent	In 1970, Madison became an independent church. This meant that Madison could make its own decisions in administration, finances, and vision.
Have the First Black Pastor	In 1974, Madison hired Rev. Virgil Patterson, the first black pastor in the Grand Rapids area. He was the third black ordained pastor in the Christian Reformed Church.
Add a Black Staff	In 1975, Madison hired a second black staff member. In July of that year, four African-American families were baptized into the church.
Vision & Diverse Leadership	In 1978, Madison decided to have diverse leaders from different ethnic groups, and made a written policy[35] of multicultural leadership. As a result, from that year on, Madison has had racially diverse leadership including both black and white pastors.
Ministry for Neighbors	In order to help their neighbors and share the gospel with them, Madison began offering various kinds of community services through the non-profit organization "Restorers." This organization was established in 1997 and has expanded the outreach capacity of Madison by meeting the neighborhood's felt needs.
Have Diverse Praise Teams	As Madison continued to grow, it not only incorporated diverse praise team members, but also multiple praise teams with different cultural flavors, such as Anglo style, African-American style, and other styles of music. For Madison, music became very important for embracing different cultures and people.
Cultural Intelligence Training	Madison continually provides multiple training programs in order for whole church staff and congregation can grow in understanding persons of different races and their cultures.
Launch a Multiethnic Campus	Due to the limitation of facilities and the desire to share the gospel with more people in the area, Madison launched a second multiethnic campus in a nearby school in 2008.

---

35. See Appendix D, the "Multicultural Leadership" written policy of MSC. MSC has continually developed and renewed this policy.

Characteristics of Madison Square Church's T-process

The T-process of Madison has some unique characteristics that can be beneficial to other churches: stay with neighbors of different race, systematic care for neighbors, strict diversification of leadership, and cultural intelligence training.

Stay with Neighbors Different from Us

The multicultural characteristics of Madison began with the decision to stay in an area that saw a Caucasian neighborhood become African-American. If relocation was necessary for the KIM churches of Lakeview and Renewal, the decision to stay in the Madison area, where a different racial group took over, was crucial in Madison's T-process. When Madison began its ministry in the area, it did not plan to be a multicultural church, but anticipated sharing the gospel with the local poor white population. However, as the neighborhood changed from white to black, Madison needed to decide to what to do with an unexpected people group. In the history of the American church, it has been a common phenomenon that as urban neighborhood populations would change to a different ethnic/racial makeup, many churches would consequently move to a suburban area. Unlike other churches, Madison decided to stay in the area with their new neighbors. Manuel Ortiz has named this attitude "permanence," referring to the acceptance of significant and rapid change, such as economic or racial changes, welcoming the change, and properly responding to it.[36] Denying the reality or focusing on feelings of fear will cause congregants to be hostile towards their new neighbors and will not win souls. Thus, in terms of becoming a multicultural church, Madison's decision to stay and minister to them became a foundational step for its moving forward. If Madison decided not to stay, the current multicultural Madison would not exist. Madison wanted to stay in the same place not to intentionally become multicultural, however, but to serve its neighboring African-Americans with the love of God. In the same way, Madison also embraced its Hispanic neighbors for the same reason.

Systematic Care for Neighbors

The importance of loving neighbors in the T-process of Madison can be found in the establishment of the non-profit organization called "Restorers" in 1997. Even though Madison had served its neighbors in various ways even before 1997, it started "Restorers" in order to serve its neighbors more effectively and systematically. The ministry of Restorers has been

---

36. Ortiz, *One New People*, 120–122.

developed through the collaboration of Madison and Hall area churches with the leadership of Madison. As a church, Madison has tried to reach out to its neighbors for evangelism; through Restorers, Madison has provided diverse community services in order to meet its neighbors' felt needs. As of 2012, through the ministry of Restorers and in collaboration with it, Madison provides ESL (English as a Second Language) classes, employment assistance, a financial freedom class, tutoring for middle school and high school students, a women's help program, and so on. Even though it cannot be measured how much these direct and indirect community services enhance Madison's multicultural make-up, here is a good example of how community service and the desire to serve neighbors bring diverse people to Madison. When I interviewed Rachael, a single mother who was formerly a drug addict and is now fully recovered, she shared how she became a member of Madison and a Christian. As to the question, "What were the main reasons you first visited Madison? Why did you go and visit Madison for the first time?" she answered:

> I'm in rehab from drugs. I was addicted for about a year, and I was living downtown. I was in recovery, and I was looking for a church to go to, and somebody recommended Madison, [saying] that they were very high and very well-known with the recovery with people in the area, and they supported that very well. Somebody picked me up and took me there. And Teen Challenge was there, are you familiar with them? Teen Challenge is a recovery base program in Muskegon, Michigan, and Madison supports them. They visit Madison a couple of times a year. And they were there visiting the first day I was there, and it was just amazing. I just knew that's where I was supposed to be.

Rachael visited Madison and became a member of it because the church was not only well-known among the needy like her but also overall very supportive. As she shared, Madison made every effort to meet the needs of neighbors as a way of sharing the love of God, sometimes through direct ministry and sometimes through cooperation with others like the recovery ministry team in this story. These continuous efforts to serve neighbors who are in need and the shared vision in the church made Madison hospitable and welcoming.

Strict Diversification of Leadership

The other big step was to hire an African-American pastor and staff member in 1974 and 1975. Even though Madison was a daughter church of a

Dutch church, it decided to have African-American pastors in order to reach out to a changed neighborhood effectively. This approach was successful and consequently accelerated the T-process of Madison. In "We've Come This Far by Faith: The History of Madison Square," the church interprets the impact of this decision positively: "Apparently it [having two African-American pastor and staff] was also 'paying off'. In July of 1975, four black families were baptized into the church—a very positive move toward a well-integrated fellowship."[37]

Later, it further developed such multicultural leadership so that it also included lay leaders such as deacons and elders. In 1978, Madison made an official policy regarding multicultural leadership, formally establishing what had previously been a strong but unwritten value. Multicultural leadership means shared leadership in the church with ethnically and racially diverse people groups. In its written statement regarding this "Multicultural Leadership,"[38] the church describes "why and how Madison considers ethnic and racial diversity in nominating council members and in hiring pastors and staff."[39] It says, "Our commitment to multicultural leadership is tied directly to God's call upon us as a multicultural church. One of the most strategic behaviors of a multicultural church is to ensure multicultural leaders. This is true for council, for staff, and for worship team as well as for other service opportunities." This statement shows how Madison's policy on leadership diversity, in terms of ethnicity and race, extended at that point from having non-Caucasian paid staff to having diversity among all of its leaders, including volunteers.

Along with the intentional multicultural leadership policy, the uniqueness of the T-process of Madison is also reflected in having diverse praise teams. Whereas the other three Korean-initiated multicultural churches play a contemporary style of worship music, Madison has had nine diverse praise teams which reflect different cultures through music. Each worship team, consisting of ethnically and racially diverse members, plays different styles of music with different worship leaders, including a female African-American, a female British-American, a male Anglo-American, and a female Indian-American. In addition, in the 1980s, Madison had two choirs: a traditional choir and a gospel choir. One was primarily white with traditional European choral music, which was led by the Caucasian pastor's wife, and the other was the gospel choir with black gospel music, which was

37. Madison Square Church, "We've Come This Far by Faith: The History of Madison Square."
38. See Appendix D.
39. See Appendix D.

led by an African-American choir director. These diverse praise teams have helped people to experience diversity and have trained congregations to be open to other cultures. A long-term member of Madison since 1969, Robert shares how diverse praise teams and their music have led him to appreciate different cultures and diversity:

> Because of the way I grew up, very traditional and everything else, having a college education, I've always had in my head that what I would prefer would be a High Church. I would like to have a choir sing an introit, as it's called as we're beginning the worship, organ music, the Bible processing down the aisle. And so for a long time, I had a love/hate relationship with Madison, because I don't feel comfortable with saying Amen and Hallelujah, I don't dance around, I don't wave flags [when singing gospel], and when he says, 'Raise your hands,' I'm saying 'Let me worship the way I want, don't tell me what I need to do.' So that's one side, but it's real that is as uncomfortable as I am with a lot of stuff like a lot of the folks worship in a way that I would not normally choose to worship. God is there and He changes lives . . . I meet God there, and as beautiful as the other church is . . . so I can get my fix and I meet God there too . . . I think Madison is closer to God's vision for the church. It's closer to what heaven's gonna be, it's real.
>
> And even though I am not Mr. Whatever, I enjoy the dynamism, I guess maybe I worship that way through them . . . And then the diversity, the multicultural is a blessing and I feel sorry for folks that don't have that. I really do, it's a point of growth.[40]

According to Robert, multicultural music by multiethnic/multiracial music teams has helped him grow in comprehending multiculturalism in the church. Multicultural music helps people to overcome the desire to stay in their comfort zone and leads them to appreciate other cultures and people as well.

Cultural Intelligence Training

One of the unique characteristics of Madison's T-process is in intentional and ongoing "cultural intelligence training" for the congregation as well as staff. Madison's this approach differs significantly from other KIM churches that are focusing on Christian identity as a common ground without taking a serious consideration of the diversity of each people group and

---

40. Interview with a long-term member, January 21, 2012.

culture. Three case study KIM churches try to avoid cultural distinction among diverse people. In contrast, to pursue its vision "to build a community of diverse people who are being transformed by Christ," Madison continually provides multiple training programs focusing on diversity and racial reconciliation such as Breakfast Club, Understanding Racism workshop, Understanding Racism Grow Groups, and New Community Living Conversations, 8-week Sunday School classes, and 8-week sessions of Institutes for Healing Racism.

Several distinctions can be found in Madison's "cultural intelligence training." First, Madison puts priority in diversity and diversity training. To this effort, Madison has assigned a staff to heighten understanding of cultural diversities and differences. Laura Carpenter, an African American woman and director of diversity, finished two-years of anti-racism training, and has been leading the ministry of diversity. Also, all staff and most council members took the Anti-racism workshop. This is important because Soong-Chan Rah says, "If change is to come to the level of cultural intelligence in the church, then significant group learning, particularly for the church leadership, must occur."[41] Second, most programs are not passive informative learning, but participatory and conversational in character. Third, cultural intelligence training in Madison involves group learning such as workshops rather than individual learning. Group learning is important because it brings changes to the entire community. In this regard, Rah says, "One of the lessons of cross-cultural competency, cultural intelligence, and multicultural learning is the importance of group learning. An individual may learn lessons the rest of the community is not learning, which can bring about personal change in an individual without any guarantee of significant changes to the entire community."[42] Fourth, these training events are not one-time occurrences but rather ongoing programs that repeat annually or even several times in a year so that people could have more than one opportunity to participate in the training. In other words, through those programs, Madison continually brings people to the learning circumstance in order that congregants can grow in understanding persons of different races.

Summary of T-processes of Four Multicultural Churches

Based on the information obtained through my field research, the T-processes of all four multicultural churches can be summarized in one chart. In Figure 1 below, we can see what kinds of transition process each church

41. Rah, *Many Colors*, 148.
42. Rah, *Many Colors*, 147.

took intentionally and unintentionally. Based on the analyses of the four transition processes provided in this chapter, I will propose a model transition process in chapter 6. Before offering this model transition process, in chapter 5 I will discuss key findings that are important in understanding multicultural churches, especially KIM churches.

Conclusion

Because one church cannot be the same as any other, these four multicultural churches show very different T-processes demonstrating how they have moved to being a multicultural church from a mono-ethnic, monocultural situation. One thing in common between the KIM multicultural churches' T-processes is their being rooted in the English ministries of Korean immigrant churches and their beginning with an influx of non-Koreans before they decided to become multicultural churches. For these KIM churches, becoming independent was the pivotal point in their T-process. Some steps are predictable such as casting a vision for becoming a multicultural church, having non-ethnic names, and having diverse multicultural staff members. Some are unexpected and surprising, like starting community services for neighbors of different ethnic/racial groups. Each T-process and its unique characteristics give us a glimpse and insight into what such a process looks like in the United States. Based on these T-processes, I will propose a model T-process that will be applicable for any local church that wants to become multicultural.

STUDY OF FOUR MULTICULTURAL CHURCHES   121

Name	CFC	Lakeview	Renewal	Madison
Transition Process	Korean-Am Campus ministry ⇩ Influx of Non-Korean Students ⇩ Change Church Name (remove "Korean," make it neutral) ⇩ Train People ⇩ Adopt Strategic Inequalities ⇩ Diversify Front Faces ⇩ Provide Ethnic Ministries/ELS ⇩ Hire Indian-Am Intern Pastor	EM in a Korean Church ⇩ Influx of Some Non-Koreans ⇩ Have Autonomy ⇩ Become Independent ⇩ Relocation & New Name ⇩ Vision for Multiethnic Church ⇩ Vision Casting ⇩ Hire Non-Asian Staff ⇩ Grand Opening Event ⇩ Vision for Multisite ⇩ Have a Vision-Night ⇩ Fundraising ⇩ Launch a Multiethnic Campus ⇩ Send out Mailers	Start English College Ministry ⇩ EM in a Korean Church ⇩ Start Community Services ⇩ Influx of Some Non-Koreans ⇩ Become Independent (stay in the Korean church) ⇩ Vision for Multiethnic Church ⇩ Vision for Multisite Church (Church-wide vote) ⇩ Relocation ⇩ Hire a Caucasian Pastor ⇩ Launch a Multiethnic Campus ⇩ Diversify Leadership	Outreach of a Dutch Church ⇩ Community Change (Caucasian to African-Am) ⇩ Decide to Stay ⇩ Outreach to non-Caucasians ⇩ Influx of African-Americans ⇩ Become Independent ⇩ Have the First Black Pastor ⇩ Add a Black Staff Member ⇩ Vision & Diverse Leadership ⇩ Ministry for Neighbors ⇩ Have Diverse Praise Teams ⇩ Cultural Intelligence Training ⇩ Launch a Multiethnic Campus
Supplemental Ongoing Process	- Emphasize evangelism - Extraordinarily strong/frequent prayer meeting - Strong training for small group leaders	- Weekly teaching staff meeting - Weekly staff meeting - Send invitation mailer (4/yr) - Having joint worship/events	- Having joint worship/events	- Anti-racism workshop - Worship workshop with emphasis on diversity

Figure 1. Transition Processes of Four Multicultural Churches

5

Key Findings

I WILL NOW DISCUSS the key findings which emerge from my analysis of the case study churches' transition processes as presented in chapter 4. In this chapter I will also discuss the relationship between multicultural churches and evangelism, seeking to determine any connection between a church's multicultural character and its growth, and then describing how multicultural churches can wisely and faithfully do the work of evangelism.

Key Findings from the T-processes of Four Multicultural Churches

I found four key findings related to the case study churches and the characteristics of the T-process among them: 1) the importance of the first-generation's vision and support for the next-generation, 2) the preferred qualifications for the senior pastor of a multicultural church: sharing the pulpit and having a multicultural family background, 3) the impact of having younger church members, and 4) the relationship between multicultural churches and evangelism.

The First-Generation's Vision and Support for the Next-Generation

Even though first-generation Korean-American Christians have limitations in reaching out to non-Koreans in the United States because of language and cultural barriers, still there is room to participate in the multicultural church movement by raising and supporting the generations which will follow them. The T-processes of Lakeview Church and Renewal Presbyterian Church show the importance for these churches of having the first-generation's vision and support for the next-generation, working through the intergenerational conflict that often arises, rather than allowing it to polarize the two generations within the church. In general, second-generation Korean-Americans "characterize the first-generation's religious participation as hierarchical, patriarchal, and static," whereas they consider themselves to be "democratic, egalitarian, and dynamic."[1] Additionally, in many cases, second-generation Korean-Americans believe that first-generation Koreans are indifferent towards them and treat them as children, regardless of their social positions and achievements. These perceived mistreatments and the resultant bitterness often cause conflicts between first and second-generation Korean-Americans in the church. Eventually, because of these conflicts, many second-generation Korean-Americans end up leaving their parents' churches.[2] Regarding this situation, Yoo, lead pastor of Renewal West Philly campus, states,

> Most of my friends, in my generation, a lot of them are bitter and they want nothing to do with the Korean churches and I think part of the reason is because there definitely is the sense of feeling controlled and not treated like an adult. I think obviously in Korean culture, age matters . . . So a lot of guys, my age, my generation, they're like just forget it, I'm done. Even recently a friend of mine who is serving as an EM pastor, and the church loved him, it was growing but he just couldn't take it anymore, the relationship with the KM master.[3]

In the midst of these sorts of tense relationships, it is difficult to expect good fruits to come from Korean churches' EM congregations or from second-generation Korean-American churches, because it takes a long time for both to recover from these wounds, and it takes a great deal of energy. Because of this tension, in addition, we can easily find a lack of vision

---

1. Kim, *God's New Whiz Kids?*, 43.

2. Sharon Kim, for instance, after studying twenty-two second-generation Korean-American churches in the Los Angeles area, provides two reasons why the generational gap between first- and second-generation Korean Christians often causes generational conflicts and splits accordingly. First, younger-generation Koreans, influenced by western horizontal egalitarian culture, feel frustrated and offended by the older generation's hierarchical leadership style. A second-generation lay leader says, "The first-generation leadership had the final say over all our decisions . . . I'm respected at my job and have very important responsibilities. However, at my church the first-generation treats me like an incompetent child." Second, often second-generation Koreans feel that the "[Korean] immigrant churches exist to cater exclusively to first-generation needs." As a result, Rebecca Kim states, "many SGKAs [second generation Korean Americans] do not view the immigrant church as their own and are leaving them." See Kim, *A Faith Of Our Own*, 30–33; Kim, *God's New Whiz Kids?*, 43.

3. Dwight Yoo, interview by author, January 26, 2012.

and support from first-generation church leaders for the next-generation in many Korean immigrant churches.

The experiences of Lakeview Church and Renewal Presbyterian Church regarding the relationship between first-generation and second-generation immigrants, however, have been different from those of many other Korean churches in the United States.[4] The atypical and positive experiences displayed in Lakeview and Renewal in this area stem from the first-generation church leaders' efforts which included the following characteristics: 1) having a clear vision for the next-generation, 2) sacrificing for and investing into the next-generation, 3) placing a priority on the second-generation, and 4) providing mentoring for EM pastors by the first-generation senior pastor. These distinct actions need to be discussed, as they provide valuable insight.

First, Jong Min Lee, retired senior pastor of Lakeview Korean Presbyterian Church (LKPC), had a clear vision for the next-generation from the beginning of his church-planting. When Lee came to America in 1973 for further study, he had a desire to get a PhD degree in order to become a seminary professor in Korea. However, when a group of Korean immigrants pleaded with him to start a church in Chicago, he accepted the idea with one restriction—that they were to establish a church for the next-generation. So, Lee and about fifteen young Korean-Americans planted LKPC in 1977. To accomplish his vision "to establish a church for next-generation," Lee proposed five action plans. The first was to join a mainstream denomination. Since he believed that the second-generation of Korean immigrants should become an influential part of American society, he insisted that the church join not a Korean denomination, but a mainstream denomination. For this purpose, he chose the United Presbyterian Church, which had sent missionaries to Korea. In taking this step, he believed that their children would not remain in an ethnic ghetto, but would become main actors on the American stage.

The second action plan was for the church to have its own church building(s). Lee believed that without its own building, it would be difficult to provide a stable and good environment for the next-generation. The third action plan was to have 1,000 congregants. Even though this number did not come from scientific research, Lee believed that to provide good education, the church would need to have enough human resources and power. The fourth action plan was to send missionaries. Lee's ideas on mission were ahead of their time in a Korean church setting, because Korean churches have been interested in missions only since the 1980s.

---

4. Kim, *A Faith Of Our Own*, 30–33; Kim, *God's New Whiz Kids?*, 43.

The final action plan was to build a Christian school. As the American public school system had changed in that Christian elements such as prayer and Bible reading were prohibited in public schools by law in the early 1960s, Lee felt it was necessary to establish a Christian school in order to protect children from secularization and to provide a biblical education. As we see in these five action plans, the vision of LKPC was very clear, very thorough, and was tied into the next-generation from the beginning.

The retired senior pastor of Emmanuel Church of Philadelphia (ECP) Rev. Henry Koh (In Ho Koh) also had a clear vision for the next-generation. The reason for this vision came from his personal experiences. His family immigrated to the United States just after the Korean War in 1954, right after Pastor Koh had finished high school in Korea. He was not a Christian at that time, and he did not become a Christian until he went to college. He entered college wanting to become an engineer, seeking to participate in the reconstruction of a destroyed Korea. However, as a student, Koh met Jesus Christ through the ministry of InterVarsity Christian Fellowship, and this encounter caused him to find his identity in Christ. As a result, Koh changed his life direction and became a pastor. Through this unique experience, Koh received a clear vision to raise the next-generation of Korean-Americans according to God's will. Koh believed that the Korean immigrant church should be a place that would nurture and train these next-generation Korean-Americans in order for them to contribute to the evangelization of the world and the United States. To make this vision possible, Koh felt that instead of remaining a ghetto, first-generation Korean-American Christians needed to raise the second-generation so that they could be influential within mainstream society in America.[5] We can see that the leadership of both LKPC and EPC had a vision for the next-generation from the very founding of the churches.

The second characteristic of LKPC and EPC is that the first-generation congregations sacrificed for and invested in the next-generation. In the early period of LKPC, the church hired a bilingual children's Sunday School director, even though LKPC did not have enough money in its budget for the expense. Due to this shortness of finances, for approximately two years LKPC paid the salary of the bilingual director, but not that of Senior Pastor Lee. During that time, Pastor Lee voluntarily gave up his monetary compensation and worked a paid position as a social worker during the week. As LKPC grew, the church started an EM for young adults, but it did not grow with due at least in part because the EM pastor was only

---

5. In Ho Koh, *Open Talk Show*, "Identity," episode 16, http://ny.cts.tv/ (accessed December 13, 2012; originally aired September 27, 2011).

part-time. Hence, Lee and LKPC decided to hire Rev. Joshua Kang to lead the EM, paying him a relatively high compensation equivalent to the senior pastor's. This act was exceptional, but Lee considered it to be an important investment sowed into the next-generation.

The third characteristic of the first-generation was that these churches put a priority on the second-generation in their ministry decisions. The best example of this prioritization can be found in LKPC's worship times. Even though the first-generation Korean-speaking congregation was in the majority and had authority in decision-making for every aspect of church life, LKPC assigned its best worship time to the EM congregation. While the Korean-speaking congregations had three Sunday morning worship services at 5:30 am, 8:00 am, and 10:30 am, the EM of LKPC had it at 11:45, which was the prime time for Sunday worship in the given situation. By doing so, the EM was able to have various programs and activities in the afternoon, which helped the EM congregation to grow. In addition, when LKPC was able to buy a church building, it also bought a school building that had 29 classrooms. This happened only seven years after LKPC's planting. Because of these classrooms, LKPC was able to start Niles Korean School in 1985 in order to teach the Korean language and culture. Niles Korean School later became one of the largest Korean schools in the United States, having about 500 students. This was possible because it was decided that the education of the second-generation would be the top priority of LKPC. Because of the investment in, and priority given to, the next-generation, LKPC earned a strong reputation for its provision of second-generation Korean-American education, which resulted in more Koreans joining LKPC. Similarly, ECP, too, demonstrated a strong commitment to its second-generation by founding the "Philadelphia Korean School" in 1990.

The fourth characteristic of Lakeview and Renewal is the mentoring provided for the EM pastors by the first-generation senior pastors. In response to the cases of many second-generation Korean-American pastors, who had bad experiences with the first-generation church, Rev. Lee of LKPC and Rev. Koh of ECP made sure to personally mentor their EM pastors. In the case of ECP, Koh worked hard to have a good relationship with his EM pastor, trying to avoid authoritarianism. He believed that to raise a strong next-generation of church leaders, the first-generation senior pastor must share in their daily lives, such as in eating and praying together regularly. Koh encouraged his full-time EM pastor to participate in early morning prayer, as part of the heritage of Korean Christianity, but he also insisted that the part-time EM pastors, who were in seminary, focus on their studies (instead of attending early morning prayer). In ministry, Koh provided critiques and comments on the EM pastor's sermons after listening to sermon recordings. In terms of mentoring, Lee also has been a great mentor to EM pastors. Even now, after being independent of Lakeview, Kang considers Lee to be a spiritual father and often asks for advice regarding his ministry.

Another aspect of the mentoring provided by Lee and Koh, which was strategic and essential for the T-process, was to give the EM pastor both the freedom and opportunity to practice self-governance. In both churches, the first-generation provided for all expenses until the EM congregation was able to pay for the compensation of its own staff. However, even when the EM congregations grew and were able to pay their staff members, the first-generation congregation still did not ask that the second-generation cover various additional payments, such as utility charges and maintenance fees. Therefore, the EM congregations were able to both gradually acquire ownership and also to save up money. As a result, when they became independent, they had enough savings to move out to their new locations. In fact, Renewal was able to buy its own church building when it became independent, a step which was a great advantage in starting a new church.

In addition, Lee and Koh encouraged the EM congregations both to have their own elders and to form their own sessions. By doing so, under the mentoring and supervision of Koh and Lee, the EM pastors were able to safely experience the process of operating a board and the whole aspect of ministry governance. Yoo recalls,

> to give a lot of freedom, I think that was the difference in our church. Our times, like my father [an elder at ECP], they tried their best to encourage like you have to become independent, "you have to financially become independent" and to encourage them "this is how you run a session meeting." And to train them and encourage them to grow up and be independent instead of no, "do it this way, do it this way." "Just think for yourself. You come up with your own elders. You guys make the decision" and just getting a lot of freedom . . . I think that's why it worked for us.[6]

Mentoring provided both the foundation and the momentum for the EMs to become independent smoothly. As Lee and Koh incrementally gave the EM pastors more authority and power to run their own ministries, this process eventually prepared and led the EM congregations to become independent.

In fact, even now Koh is helping second-generation Korean-American pastors in the PCA (Presbyterian Church in America) throughout the United States. He has been serving as the Korean Ministries Coordinator of MNA (Mission to North America) in the PCA and as chairman of Next-Generation Leader Development Committee in the Korean World Mission

6. Dwight Yoo, interview by author, January 26, 2012.

Council for Christ (KWMC[7]). Based on his successful ministry experience, as a respected elder among thousands of first-generation Korean-American pastors, he is still serving, on the one hand, to equip second-generation Korean-American pastors, while on the other hand, he is also trying to help first-generation Korean-American pastors to meet their responsibility to mentor second-generation church leaders.

In many cases, Korean immigrant churches and their first-generation senior pastors and elders treat EM pastors/congregations as children, no matter how old they are and how high they advance in their work places; they do not give them autonomy. In finances and governance, the session or senior pastor of most Korean churches makes every important decision, which, in many cases, does not reflect the EM congregation's voice. The desire to have a voice in decision-making among second-generation Christians, thus, is one of the common reasons why they often look for their own second-generation church, having continually experienced invisible walls and discrimination in this regard.[8] In contrast to this normal predicament, Lakeview and Renewal became independent with the blessing and sacrificial support of the first-generation congregations. This shows the importance of the first-generation senior pastor's vision for the next-generation and his mentoring of the EM pastor in developing KIM churches.

Preferable Qualifications for the Senior Pastor: Sharing the Pulpit and Having a Multicultural Family Background

Are there any advantageous qualifications or methods needed for a senior pastor to be successful in leading the transition from a mono-ethnic church to a multicultural church? If yes, what are they? Can a pastor change something to improve the multicultural character of a church in this regard? Since Korean culture affords senior pastors much more power than pastors in Western culture, the influence of the senior pastor is essential in pursuing the goal of a KIM church becoming a multicultural church.

My field research has found that two things stand out as advantageous qualifications or methods for a senior pastor of a church which is moving toward becoming multicultural. In addition, Yancey offers the helpful principle of "personal skills" in order to be successful in leading a multiracial

---

7. An interdenominational worldwide Korean Christian organization for world mission. See http://www.kwmc.com/.

8. Kim, *A Faith Of Our Own*, 31; Goette, "Transformation of a First-Generation Church," 134.

church.⁹ Personal skills mean 1) sensitivity to different needs, 2) patience, 3) empowering other individuals, and 4) relating to those of different races. These would be universally helpful advice for other churches regardless of any cultural/racial difference. Through my study, instead of personal skills, I found two qualifications for a senior pastor, especially a second-generation Korean-American pastor, to overcome the cultural barrier in developing multicultural character: sharing the pulpit and having a multicultural family background.

First, the senior pastor's sharing the pulpit is one of the most influential ways for promoting multicultural character in the church. In other words, the degree to which the senior pastor can give up and share his intrinsic authority in this area can influence the extent to which the church can develop a multicultural character. The more the senior pastor shares preaching with another pastor of a different race, the more the church becomes multicultural. Since Korean culture is more hierarchical (due to the influence of Confucianism) than Western culture, no matter how much the second-generation Korean senior pastor tries to share power with other leaders there will always be a limit to how far such power-sharing can go. Korean-American pastors who grew up in a Korean family have been greatly exposed to Korean culture but they also live in America. So Korean-American pastors are often bicultural, which is greatly advantageous in the beginning of the transition process of moving from being a mono-ethnic to a multicultural church.¹⁰ Nevertheless, non-Koreans and non-Asians often feel that the Korean-American senior pastor is still too Korean or too Asian in leadership style, which means hierarchical.¹¹ When Korean American senior pastors share the pulpit, this step of power-sharing can enormously help non-Korean and non-Asian members break their perception that Korean American pastors are overly hierarchical. A comment made by Holiday, a Caucasian woman who is the Director of Community Life at Lakeview church, shows how non-Asian members

---

9. Yancey, *One Body*, 118–127.

10. Jana Holiday, a Caucasian female and Director of Community Life at Lakeview church, shared how Rev. Kang's bicultural personality has been advantageous in Lakeview's transition process. She says, "We have seen a lot of situations where many of Pastor Joshua's leadership strengths have really helped us stick it out, so I think we are always in the process of trying to grow as church leadership and then kind of understand where our church's culture is, and because Pastor Joshua is 1.5, he really can be that quasi-father figure, like pastor to a lot of the 1.5 generation, second generation people, so that works really well."

11. Kim, *A Faith Of Our Own*, 30–33; Kim, *God's New Whiz Kids?*, 43; Kwon et al., *Korean Americans and Their Religions*, 14, 83; Kang and Lee, "Differentiation of Self," 23.

perceive the Korean-American senior pastor in terms of his leadership style. Holiday says,

> So when I first came on staff one of the elders [second-generation Korean-American] was talking to me about how things were going and I was like "Fine. Pastor Josh and I", back then we had this one big office all together and I was like "Yeah, you know, we are here, and we work together and it's nice to talk about stuff and its really good and we can communicate pretty well." And the elder looked at me like [saying] are you serious? You can work with him? Because he had this picture of Pastor Joshua in his mind where he was like this traditional Korean pastor and hierarchical and wouldn't be able to relate to me who is a white female. But I was like we have to make it work and we did.[12]

Even though the Korean-American senior pastor and other staff from different races work together harmoniously, people may consider him to be too hierarchical, regardless of his effort and reality. That is why the senior pastor needs to make a strategic change that is "sharing the pulpit" with others who have different racial backgrounds in order to overcome this limitation and misunderstanding for the sake of growing the Kingdom of God.

When the senior pastor shares the pulpit in this way, the church can expect two effects. First, sharing the pulpit with someone of another race/ethnic group helps the congregation to see that this church is not dominated or led by one ethnic or racial group alone. In contrast to these efforts, the respective main campuses of both Lakeview and Renewal did not progress much in this area, as their pastors, though sharing power in many other ways, did not engage the strategy of sharing the pulpit with non-Asian pastor(s). In the case of the Lakeview Northbrook main campus, hiring several non-Asian staff members, though helpful, did not seem to strengthen its multicultural character as much as the Lakeview Vernon Hills campus' choice to employ a Caucasian teaching campus pastor. In other words, if a church wants to become a multicultural church, it must go beyond just employing diverse staff of different racial/ethnic backgrounds to "sharing the pulpit" with them. In this regard, an African-American pastor of a large congregation gives us a clue as to why hiring other staff from different races is less effective if the senior pastor does not share the pulpit. In a discussion with Mark DeYmaz (white), one of the leaders of the multiethnic church movement and author of *Ethnic Blends* and *Building A Healthy Multi-Ethnic Church*, the African-American pastor said,

---

12. Jana Holiday, interview by author, January 18, 2012.

> Mark, if you hire or otherwise empower African Americans only to lead your church in worship, you may inadvertently suggest to people, "We accept them as entertainers." Or if you hire or otherwise empower African Americans only to work with your children, you may inadvertently suggest, "We accept them to nanny our kids." And if you hire or otherwise employ African Americans only as janitors, you are quite clearly stating, "We accept them to clean up after us." It is only when you allow us to share your pulpit, to serve with you on the elder board or alongside you in apportioning the money that we will be truly one with you in the church.[13]

In other words, unless the senior pastor shares the pulpit, people will not believe that the senior pastor and the church really intend to pursue becoming a multicultural church.

Second, sharing the pulpit can meet the needs of diverse people who have different preferences in preaching styles. David Anderson is a good example in this case. As a black pastor of a multicultural mega-church, he strategically shares the pulpit with others. Anderson says, "As the senior pastor, I preached about 65 percent of the time . . . The remaining 35 percent of the time is taken by the other speakers on my team, which consists of one Latino, three whites, and a black."[14] The reason is people's different preferences. He found that white congregants focus on "teaching/information," and black members prefer "preaching/inspiration." In addition, in his church, Bridgeway Community Church, "Hispanic attenders tend to react similarly to the way blacks do. They prefer preaching that inspires. Asians tend to react similarly to whites, preferring teaching."[15] In other words, in a multicultural setting, even if a pastor is excellent in his or her own preaching style, he or she cannot meet the desires of different groups of people. Sharing the pulpit is not easy for most senior pastors, but it is surely a powerful catalyst for improving the level of multicultural character in the church.

For the same reason, a church that wants to become multicultural or to deepen its multicultural character might consider adopting a co-pastor system. When Madison had such a co-pastor system, with two lead pastors from different races (black and white) from 1982 to 2005, it grew dramatically and deepened its multicultural character in many ways. Under this co-pastor system, the two different pastors shared responsibility equally. It gave the impression that each ethnic/racial group was equally important and allowed

---

13. DeYmaz, *Healthy Multi-ethnic Church*, 74.
14. Anderson, *Multicultural Ministry*, 107.
15. Anderson, *Multicultural Ministry*, 107.

people to have ownership in this multicultural church. Therefore, to a pastor who wants to overcome cultural limitations and lead the congregation in moving toward a deeper level of multicultural character, sharing the power and responsibility of the senior pastor with a pastor from a different racial background is a revolutionary, but effective way of bringing change.

Another advantageous qualification for the senior pastor of a multicultural church is having a multicultural family, which includes either having a biracial marriage or having children from different racial backgrounds. While visiting the four case study churches, I felt that the extent of the multicultural character of Madison was much deeper than that of the three KIM churches, largely because it was racially well-mixed both in the pews and on the stage (having whites, blacks, Hispanics, and Asians present). In addition, the music and the general atmosphere during its worship time were both very culturally diverse. Also very important for the strength of the multicultural character at Madison, however, was the senior pastor's culturally diverse family background. Michael O. Emerson and Edward J. Blum, the authors of *People of the Dream: Multiracial Congregations in the United States*, discovered through an in-depth study that twelve percent of the senior clergy members of multiracial congregations have a mixed racial background, whereas only one percent of senior clergies of mixed racial background led uniracial congregations.[16] In terms of cultural/racial background, Madison's lead pastor belongs to the 12 percent. Furthermore, when Emerson and his colleagues visited churches to study multiracial congregations, sixteen pastors among twenty-two senior pastors of these churches had multiracial backgrounds.[17] Whereas all of the senior pastors of the three KIM churches were married to Korean-American wives (i.e., spouses of the same ethnicity) and had Korean-American children, Rev. Beelen, who is white and is still the lead pastor of Madison, was married to a white wife (i.e., also a spouse of the same race), but had three African-American adopted children. In addition, former co-pastor of Madison, Rev. Venegas, who was black Puerto Rican, married a white American wife. In my observation, the senior pastors' multicultural family background speaks to the congregation more loudly than any eloquent sermon, communicating that the pastors belong to all, rather than only to a certain racial group.

Likewise, I found that there are many pastors of successful multicultural churches that have multicultural backgrounds themselves. Dave Gibbons, the

---

16. Emerson and Woo, *People of the Dream*, 88; Woo, *The Color of Church*, 206. For Emerson and Blum, "mixed racial background" includes interracial marriage, grown-up in a mixed-race environment, or having cross-race experiences.

17. Emerson and Woo, *People of the Dream*, 88.

founding pastor of Newsong Church[18], which is one of the largest multicultural churches in the United States, was born to a Korean mother and an Irish-American father.[19] Gibbons then married Rebecca, who is Caucasian. In other words, both from his parents and through his marriage, Gibbons is multicultural. Dirwin L. Gray, the founding and lead pastor of Transformation Church in South Carolina, a multicultural church as well as the second fastest growing church in the United States in 2010, has a biracial marriage background. He is African-American, and his wife Vicki is a Caucasian. People can easily see his multicultural marriage background on the front page of the church's website.[20] David Anderson, founder and senior pastor of Bridgeway Community Church located in Columbia, Maryland, has a biracial marriage too. Anderson, an African-American, married Amber, a woman who is half American and half Korean. Anderson not only ministers to a large multicultural church that has about 3000 multicultural worshippers every Sunday, but is also an author of several books about multicultural churches. Anderson describes his wife's ethnicity as follows in *Multicultural Ministry*:

> My wife, Amber, is Amerasian, which means she is part American and part Asian. Her biological father was an American soldier, and her mother was full-blooded Korean... Most Koreans would never guess Amber is Korean because her almond-shaped eyes are not slanted enough. Most Anglos or African-Americans on the other hand wouldn't see her as "American" because her eyes have just enough slant to them to make her look Asian. Because of her cinnamon-colored skin and dark hair, she has been mistaken for Hawaiian, Latina, Filipino, and a host of other nationalities.[21]

No matter how people assess her ethnic/racial background, no one perceives her as being of the same race as her African-American husband.

Rodney Woo and his wife Sasha are another example of a successful multicultural ministry with a multicultural family background. Rodney Woo, former senior pastor of Wilcrest Baptist Church in Houston, Texas (1992–2010) and the author of several books, including *The Color of Church: A Biblical and Practical Paradigm for Multiracial Churches*, was born with Chinese heritage through his half-Chinese father. Woo's wife Sasha has Hispanic heritage. In one of his books, Woo describes how his biracial and multicultural family

---

18. See http://global.newsong.net/ and http://irvine.newsong.net/.
19. Woo, "Dave Gibbons Is a Church Misfit."
20. See http://www.transformationchurch.tc/ (accessed Dec. 15, 2012).
21. Anderson, *Multicultural Ministry*, 66.

background gave him a strong foundation and advantage for understanding people and growing a multicultural church.[22] Woo says,

> God showed me how the variegated pieces of the puzzle of my own personal life formed a God-shaped pattern and vision. One of the subtle pieces of my puzzle was my own family heritage. My half-Chinese father served as a missionary to Hispanics, African-Americans, and Vietnamese in Port Arthur, Texas . . . My wife, Sasha, also brings a diverse perspective into the ministry with her Hispanic heritage . . . In this divine orchestration of bringing our racially diverse families together, God taught me how important personal relationships are in crossing racial barrier.[23]

Using Woo's racially diverse family background, and under his leadership, God transformed Wilcrest Baptist Church, an all-Anglo declining congregation in a transitional neighborhood, into a multicultural congregation that has more than 60 percent non-white and represents over 44 different countries within its membership.[24]

Based on these findings, we may assume that the senior pastor's multicultural family background can be advantageous in leading a multicultural congregation. Two reasons for why the senior pastor's multicultural family background is advantageous in multicultural churches can be conceivable. First, by providing a deeper understanding on multicultural dynamics, having a multicultural family background can make the senior pastors adept at leading multicultural churches.[25] Second, a senior pastor's multicultural family background could also be advantageous because it can give an impression to the congregation that the senior pastor does not belong to a single racial/cultural group but identifies with more than one culture and/or race.

Young Membership

One of the most outstanding characteristics of the KIM churches is that the congregants in these churches are relatively young. These three churches have two similarities in this regard, as first, the majority of their attendees are in their 20s, and second, the average age is in the 30s. In terms of age distribution, over 90 percent of CFC's members are under 30 years old (18–22 years old: 73.3 percent, 23–29: 14.0 percent, and 0–17: 3.8

---

22. Woo, *The Color of Church*, 4.
23. Woo, *The Color of Church*, 4.
24. Yancey, *One Body*, 35–36.
25. Emerson and Woo, *People of the Dream*, 88.

percent).²⁶ Members who are over 40 years old make up only 1.5 percent. Even though CFC as a church is already 22 years old, most of its members are college students, graduate students, and young professionals. In the past 10 years, the number of children and youth has grown, and CFC is slowly becoming a family church where different generations worship together. Lakeview church also has a young membership. The average age of Lakeview's Northbrook campus members would be in their early 30s, with many college students and singles; on the other hand, the average age on the Lakeview Vernon Hills campus would be 35 years old, with more families than singles. In terms of age distribution, the makeup of Renewal Presbyterian Church is very similar to Lakeview Church. Renewal's West Philly campus has mostly college students and singles; on the other hand, Renewal's Devon campus has more family-oriented members and is multigenerational, although the average age is still young. A shared characteristic of both Lakeview and Renewal churches is that the second campus, which was planted later for the purpose of pursuing the multicultural church model, is more family-oriented than the main campus.

All in all, these three KIM churches consist of principally young members mainly for three reasons. First, the English ministry (EM) of Korean immigrant churches in the United States is still in its early stages. Even though Korean immigration started in 1903, the vast majority of Korean immigrants entered the United States after 1965 due to the Immigration Act of that year.²⁷ Because of the small number of English-speaking Korean-Americans (both pastors and congregants), Korean immigrant churches in the United States began their English ministries (EM) for the next-generation beginning in the late 1980s to early 1990s. LKPC and ECP were forerunners of such English ministries, which they started in 1990. It took time, however, for these to grow because of the lack of English-speaking Korean-American pastors and because most English-speaking second-generation Korean-Americans left the church to study or work. As the number of second-generation Korean-Americans and their pastors increased, the EMs of LKPC and ECP grew and became independent in the 2000s. Another reason why KIM churches (except for the second campuses of Lakeview and Renewal) are young in membership is due to the fact that their members are mainly college or graduate students. CFC started its ministry in 1990, but is the same in this regard. Since college students leave for employment after finishing their studies, it is difficult for all of the three KIM churches which I

---

26. Covenant Fellowship Church, *2011 Annual Report*, 4.
27. Min, *Koreans' Immigration*, 7; Hurh and Kim, "Religious Participation," 19.

studied to have families with children. In other words, the frequent turnover of church members contributes to the young average age.

The third reason why the congregants of the KIM churches are young is in the characteristic of multicultural churches. The multicultural church requires a passion and acceptance for change and for new things, which is more likely to be present among young people. A multicultural church means worshipping together with people who are different from oneself. Without tolerance or passion for embracing differences or change, members of a multicultural church will find it difficult to stay at that church, because a relatively new multicultural church requires frequent changes and many adjustments for it ultimately to progress. In an interview, Holiday, a staff member at Lakeview, mentioned that quick change is one of the main characteristics of Lakeview Church. Such transitions are only possible when people welcome change. According to Gerardo Marti, one of five characteristics of Mosaic, which is one of the largest multicultural churches in the United States, is the young age of its membership.[28] The ages of Mosaic's members are in between peoples' twenties and early thirties. Among several reasons why Mosaic is dominated by young members, one is about rapid change and the acceptance of members. Young people have a relatively change-friendly ideology and try to take advantage of changes in culture. An observation made by an older member of Madison helps us understand how it works. A long-term member said,

> I think one of the reasons it [transition process] worked for Madison, is we started as a mission, and we didn't have a lot of old people. I'm sorry. Well, I'm old now, so I can say that. Because if you have an older congregation for example . . . older people are not going to start saying drums and saxophones and transitioning to gospel music as much. So we didn't have that, these old people at Madison, ever, with this long tradition of worshipping in this European way. And so in the 70s especially, the people who are coming are people who are saying I'm sick of that traditional stuff. I want to reach out and I'm into Levis [jeans] and guitars . . . So I think it's tougher for a church like Oakdale or Fuller [old congregations] to transition than it was for Madison.
>
> Now, . . . folks like myself and Marty we've been around since the late 60s early 70s. So there are many more older folks now but these are folks that bought into it at a much younger age. So we're not the typical older folks. We grew old in this

---

28. Marti, *A Mosaic of Believers*, 153–154.

environment [enjoying new things], not in the traditional environment.[29]

The multicultural church seeks to go beyond tradition and try new things in worship and ministry. This is often difficult for those who are more traditional and for those who want to participate in worship and ministries in the ways that they are used to. Even though Madison has many older people, they are not the typical older generation; they were the people who grew old in an environment that required them to regularly accept new things in their church life. In other words, openness to trying new things in the church became part of their DNA. Therefore, they may be older in terms of age, but they are young in spirit in terms of acceptance of change and differences.

Some Issues of Evangelism in the Four Multicultural Churches

One of the concerns of this study is to find out how a church can effectively reach out to diverse people, who can be difficult to integrate if a church is monocultural, by becoming multicultural. If we can find out why people visit and stay at multicultural churches, this information can help multicultural church leaders to maximize their capacity for evangelism. For this purpose, I will examine the *pull factors* (things that attract people to visit the multicultural church) and *stay factors* (things make visitors stay and become members of the multicultural church) evident within the case study churches. Based on the findings of my research, I will then discuss any correlation between multicultural churches and evangelism.

Pull Factors

To find out the case study churches' pull factors, I interviewed people as to why they visited the multicultural churches. Some of them came without knowing that the churches were multicultural. Others shared reasons that were varied—invitations by church members such as family members, roommates, friends; a good reputation for certain ministries such as college ministry, small group, international ministry, preaching, worship, etc; to make friends; to learn American culture; to be trained; proximity; the denomination; and so on. These reasons are listed in Table 2, which indicates

---

29. Interview with a long-term member, January 21, 2012.

that most people (about 90 percent) become members of CFC through many kinds of human networks, especially friendships.

Table 2. Avenues of Hearing about CFC[30]

1	Friends	328
2	Home Church/YG	166
3	Event	47
4	Dorm-mate	28
5	Family	22
6	Flier	22
7	Quad Day	14
8	Co-worker	2

These survey results in Table 2, however, do not include any references to how much the multicultural character of CFC influenced people in this regard. In other words, I found that cultural/ethnic/racial diversity was not the primary reason for people's choosing to visit the three KIM churches. For example, when I asked, "Did you know that this church was multicultural? Did it matter?" a Chinese international student said, "No, it doesn't matter because whether it is multicultural or not, it would be new to me since I am a foreigner." Rather, CFC's survey results displayed in Table 2 show how people became members of CFC.

On the other hand, I did find that mixed-marriage[31] couples prefer to attend multicultural churches over monoethnic/monocultural ones. When people marry someone from a different ethnic/racial background, a multicultural church is a better choice for both husband and wife because they are both more ethnically "normal" in the church. If a mixed couple goes to

30. Covenant Fellowship Church, "2012–13 CFC Census," 38. YG indicates nationwide Youth Group conference.

31. Mixed-marriage indicates the case that a husband and wife have different ethnic or racial backgrounds.

a monocultural church, one or both of them can be considered to be the stranger. Likewise, when people have a multicultural family background or have experienced cross-cultural relationships extensively, it seems they are more likely to join multicultural congregations. For instance, a white couple chose to join Madison because the husband has many extended family members from different ethnic/racial backgrounds. The white husband stated, "You know we have African-Americans, Jewish, . . . Chinese, Korean in our extended family, not our immediate family. But cousins, uncles, aunts, brothers, sisters, you know, married into all these different races." In addition, there can be a kind of people who want to experience diversity. He also stated,

> In our newcomers' group, it seemed like most of the people in our newcomers' group when we first came here [Madison] last year, with everyone they pretty much came here because it was multi-cultural. That was the thing that drew it. Not just because they were like us that had a lot of different races and ethnic background in the family, but they just wanted to be a part of that. They wanted to experience that even though they themselves were not. But in our newcomers' maybe eight, ten people in it, every single one came here. One of the reasons they came was multi-cultural. And so, that's obviously the big draw at Madison.[32]

In other words, there are different kinds of people to consider in terms of pull factors. One is those who join the multicultural church because of its multicultural character; another is those who join the multicultural congregation due to other factors. Thus, it is difficult to generalize whether being a multicultural is advantageous in evangelism or not. Nevertheless, two things are outstanding in respect to pull factors. First, mixed-marriage couples prefer to join multicultural congregations. Second, human networks—such as friends, family members, coworkers, neighbors—play a crucial role in drawing people into multicultural congregations by inviting or introducing them.

Through my field research, I met and observed several mixed-marriage couples who preferred to attend a multicultural church, because in general, members of multicultural churches seemed to be more open and hospitable to them. Because of this attraction that multicultural churches have for mixed-marriage couples, Rev. Beelen emphasizes the importance of having mixed-marriage couples as a core group. Beelen said,

---

32. Interview with a member, January 20, 2012.

> Over time, people that like the idea and don't know how difficult it is, they come and go. So you have [to have] a core group of people. So that's why marriages are so important. The married couples who are married across race, they can't just pick up and go. I mean they can, but they'll go to a white church or a black church but they don't want either one. They want a mixed church. And because they're married to each other, their commitment is usually deeper than other people.[33]

In other words, mixed-marriage couples are strategically important in terms of developing and deepening a church's multicultural character. Their extraordinary commitment by nature to a multicultural church can blossom when the leaders, especially the pastors, understand their importance and give them more opportunity to participate in ministry. In Madison, one or both of its mixed-marriage couples often stands before the congregation as announcers, prayer servants, and communion servers, and some of them serve as a deacon or elder. Thus, if a church wants to become a multicultural church or to deepen its multicultural character, pastors not only need to understand the importance of these mixed-marriage couples but also to help them find areas where they want to serve.

Stay Factors

Another consideration in relation to multicultural churches and evangelism has to do with *stay factors*, especially in relation to racial/ethnic non-majority[34] visitors. To develop or become a multicultural church, it is crucial to know why non-majority visitors decide to stay at multicultural churches. Knowing stay factors is important because if non-majority visitors do not stay, a monocultural church will not become a multicultural church, and a multicultural church will revert to being a monocultural church.

Through my research, I found several stay factors. I discovered that visitors decided to stay at the multicultural churches for various reasons including good preaching, good worship, the hospitality of the congregation, genuine relationships in small groups, strength in prayer, the probability to grow in the Spirit, conviction by the Holy Spirit, etc. Significantly, these reasons are not unique to multicultural churches, but can be found in monocultural churches too. In other words, I found that visitors stayed and became members of the multicultural churches because of the churches'

---

33. David Beelen, interview by author, January 20, 2012.

34. In this paper non-majority means those who are not dominant in the church. For instance, non-Koreans are the non-majority in the KIM churches.

strength and vitality rather than because of their multicultural characters. Specifically, I can identify two important stay factors from the four case study churches: excellence in preaching and strong small groups.

Excellence in Preaching

The first common stay factor among the four multicultural churches was excellence in preaching. For instance, Rev. Chung, senior pastor of CFC, had been a well-known speaker even before he went to seminary. When he was the leader of a gospel band, he traveled extensively throughout the United States and held evangelistic meetings for second-generation Korean-Americans. Through my participation in a family retreat and the observation of his Facebook account, I easily found testimonies from many people that Chung's messages had changed their lives in dramatic ways. Many of them still remembered messages that Chung had shared many years ago. Also, several CFC members—Koreans and non-Koreans, Asians and non-Asians, long-term Christians and new converts—regardless of their different backgrounds, told me that his message was powerful and touched their lives. One interviewee said that his preaching was more like counseling in the sense that his sermons addressed the points they were struggling with and then gave them biblical answers. Due to his excellence in preaching, Rev. Chung has often served as a main speaker for large-scale Christian meetings. For instance, he was one of the main speakers alongside John Piper and Loren Cunningham at the GKYM Fest (Global Korean Young Adult Mission Festival) in 2012.

In addition, Rev. Kang, too, has been a main speaker for many second-generation Korean-American Christian conferences and other church events. His father, Rev. Dal-Hee Kang, was an especially well-known evangelist, and as a PK (pastor's kid), he has maintained this heritage of being an influential preacher. Rev. Paul Kim, the first senior pastor of Renewal and currently a teaching pastor at Pacific Crossroads Church[35], which is a fast-growing large church in Southern California, is also an excellent preacher. Not only those three KIM churches, but Madison, too, has grown due to its having excellence in its preaching. This group interview at Madison shows how much excellent preaching influenced visitors to stay, even when the visitors initially came because of the multicultural character of the church:

> Shawnee: I want to say this, it [the multicultural factor] brings people here [to Madison] like it brought us here. We were told about this, but it didn't keep us here.

---

35. See http://pacificcrossroads.org/.

Doug: Right, that doesn't keep you.

Shawnee: We came to try it, but that wasn't what we necessarily love about it. It was the word being fed and all of those other things. The multi-cultural was part of the experience and it did bring us through the doors, but it's not enough to keep someone there.

Doug: There have to be other things.

Lora: And you have to feel spiritually fed.[36]

In the case of Madison, even though it experienced substantial growth after becoming a multicultural church, especially since the 1980s, the foremost reason for its growth was the excellent messages of its two co-pastors, Pastor Venegas (black) and pastor Beelen (white). When I visited Madison, Rev. Beelen was teaching homiletics at Calvin Theological Seminary, and Pastor Venegas was known to be particularly gifted in evangelism. Both were skilled, energetic, and passionate in their preaching, and the church grew as a result.

Throughout my interviews, I found that congregants mentioned the importance of high-quality preaching by the senior pastor or campus pastor in deciding whether or not to stay in the church. In other words, one common reason for the growth of the four multicultural churches is excellence in preaching.

Strong Small Groups

Another strong stay factor among the three KIM churches was the strength of their small group ministries. All three KIM churches had particularly strong and diverse networks of small groups. CFC, as a campus church, has a multitude of small groups for college students, singles, couples, couples with children, various ethnic groups, etc. According to their statistics, the number of small group participants in the church is higher than the number of Sunday worship participants. In my field research, CFC members stated that the small group was the primary reason why they stayed at the church. Table 3, "Factors for Staying at CFC," clearly shows that the small group is the most important reason why visitors decide to stay.

---

36. Interview with a group, January 20, 2012.

Table 3. Factors for Staying at CFC[37]

Factor	2009	2010	2011	2012
Small Group	4.11	4.13	4.17	4.07
Sermons	3.65	3.66	3.82	3.81
Friends	3.68	3.71	3.79	3.77
Music/Praise	3.37	3.41	3.54	3.59
Special Events	2.84	2.89	2.87	2.76

[Scale] 5: very important, 4: important, 3: moderately important, 2: somewhat important, 1: not important

Lakeview Church also has diverse small groups based on ages, residential areas, marital statuses, etc. Along with the Sunday worship service, the small group ministry is an essential part of Lakeview Church. According to Jana Holiday, Director of Community Life at Lakeview Church, each week, about 80 percent of the congregation participates in a small group. Rev. Kang's statement provides a glimpse into the importance of small groups at Lakeview Church. He said,

> Small group, we call it the backbone of our ministry. It is through the web of relationships in small group that people feel at home. So each campus have their specific small groups, but some small groups have people who attend both campuses, different campuses, the content of small group time is the same, come together, have fellowship, the main meat of the small group is sharing the Word, how did God speak to you through your private time and praying for one another. And then outside of small group, they get together to celebrate each other's birthdays and small groups take turn visiting the homeless church in Chicago that we have been partnering with for a long time. Every Saturday they have prayer meetings, prayer services so our small groups take turns volunteering to provide meals and their worship together.[38]

Renewal, too, has a strong small group ministry that they have named "community group." When I took part in a community group meeting at Renewal, I was surprised because of the openness and acceptance among

---

37. Covenant Fellowship Church, "2012–13 CFC Census," 39.
38. Joshua Kang, interview by author, January 16, 2012.

its members. In the beginning of the meeting, a female member shared her testimony with tears regarding how she came to believe in Jesus Christ, and who He is in her life. Among its thirteen racially diverse participants, the group leader was Caucasian and there was one biracial couple (Caucasian husband and African American wife). This group also had one seeker Caucasian couple who had left another church several years ago and was looking for a new home church. All in all, this community group looked very healthy in many ways, including racial balance, openness and depth of sharing among its members, and sincerity and eagerness in participation. For these three KIM churches, then, the strength of the small group is a pivotal component in many ways and contributes toward these churches' growth.

There are several important similarities among the small groups of the KIM churches that I studied. First, most small groups met every week or at least every other week. In particular, CFC, which had the highest number of non-believers and seekers among the four case study churches, had small groups which met on a weekly basis. In my personal experiences, I have found many churches that have small groups which meet only once a month because of members' busy schedules. In contrast to this trend, I found that the members of the KIM churches which I studied were eager to take part in small groups, because they believed that it was worth investing their time in this type of authentic Christian community.

Second, one of the main emphases of the small group meetings for these churches was Scripture. For instance, each month Lakeview publishes a daily devotional book named "The Dew," which the congregation uses for both personal QT (quiet time) as well as for small group meetings. Because of this, people focus on the word of God more and share in their groups how they understand the word and apply it. Even though there is a leader for these meetings, the meetings are different from a typical Korean Bible study in the sense that each member has ownership and shares what they have discovered and learned. Within this atmosphere, the leader functions as a facilitator instead of a teacher.

Third, the attitude of small group participants was very sincere in openness and love for one another. As I mentioned earlier, when I went to a small group meeting at Renewal, a female member in her late 30s or early 40s prepared a written testimony and shared it with the group with tears. It seemed to me that such an occurrence was common for these meetings. Her tears and those of other participants demonstrated how much they valued the meeting and invested their time in it.

Fourth, the small group played a crucial role in providing a genuine family-like community where everyone could taste God's love and experience a sense of belonging. George Hunter, one of the leading scholars of the church growth movement, insists in *The Celtic Way of Evangelism* that "belonging comes before believing."[39] Through his research into Celtic evangelism, he found that "Christianity is more caught than taught."[40] Specifically, he asserts that "for many people, the faith is about three-fourth caught and one-fourth taught."[41] Practically speaking, to experience belonging, unchurched people need small communities of believers which small groups can provide.[42] For example, a Japanese member of CFC experienced God's extraordinary love through her small group members. She recalled,

> They threw a baby shower for me when I was pregnant with my first child. CFC baby showers would welcome guys too. I received a gift from a guy who I didn't even know, and he and other guys were actually enjoying hanging around with each other in the baby shower setting. That was an unexpected thing to see, because baby shower should be the most boring event for single guys. So, I got to see something beyond human nature living in them. I got baptized a few years later.

To summarize, I found four similarities in the small group ministries among the three KIM churches which made them strong: frequent participation (every week or at least every other week), Scripture-centeredness, members' genuine and sincere attitudes, and a family-like atmosphere. Encompassing these characteristics, it is apparent that having a strong small group ministry played a major role behind evangelism in the three KIM churches.

Challenges in Evangelism

In addition to looking at the pull and stay factors, it is also important to ask what difficulties KIM churches face in relation to evangelism. Through my interviews, I found that most Asians feel comfortable visiting and attending (English-speaking) KIM churches. Similarly, sociologist Rebecca Kim found that second-generation Asian-Americans feel comfortable with each other because they have several similarities. Second-generation Asian-Americans have a similar story that their parents gave up much and immigrated in order to "give their children a 'better life' and greater educational

---

39. Hunter, *Celtic Way of Evangelism*, 54; Hunter, *Contagious Methodist Movement*, 21–22; Gibbs, *ChurchNext*, 197–201.

40. Hunter, *Celtic Way of Evangelism*, 54.

41. Hunter, *Celtic Way of Evangelism*, 54.

42. Gibbs, *ChurchNext*, 197.

and occupational opportunities in America."[43] Also, Asian immigrant parents are more "strict, conservative, and controlling in their interactions with their children compared with the average white American parents."[44] In personality, second-generation Asian-Americans are usually "quieter, less assertive, and more conservative than non-Asian Americans."[45] According to Kim, Asian-Americans often find similarities in food such as rice, soy sauce, fish sauce, hot pepper paste, sesame oil, ramen noodles, dumplings, and tempura, and so on.[46] In addition to food, Asian-Americans share popular culture and products revealed through Asian-American magazines, films, restaurants, video games, dress codes, etc. In short, Asian-Americans share many similarities compared to the relationship with non-Asians; other Americans treat them as strangers and foreigners regardless of the fact that they were born in America and English is their first language. It is a common question that almost every Asian-American has in an encounter with other Americans: "Where are you from?"[47]

It is culturally difficult for the three KIM churches to reach out to non-Asians. Even though the three KIM churches are multicultural, Koreans and Asians are still more than eighty percent. The high percentage of the Korean and Asian population itself is a big hindrance for both church members and non-Asian visitors. Members often hesitate to invite non-Asians. Some KIM church members think their churches are a Korean church or an Asian church instead of a multicultural/multiethnic church. The hesitation of the members often cools down the activity of evangelism toward non-Asians.

Another difficulty in evangelizing unchurched non-Asians is in the KIM churches' unintended ethnocentrism. Yoo said, "They [Korean-Americans] are not rude, they're not mean about it or anything like that, but I think sometimes they just are more comfortable sticking with Korean friends . . . they're very ethnocentric, without even realizing it, you only hang out with Koreans, you only talk to Koreans." This tendency is especially strong among those who grew up in places that have many Koreans, such as Los Angeles or New Jersey. Some Asian members admit to having a strong Korean culture in KIM churches, but they do not think it is a hindrance for them.

43. Kim, *God's New Whiz Kids?*, 91.
44. Kim, *God's New Whiz Kids?*, 91.
45. Kim, *God's New Whiz Kids?*, 92.
46. Kim, *God's New Whiz Kids?*, 93.
47. Kwon et al., *Korean Americans and Their Religions*, 59; Takaki, *A Different Mirror*, 1, Takaki also shares his experience that he was often asked "How long have you been in this country?".

KIM churches can overcome these difficulties when they have enough non-Asians in leadership positions and in the congregation's membership at large. When Lakeview and Renewal launched their second campuses with a relatively high percentage of non-Asian founding members, visitors felt comfortable coming to the campuses and easily joined the congregations. Both the Lakeview Vernon Hills (second) campus and the Renewal Devon (second) campus started with a Caucasian teaching pastor which made the campuses more multicultural because of their balanced leadership.

Importance of Intentionality in Evangelism

Even though I could not find a causal link between evangelism and churches' being multicultural except for in the case of mixed-marriage couples,[48] I did find through these case study churches that evangelism is possible when intentional efforts have been made through the cooperation of the church's leadership and its members. For example, Renewal started a small group several years ago named the "Perspectives Group." According to Rev. Yoo, about 80 percent of the church's conversions and baptisms are from this group. Members invite people to this group, saying, "Hey, if you're interested in learning more about Christianity, come to this group, no pressure, we can debate, you can bring up your issues, you can ask any questions you want." Because of such an invitation, Jefferson, who became a Christian through this group, is now one of its leaders.

In comparison to the other three multicultural churches, CFC is more serious about evangelism, and it reveals this intentionality in many ways. First, CFC emphasizes evangelism continually through preaching and other

---

48. An expert and leading scholar of the multiracial church movement, George Yancey argues that according to research, multiracial churches (including multicultural churches in my definition) show higher growth rates than homogeneous churches in the United States. Specifically, Yancey found that "multiracial churches are more likely to have grown over the past year than monoracial churches (66.1 percent [of] multiracial churches have grown versus 57.1 percent of monoracial churches have grown)." Though this statistic is based on a large-scale survey as part of a Lilly study, I am curious about whether one can generalize that multicultural churches are more likely to grow than monoracial churches *because of* their multicultural characteristics. Yancey tests two things—the size and age of churches—because smaller and younger churches might grow faster than larger and older churches. According to him, multiracial churches are larger than monoracial churches. Also, even after adjusting founding dates to compare both multiracial and monoracial churches, the growth rate of multiracial churches is higher than that of monoracial churches. Nevertheless, it is difficult to say that multicultural churches are more likely to grow than monocultural churches *because of* their multicultural characters, as Yancey's data seems to be more correlational. See Yancey, *One Body*, 35–36.

means, so that evangelism becomes for CFC members a core value in their daily lives. During my visitation, I found that Rev. Chung and church members occasionally mentioned the same phrase, "Whoever you meet in your neighborhood, in class, in the office, or elsewhere, love them, pray for them, share with them the gospel." It was more than a catchphrase as it represented both a commitment and a lifestyle. Second, CFC offers several training classes that members can take in relation to evangelism, including understanding the Bible, systematic theology, mission, etc. These classes are led by a pastor or an older member who is usually a seminarian, so that members can be equipped for outreach. Third, CFC offers many programs for evangelism such as ethnic small groups, International Student Connection (conversation partner), Muslim women's group, Moms' group, American culture class, mini Olympics, basketball league, "How to Survive at the U of I," etc. Interview statements by Mark, a Caucasian leader at CFC, and David Kang, Associate Pastor of CFC, give us a deeper understanding of how much CFC as a faith community commits to evangelism. Mark states,

> Connection Groups (which was formally Conversation Friends) is a ministry where volunteers from CFC meet with international students for an hour once every two weeks in a group that normally consists of two volunteers and three international students . . . There are other branches of ISC [International Student Connections] that minister in other ways, including a class that focuses on learning American culture, introductory bible studies for those not familiar with the Bible, a group focused on cultural exchange with Indian international students, a group focused on building relationships with Japanese international students, a group focused on building relationships with Muslim women, and a group of moms that arranges play dates with mothers who are international and married to someone attending school or are attending school themselves. The American culture class meets about every other week for an hour a half and the introductory bible study group meets weekly for an hour and a half. All other groups meet more informally throughout the year.[49]

In addition to these, Kang adds,

> We have many events to invite people, but small group is one of the main avenues where people join our church. With that being said, our whole first month is dedicated to reaching our campus through events such as area info night (we introduce people to what small groups are like), mini-Olympics (this is an

---

49. A Caucasian leader, e-mail message to author, December 1, 2012.

all-day event where small groups participate in events against one another), How to Survive at the U of I (a program on the first day of school that our church provides tips for how to survive at the University. This is a great event to invite new students and people to the campus.) We also have other events such as the variety show (people in our church showcase their talents and this provides an avenue to invite friends/ coworkers who are not a part of our church). During the summer time, we also do outreach since the summer affords more time to invest into the people in our community. So we have picnics, fellowships, and a basketball league to foster outreach.[50]

The purpose of these ministries and events is to build genuine friendships and to "seek opportunities to have deeper spiritual conversations and hopefully have an opportunity to share the Gospel."[51] In CFC's evangelistic endeavors, two things are prominent: variety of outreach programs and intentionality. CFC is exceptionally intentional in reaching out and integrating its target population into its community. CFC also provides countless events, programs, and small groups that try to meet its target population's needs. Through these kinds of cooperative efforts between members and the church, evangelism is very productive. For example, approximately 150 newcomers join CFC each year. In other words, evangelism is in the center of CFC not only in vision or preaching but also in action.

All in all, as to evangelism, becoming multicultural is meaningful for providing a welcoming environment in order to embrace all different kinds of people in a globalized multicultural society. If we understand mission and evangelism as obedience to our calling, as in the story of the Good Samaritan in Luke 10:29–37, we should ask how we can wisely and faithfully reach out to diverse people through local churches in multicultural neighborhoods. Through this study's examination of multicultural churches and evangelism, I came to the conclusion that evangelism must be intentional, and that multicultural churches should provide two things: evangelism training and many entry points (programs, events, small groups). This study, too, shows how human networks such as friendships and kinships are crucial in the multicultural church.

---

50. David Kang, e-mail message to author, February 20, 2013.
51. Interview with a member, December 20, 2012.

Conclusion

Even though all three KIM churches became multicultural after becoming independent, the first-generation's vision and support for their second-generation Korean-American church members, especially among the senior pastors, was crucial in their T-processes. It shows a desirable way for how first-generation Korean-American Christians, who have an extraordinary passion for missions but also have cultural and language barriers at the same time, can actively participate in the multicultural church movement by raising and supporting the second-generation. In fact, the T-processes for the KIM churches, especially Lakeview and Renewal, were the result of the cooperation between the first-generation's laying the foundations and the second-generation's standing on them. In terms of leadership, the senior pastor's willingness to share the pulpit was highly influential, even more so than having diverse leadership. In addition, a senior pastor's multicultural background, such as having a biracial marriage, was also found to be of great advantage in pursuing the T-process. Because a multicultural church demands that its members be more open-minded and have the ability to adjust to many changes, all three KIM churches tended to have younger memberships. Nevertheless, we found that many of these young members, as they aged, remained young in spirit, as the one hundred-year old Madison now has many older congregants who are non-traditional with respect to the acceptance of change and diversity.

With respect to evangelism, this study shows that becoming multicultural is valuable for providing a safe and welcoming community that can integrate diverse people within the globalized multicultural American context. However, it is difficult to find how much this multicultural character is effective in outreach, especially for people of different racial backgrounds. Although this study shows that some people groups, such as mixed-marriage couples and people with diversity in their backgrounds, prefer multicultural churches, being multicultural does not guarantee that people of different ethnic/racial backgrounds will automatically come and join the multicultural church. In other words, even after becoming a multicultural church, the church needs to make every effort to provide reasons for people to come and to invite diverse people. Similarly, it is also apparent from the field research that when people do visit multicultural churches because of their multicultural character, they stay not because of this multicultural aspect, but for other reasons. In my study of four multicultural churches, two stay factors were outstanding: excellence in preaching and a strong small group ministry. If we understand that being a multicultural church is not for the sake of church growth, but for obedience in our calling to reach out to *panta ta ethne*, we must ask how we can faithfully and wisely obey the Great Commission in a multicultural society. In order to accomplish a goal—reaching out to diverse people—multicultural churches must be *intentional* in evangelism and should provide two things: evangelism training and many programs/events for outsiders. In this regard, this study also confirms how human networks such as friendships and kinships are essential in evangelism for the multicultural church. Based on the analyses of the transition processes of the four multicultural churches and the key findings as presented in chapters 4 and 5, I will next propose a transition process model for the churches to become multicultural in chapter 6.

6

The Windmill T-process Model

How to Move toward Becoming a Multicultural Church

BASED ON THE DATA and findings presented in chapters 4 and 5, I will now discuss the applications for Korean immigrant churches and other mono-ethnic/monocultural churches who seek to reach out to their neighbors of different ethnicities/races. The primary application is a proposed transition process that I have developed from my field research and the relevant literature. I call it the "Windmill T-process," and my hope is that it will help monocultural churches move toward becoming more multicultural.

The Windmill T-Process Model

The Windmill T-process consists of ten steps which can be divided into two different groups. The first group includes the steps that are basic and common to the T-processes of most of the KIM churches in my study: checking for feasibility, casting vision, becoming independent, adopting a non-ethnic church name, and relocating. The second of the two groups includes steps that are much more directly connected with and influential in the process of becoming multicultural: serving the neighbor, refreshing the vision, diversifying leadership, promoting cultural intelligence, and having multicultural worship teams.

Group One: 5 Basic Steps

Each step in this first group is a one-time event that can be accomplished at any point in the church's early transitional stages, and the order in which they are to occur can vary in accordance with the unique circumstances of the particular church.

Checking for Feasibility

This step is a prerequisite process that is designed to give an assessment of whether a church will be able to become multicultural or not. Through my field research, I found that churches need to check two important aspects of their fellowships: multicultural friendships and demographics. In a case where a church wants to become a multicultural church, this transition is likely to happen when the pastor(s) and leaders—those who have both power and a voice in the decision-making process—have multicultural friendships and multicultural family backgrounds. McIntosh and McMahan point out that the senior pastor's cross-cultural experience is one of the most crucial factors in the success of becoming multicultural.[1] All of the pastors and leaders from those four multicultural churches came to the same conclusion that pursuing a multicultural church is an extremely hard job that needs lots of energy and time. Having a theology or a sense of conviction of the church's calling to be a multicultural church is not enough to sustain the church through this difficult process. This is why church leaders need to have a sharp assessment of their own multicultural friendships before taking any plans into action. Rev. Paul Kim emphasizes:

> Do you ever go to home of non-Korean-Americans? Does a non-Korean-American ever been to your home? What birthday parties do you go to or weddings you go to? . . . They themselves if the lead pastor or the session members or whatever, if all they have are Korean-American friends and if they only have Korean-American friends and they say we wanna become multiethnic church, I would say I don't think it's going to happen. Because they are not going to attract or even if they came, they wouldn't get embedded or welcome or integrated unless the leadership says hey, come over to my house, our kids will play together, I'll go to your house. These non-Asians or non-Koreans have to feel like they could be part of that community fabric so that happened and again the leadership needs, they have to have it in their personal life.[2]

Therefore, if pastors and leaders of a church want to pursue becoming a multicultural church, they need to examine their friendships and start with that. If they really want, but do not yet have multicultural friendships, they need to start to make friends beyond their ethnicities. In this regard, the senior/lead pastor is more important than the other leaders in terms of impact

---

1. McIntosh and McMahan, *Being the Church*, 169.
2. Paul Kim, interview by author, February 2, 2012.

on the congregation overall. With regard to the congregation's multicultural friendships, the feasibility of transition among second-generation Korean Americans is generally positive. According to Rebecca Kim, a large proportion of second-generation Korean-Americans have ethnically and racially diverse friends. In her survey, she found that "40 percent had mostly an ethnically diverse group of friends; 24 percent had mostly Asian American friends; 24 percent had mostly white friends."[3] Even though statistics in this regard are positive for second-generation Korean-Americans, senior pastors who want to lead their churches toward becoming a multicultural church need to examine their own lives to see if they have multicultural friendships before taking steps toward transition.

Furthermore, if a pastor or leader, especially the lead pastor, has a multicultural family, this, too, is of a great advantage to a church that is wanting to become multicultural. Rev. Beelen, the senior pastor of Madison, is an Anglo-American with Dutch heritage. In my observation, one thing which has been particularly beneficial for him as a pastor of a multicultural church is the fact that he has three African-American adopted children. This deep, personal commitment gives the impression (a genuine one) that Rev. Beelen is closely connected to African-Americans; he and his family are multicultural. Similarly, Rev. Dante, former pastor of Madison and an American with a Puerto Rican heritage, is married to an Anglo-American wife, creating a family makeup which, too, is advantageous. Building on his excellence in evangelism and preaching, his multicultural marriage furthers his multicultural credibility at Madison as a church which has Caucasians, African-Americans, and Hispanics worshiping together.

Another aspect to check before pursuing becoming a multicultural church is the demographics of the church and its neighborhood. All four case study churches had had some non-majority people join them before the churches started to pursue becoming multicultural. All of the leaders of the churches mentioned in their interviews that the transition to becoming multicultural was not easy, but they also all shared that they started by having some non-majorities in their church memberships. Therefore, if a church wants to become multicultural, the leaders need to examine their church to see if it has already some non-majority people. If the church has non-majority people worshiping in it already, it means that the church is attractive for outsiders and is likely to become a multicultural church. Rev. Paul Kim says,

> I would wanna understand their context more or I ask them about their context because some churches, let's say they are 99 percent

---

3. Kim, *God's New Whiz Kids?*, 42.

> Korean-American. They are in a Korean church building and they say we wanna be multiethnic. I'm going to say humanly speaking, that's highly unlikely. The only non-Asian who will come to your church are the non-Asians who are comfortable with and like Asians. That's a very small percentage of the non-Asian world. But even in the Korean-Koreans, you have few non-Asians who do feel comfortable with being in an Asian settings.[4]

Even if the church leaders want the church to become multicultural, but it has no non-majority members, it will be very difficult for it to become a multicultural church and hard to take the next steps in the process of transitioning.

In terms of demographics, diversity in the neighborhood is also important. This is because if different ethnic/racial groups of people are not present in the local area, a church cannot become multicultural. In this regard, Korean-American churches have a great advantage, because they are usually minorities and are often surrounded by non-Koreans and non-Asians. Even with this advantage, however, what I found in this study in relation to demographics is that if a race is dominant (especially Caucasians) in an area, it is difficult for Korean-American churches to bring them into the church. For instance, the Northbrook campus of Lakeview Church is located in a community that has mainly Caucasians, with a small percentage of Asians, based on the 2010 census. Compared to the other three multicultural churches, Lakeview's Northbrook neighborhood is fairly monoracial, and it seems that it is difficult for its neighbors to come to a church that is Asian-dominant.

Manuel Ortiz also points out that studying the demographic information of the neighborhood is the first part of the preparation process for the transition of a church into a multiethnic church.[5] For Ortiz, studying the community, specifically its demographics, is much more than just finding out information about what kinds of people live around the church. Studying the community includes investigating demographics, patterns of migration, economic transitions, racial transitions, and even spiritual transitions.[6] These are significant, because when a church acknowledges this information, the church can properly respond and move smoothly toward becoming a multicultural church like Madison Square Church.

---

4. Paul Kim, interview by author, February 2, 2012.
5. Ortiz, *One New People*, 119–120.
6. Ortiz, *One New People*, 120.

Casting Vision

To transition from being a monocultural church to a multicultural one, casting and articulating vision is an essential process. In my field research, every interviewee, no matter whether they were pastors or laymen, all agreed that pursuing becoming a multicultural church is a difficult job. Thus, if a church does not have a clear vision for the transition, staff members and congregants will not be able to handle the conflicts and issues which can develop and will eventually be hurt due to people's having different understandings of the church's direction.

Through the study, I could identify two different forms of vision in relation to becoming a multicultural church. One form is a vision to pursue to becoming a multicultural/multiethnic church as a value in itself; the other form involves a vision to go to all people in pursuit of fulfilling the Great Commission, regardless of ethnic/racial barriers. The vision of Madison belongs to the first category, and those of the other three—CFC, Lakeview, and Renewal—belong to the second category. Madison spells out its vision as such:

> To be a diverse community following Christ together.
>
> At Madison Square Church we are a community of believers that find strength in our diversity. We are called by God to share His gospel in hopes of bringing others to know him. In a racially-charged world we strive to be an example of how God's love conquers all differences and brings all types of people together to serve and glorify Him in all that we do.[7]

In this vision statement, Madison clarifies the reason for its existence is in pursuing diversity (as a multicultural congregation), to "bring all types of people together"[8] in order to share the gospel and to glorify Him. Madison intentionally pursues diversity because it believes that its strength comes from such diversity. Along with this vision statement, Madison's mission statement also supports who Madison is multiculturally: "We are a called by God the Father and empowered by the Holy Spirit to be transformed by Christ for: . . . Reaching Across!"[9] Madison defines reaching across as "reconciling in Christ for multicultural living and leading."[10] In this globalized

---

7. See http://www.madisonsquarechurch.org/vision/
8. See http://www.madisonsquarechurch.org/vision/
9. See http://www.madisonsquarechurch.org/vision/
10. See http://www.madisonsquarechurch.org/vision/

and multicultural context, Madison dreams of being a community which reflects God's multicultural vision to embrace all.

The other type of vision in relation to becoming a multicultural church is more indirect, more inclusive, and primarily Great Commission-centered. In *One Body One Spirit*, George Yancey calls it the "overarching goal." The vision statement of CFC says: "The vision of CFC is based on Matthew 9:37–38 . . . The heart of CFC's ministry is thus to produce Kingdom workers, trained to take the Gospel into all the nations, and who will in turn produce more workers."[11] In interviews, the pastors and members of CFC shared the same belief that producing more Kingdom workers is an essential task and is the core commitment of CFC. Producing Kingdom workers goes with being concerned for all nations. Thus, without saying explicitly that they wanted to be multicultural, CFC became a very diverse community in terms of ethnic backgrounds as a byproduct of its overall Kingdom-centered vision. Tony Thomas, an Indian-American intern pastor, says: "More and more different ethnicities started to come . . . the church always emphasized learning to pray for your own people group and have a heart for them." There is no concern about being a multicultural church, but CFC focuses on the opportunity to train its diverse people to accomplish the Great Commission with the result that many non-Koreans of a variety of ethnicities become a part of it.

Lakeview, in contrast, has had some changes in terms of the degree of emphasis on multiculturalism and the Great Commission. When Lakeview became independent, it deliberately emphasized the vision of pursuing becoming a multi-ethnic church, but the emphasis has since moved to fulfilling the Great Commission with different expressions. The short version of the vision statement of Lakeview is "Transformation: Making disciples of all nations."[12] Being multi-ethnic is still in the vision chart, but is not the top priority as it was in the past. While still pursuing being a multicultural church, Lakeview emphasizes "transformation," which refers to making disciples of all nations. Being a multiethnic church now stands underneath transformation.

Renewal's vision is "to ignite a gospel-spreading movement through multiple local congregations in the greater Philadelphia area and the world, so that individuals, communities, and cultures are renewed in Christ."[13] According to one of Renewal's core values, gospel-spreading involves sharing the gospel with diverse people in our society, stating, "In a vibrant

11. See http://cfchome.org/beliefs
12. See http://www.elakeview.org/our_vision.php.
13. See http://devon.renewalchurch.org/about/vision-core-values/.

gospel-spreading congregation, members work together to share the gospel with neighbors, classmates, co-workers, and friends, and embody the gospel in their love for one another and for their neighboring communities."[14] The description of the recipients of their ministry—"neighbors, classmates, co-workers, and friends"—implies diverse people who in many cases have different ethnic/racial backgrounds.

Regardless of which form of vision the case study churches adopted, the senior/lead pastor of each took the initiative in vision-casting. Rev. Kang of Lakeview took one month off to seek God's will regarding what kind of church Lakeview should be as soon as the church became independent. He emerged from this time with a three-word vision: seek, transform, multiply. He said, "In terms of multiply, we were pursuing multi-ethnic so that we can multiply God's kingdom beyond the ethnic barrier." During this period of vision-seeking, Rev. Kang talked to different people—staff members, and members of the congregation—to seek God's will. Rev. Kang said, "they [the congregation] wanted Lakeview become a church where they would feel comfortable bringing non-Koreans." In the case of Lakeview, the senior pastor took initiative and leadership in vision-casting, other staff and lay leaders grasped the vision, and finally the whole congregation bought into the vision as their own. Renewal church had a similar step of embracing a vision of becoming a multicultural church early in its development. Even before becoming independent, there was a desire present to become multi-ethnic. After becoming independent, Rev. Kim preached and taught that Renewal should be multiethnic in order to be a welcoming place for more than just Korean-American. All pastoral staff and elders agreed; then all congregants also agreed.

Becoming Independent

To become multicultural, an EM congregation should first become independent. Otherwise, the transition from being monoethnic to becoming multicultural might not happen. The EM congregation could have some non-Koreans in the church, but there is usually a great limitation, and it will not ultimately have enough non-Korean visitors and members to make the transition. I found that it is almost impossible to be multicultural as long as the EM remains in the Korean church. A new multicultural church has lots of things which need to change, and the structure and different culture of a Korean church would not meet the church's need for rapid change. In the case of CFC, this was a relatively easy transition, even though the church did

14. See http://devon.renewalchurch.org/about/vision-core-values/.

not intend it. Renewal and Lakeview became multicultural after becoming independent, even though they had some non-Koreans already before taking this step. Madison became multicultural before becoming independent, but it did not grow much during that time. Because the mother church of Madison, Oakdale CRC, still used Dutch for its worship services and ministry, Madison could not pursue becoming multicultural because of this language limitation as well as the mother church's resistance to other cultures. After becoming independent, Madison moved forward more actively towards becoming a multicultural church and was able to have good results. Therefore, if a church or congregation in the United States does not use English in its main ministries, it is a necessary step for its English-speaking congregation to become independent in order for the church to become multicultural. If a monoethnic/monocultural church is speaking English, however, then the congregation can pursue becoming a multicultural church without separating and becoming independent.

Adopting a Non-Ethnic Church Name

If a church has an ethnic distinction in its name, such as "Korean," the church needs to remove this ethnic distinction and adopt an ethnically/ racially neutral name. Since Madison did not have an ethnic distinction in its name from the beginning, it was not necessary for it to change its name. However, the other three churches—CFC, Lakeview, and Renewal—had to change their names in order to pursue becoming multicultural. Korean Christian Fellowship became CFC without the word "Korean" in its name; the EM of Lakeview Korean Presbyterian Church was changed to Lakeview Church; the EM of Emmanuel Church of Philadelphia became Renewal Presbyterian Church. Like Lakeview and Renewal, if a church which is pursuing becoming multicultural decides to become independent from the first-generation immigrant church, the time when it makes this move is also a good time to adopt a non-ethnic, neutral name.

Relocating

When an EM congregation wants to become multicultural, becoming independent and having a neutral church name in themselves are not enough to attract and welcome non-Koreans. In the case of Renewal, even after the EM became independent, it stayed in the Korean church building for about two years. During this time, Renewal found that staying in the Korean church building was a hindrance for non-Koreans. Rev. Yoo recalled:

> Our vision was not just to stay a Korean-American church. We wanted to diversify and we realized being in Emmanuel Church was limiting because when people walk by they see *Immanuel Kyohoe* [Emmanuel Church], Korean flag, so they just assume this is for Korean people only so they kept walking. And if they visited and they walk in and it smells like *jjigae* [a Korean food] . . . For some people that's just too much, it's strange, it makes them think maybe this is not for me. We didn't want the building to be a hindrance. We didn't want the building to be an obstacle. We said because it's overcrowded and because we want to diversify we should get our own building. There was no bad relationship, it's not because we got angry or any kind of falling out, just for vision and for space we said I think we should get our own place.[15]

Even though Renewal maintained a good relationship with its mother church, Emmanuel Church of Philadelphia, staying in the Korean church building was a substantial obstacle to diversification. Ultimately, they found that moving into a new church building was necessary to attract more non-Koreans. When such a church moves to a new church building, it is wise for it to move to non-Korean church building if possible. Lakeview moved to its new location right after becoming independent, but it rented another Korean church building. In my observation, renting in a Korean church is a hindrance, as newly-independent Renewal experienced. For strangers and visitors, the presence of Korean words, Korean people, and Korean language can all give the impression that this is a Korean church.

These five steps are foundational in the model T-process of (mono-ethnic) Korean immigrant churches. Nevertheless, these steps do not make a church multicultural without the additional steps in the T-process which make up the second group. The steps in the first group can be described as a linear process as shown in Figure 2, although the order of some steps can change according to the situations encountered by the individual churches.

---

15. Dwight Yoo, interview by author, January 26, 2012

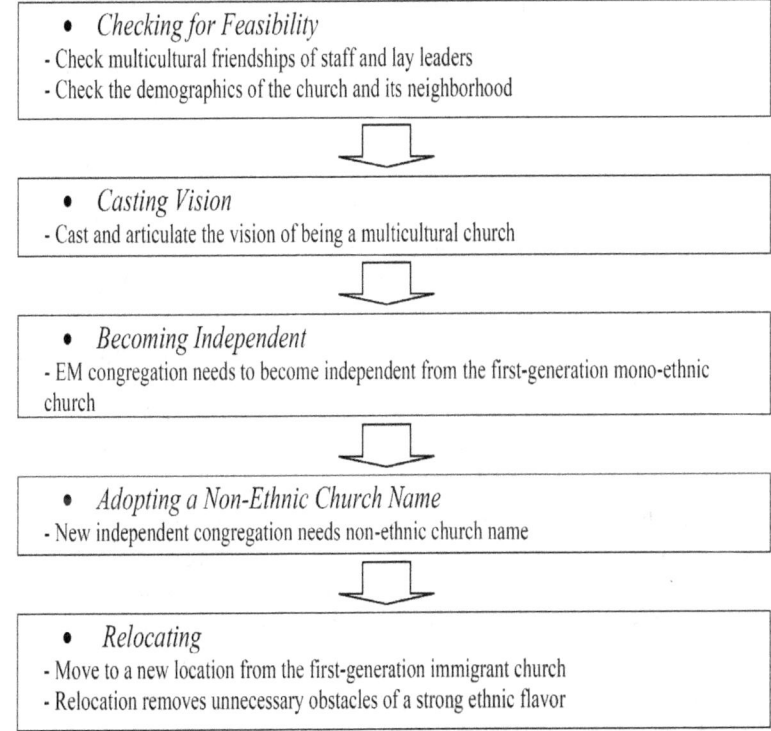

Figure 2. Basic Steps of Windmill T-Process

Group Two: 5 Ongoing Steps

The steps in the first group of the Windmill T-process are indirect in their effect on the T-process, representing the necessary "prerequisite" work, but the steps in the second group are more direct and essential to the process of moving toward becoming a multicultural church. These second group steps include serving the neighbor, refreshing the vision, diversifying leadership, and providing cultural intelligence training.

Serving the Neighbor

This is a process that has a meaningful impact on people both inside and outside of the church, even though it does not guarantee drawing unchurched (and multi-ethnic) neighbors to the church. Regardless, serving the neighborhood is helpful in two ways. First of all, serving breaks down the wall between the church and its neighbors and establishes a curiosity and an openness in its unchurched neighbors towards visiting the church. When Madison began to reach out to the neighborhood in the Madison area, the church not only provided the gospel message, but it also tried to meet its neighbors' felt needs in many ways by means of a food pantry, counseling, education regarding financial management, parenting classes, fixing and giving away cars, helping drug addicts, etc. The original intention for serving people was not to make the church multicultural, but to share the love of God with the church's diverse neighbors.

In 1993, Madison decided to establish a non-profit organization named "Restorers" in order to serve the neighborhood more systematically and effectively. This effort, I found, helped both Madison and its neighbors to break down the walls which had separated them and to become closer. Rachael, a single mother who had children through a biracial marriage, introduced herself and how she became a follower of Jesus Christ and a member of Madison. When she was a drug addict looking for a church about three years ago, people recommended that she try Madison. People in the Madison area, as well as in Grand Rapids more widely, knew about the passion and the continuing and systematic efforts of Madison for helping addicts. Rachael did not take part in the recovery program provided by Madison and Restorers, but she came to Madison because the church was working to help people like her; she could see that addicts were important to them. This is an example of one of many ways in which diverse people who are in need come to Madison.

Secondly, when a church serves its neighbors regardless of their ethnic/racial backgrounds, it helps the congregation to open their arms and have a passion for diverse people. Before Renewal became independent and multicultural, there was a murder committed by two African-American teenagers just outside Emmanuel Church. The initial reaction of the Korean congregants was a strong desire to leave the area. However, the leaders of Emmanuel Church were convicted of their sins and led the whole church to confess their sins and serve their neighbors. This was the beginning of the transition of a Korean immigrant church in Philadelphia into a multicultural church. Since these events, both Emmanuel and Renewal have consistently served their poor, mainly African-American neighbors through free summer camps, scholarships, vacation Bible school, tutoring, after school programs, etc. These services did not change the percentage of African-Americans in Renewal Church, because most church members are high-profile students studying law or medicine at the University of Pennsylvania or are young professionals. Nevertheless, one outstanding characteristic of

Renewal is that they have a passion for their poor African-American neighbors and do not stop serving them. This service helps members who are young and relatively rich professionals (and students) to maintain openness and a desire to have others in the church.

In addition to these positive effects on the transition process, the real importance of "serving the neighbor" is in multicultural ecclesiology, specifically regarding the incarnational nature of the church. As I discussed in chapter 3, the incarnational nature of the church compels us to move into the diverse neighborhoods in today's globalized multicultural society. In this regard, Ro, former executive pastor of Lakeview, emphasizes that:

> If we don't become a missionary church to our own local contact, if we can't reach our fellow coworkers, why do you want to go reach people in China or in Africa? So, my paradigm of missions have always growing up is that all these immigrant churches—Chinese or Korean, they send missionaries and spend money or sending their missionaries overseas and spend maybe fifty percent of their income budget to missions, but if they can't reach their neighbors, to me that is a wrong theology or missing something. If you can't be faithful with little, why do you want to be faithful with much? . . . To me multiethnic [multicultural] is just one step along [with] a bigger journey. Multiethnic [multicultural] . . . is a local expression of great commission.[16]

Therefore, "serving the neighbor" in the T-process is essential as well as effective, especially when the church is located in a poor neighborhood.

Refreshing the Vision

In the T-process from being a monocultural church to becoming a multicultural church, vision-casting is just the beginning of the vision-shaping process that requires continuous follow-up. Vision gives the church direction and the motivation to pursue it. However, vision-casting does not guarantee the success of the church. I found that congregations easily join the new adventure of becoming multicultural with expectation and excitement, but soon they realize that it is not just a dream but a reality that requires hard work. Rev. Kim said, "Multiethnicity is messy. It's good on paper and I like it, but it's more work, more expectation, more communication." In addition, Rev. Beelen said, "People are very individualistic especially in the United States. Well, then if they don't like what they experience, they get up and go somewhere else." Therefore, pastors have to repeat the vision in order for congregations to

16. Jon Ro, interview by author, October 20, 2012.

be refreshed and reminded that they are called to be part of this mission and it is biblical. In response to my interview question "What do you do to make sure that Madison stays multicultural?," Rev. Beelen, lead pastor of Madison, emphasized the importance of repeating the vision:

> You have to keep repeating the vision. While I'm sitting here, I'm thinking that in April or May, I will preach on Acts chapter 6 again just to remind people—here's what I would do. I would say, I'm going to preach a sermon not just on one text, although I'm going to focus on Acts 6. I'm going to go to Matthew 1, the genealogy of Jesus. OK, so the four women show up. And they're all from outside the Jewish race. And you go to the end of the book of Matthew and the Great Commission says, go to all nations, and the Greek word is *ethna*, we get our word ethnic from there. And then you go from there to Acts chapter 6.
>
> And there you see how the church made the leadership adjustment. And they actually said we need seven Greek-speaking men to be part of this. And then we go to Acts 13, that's the first missionary sending church. And you notice what happens there, same kind of thing. And then you say to people, this doesn't just happen because we get on our knees and pray. There is something very intentional about this. God intentionally tells us what Jesus' genealogy is.
>
> When he's getting ready to commission his disciples, he doesn't just say go, he says go to all the nations. And Acts chapter 6 shows you that when a church starts and there's different ethnic groups, you have to bring leadership up in from various ethnic groups on purpose. Acts chapter 13 shows you that if we don't become multiethnic like Paul who was from two different cultures, we're not going to be able to bring the gospel across boundary lines.
>
> So that, in a nutshell, would be one of the sermons I preach. So you have to repeat vision. You've got to continue to ask people whoever is in the minority, you've got to meet with them and ask them just as a minority group without the other group there, how are you doing; because the majority culture sees things as if they're normal. They don't realize that they have a culture that they're operating in a certain way. So the minority culture has to speak to the majority culture in meaningful ways and say, this is what we're saying and thinking. And if this doesn't change, because it will slide back to the majority. So you have to push against that.[17]

---

17. David Beelen, interview by author, January 20, 2012.

Rev. Yoo, lead pastor of Renewal West Philly (main) campus, mentioned the same sort of thing, stating:

> Yeah, at times during the sermon and whenever we talk about the vision, just to challenge them again, get out of your ethnic enclave we call it, get out of your ethnic pockets. God has called you. We say you shouldn't be ashamed of your ethnicity. You shouldn't run away from it. God made you who you are . . . but at the same time our main identity is Christian and that's our first culture's gospel. I think just continuously emphasizing that.[18]

Vision-casting requires follow-up. The follow-up is repeating, reminding, refreshing, and re-emphasizing the vision. This follow-up is a revolving and continuing process. Without it, people will not stay with the vision and will eventually leave the church.

Diversifying Leadership

In the model T-process, a mono-cultural church should diversify its leadership, shifting from having a mono-ethnic/mono-cultural leadership team to having one which is multicultural/multiracial. This process involves three layers: pastors/staff, lay leaders, and front-faces. Among these three types of church leaders, a church should start its leadership diversification with its pastors/staff, because they are the most influential. When a monoethnic (Korean) church wants to become a multicultural church, it is crucial for that church to have non-Asian pastors and staff members. In hiring cross-cultural pastor(s)/staff, there are certain practical suggestions that emerge from my field research.

First of all, to become a multicultural church, the church needs to hire pastor(s)/staff who have different racial backgrounds. In my research, three of the case study churches—Lakeview, Renewal, and Madison—experienced a great impact when they hired cross-cultural pastor(s)/staff. In a deeply globalized and racially diverse society like the United States, sometimes ethnic differences within the same race can be diluted and minimized for the sake of similarity when compared to larger racial differences. Therefore, as in the cases of Renewal and Lakeview, if a Korean church wants to become multicultural, the church needs to hire non-Asian pastors or staff instead of Asians. In addition, without hiring Asian pastor(s) or staff, most Korean churches in the United States could still attract and maintain Asians in the church. The three case study churches—CFC, Lakeview,

---

18. Dwight Yoo, interview by author, January 26, 2012.

and Renewal—were able to maintain a high percentage of Asian members without hiring an Asian pastor or staff member, while also being enabled to more effectively reach out to non-Asians. Thus, when a mono-ethnic/mono-cultural church decides to become multicultural, the church should have cross-cultural/multiracial pastors and staff.

Secondly, to maximize the effect of this hiring of cross-cultural pastor(s) or staff members, it is most effective for the church to hire people who reflect the target racial group. For instance, if a Korean church resides in a neighborhood that has a high percentage of Hispanics and wants to reach them, it would be effective to hire a Hispanic pastor or staff member first. In *One Body One Spirit*, George Yancey suggests that "any attempt to reach out to a group that is especially alienated in the community (e.g., first-generation immigrants, and economically deprived groups) should include a member of that group within the leadership structure of the church."[19] In my observation, it is also the same for Caucasians if the white race is not the majority in the church. When Lakeview and Renewal each hired an Anglo-American campus pastor, this step helped both campuses to become more multicultural, adding a high percentage of Caucasian members. Thus, when a church wants to become multicultural, the church should hire pastors and staff who reflect the target group's race.

Thirdly, to become a multicultural church (in relation to the hiring of pastor(s)/staff), a church should hire cross-cultural pastors first and then, as a second step, expand its multicultural diversity to staff positions. In the T-process, most churches cannot hire several pastors and staff members from various racial backgrounds at the same time. Therefore, if a church wants to take a step towards becoming multicultural, the church should start by hiring a cross-cultural pastor who preaches on Sunday morning for the adult congregation, because the impact of a pastor is much greater than that of a staff member. When Renewal and Lakeview hired Caucasian campus teaching pastors, the effect of this step for both of these churches was phenomenal and tangible. As a result, those campuses were enabled to have about half Caucasian members, although the size of these congregations was not that large. In *Building A Healthy Multi-Ethnic Church*, DeYmaz points out the importance of hiring a pastor in pursuing diverse leadership by sharing the remarks of an African-American pastor of a large congregation. The African-American pastor says:

> If you hire or otherwise empower African Americans only to lead your church in worship, you may inadvertently suggest to people, "We accept them as entertainers." Or if you hire or

19. Yancey, *One Body*, 87.

otherwise empower African Americans only to work with your children, you may inadvertently suggest, "We accept them to nanny our kids." And if you hire or otherwise employ African Americans only as janitors, you are quite clearly stating, "We expect them to clean up after us." It is only when you allow us [African Americans] to share your pulpit... we will be truly one with you in the church.[20]

This does not mean that hiring racially diverse pastors alone can make a church multicultural. However, it is true that we have to start diversity from the pastor's position, not from other staff positions. In fact, even though Lakeview's Northbrook (main) campus has two female staff members—one for administration and small group ministry and another for Sunday school— it is still difficult for the church to have non-Asian members. On the contrary, in the history of Madison, its co-pastor system of sharing preaching and other responsibilities between black and white pastors from 1982 to 2005 helped Madison to improve its multicultural atmosphere substantially.

Additionally, though, it is vital to have multicultural lay leaders, because hiring multicultural/multiracial pastors/staff in a church is not enough to accomplish the goal. In terms of leadership diversification, lay leaders must include those who can participate in the decision-making process of the church, such as elders, deacons, committee members, small group leaders, etc. In the case of Madison, more than 30 years ago the church decided to have diverse leaders not only for pastor(s)/staff but also for its lay leaders, and the church made a written statement in this regard so that it could strategically pursue being a multicultural church with consistency. As a result, in my observation, the degree of multicultural character in Madison was the highest among the four case study churches. Even without this kind of written statement and the same degree of multicultural character as Madison, the other three case study churches, too, had lay leadership teams which included multiracial elders, deacons, officers (in CFC), and small group leaders. By having multicultural lay leaders and by sharing authority and responsibilities with people of different colors, a church diversifies its ownership and overcomes its ethnic/racial barriers.

The third layer of diversification of leadership is in the "front-faces"— people who appear in front of the congregation during the worship services and other events. Diversification in this area is a very strategic and intentional process. If a monocultural church wants to become multicultural and has multicultural pastors, staff, elders, and deacons, but people of only one ethnic or racial group stand in front of the congregation during the worship services

20. DeYmaz, *Healthy Multi-ethnic Church*, 74.

and other events, how can the church expect to have a diverse congregation? Thus, front-faces can be symbolic, especially for minorities, of how much the church values diversity and wants to have different people groups in its membership. Compared to hiring cross-cultural pastors/staff and having multicultural deacons/elders, the step of diversifying a church's front-faces is less difficult, yet still very influential. Instead of just saying that we want to be multicultural from the pulpit, having a cross-cultural worship leader can demonstrate clearly and tangibly that the church actually values being multicultural. When I asked, "What kinds of adjustments did you take for welcoming others?" Rev. Chung, the senior pastor of CFC, answered,

> Sometimes for the sake of getting more [diverse] people, faces that are up there. Some of them are less qualified but still have to be up there too. Faces—presiders, praise leaders, band. You have to consider all that, not because of the inequality but because of the, you know, maximum impact for the kingdom . . . Because when you see their face, initial discomfort can be helped.[21]

In the T-process from being a monocultural church to becoming a multicultural church, the process of retaining visitors is more difficult than that of attracting them. Diverse people can come, but they can also easily decide not to come again because they feel that this church is for one group of people alone. However, when a church strategically uses front-faces, drawing on leaders who have diverse racial backgrounds, this step will help others feel that this church is welcoming and is for everyone. When I visited Madison, a praise team of multi-colored faces swayed back and forth, bellowing a black gospel tune underscored by the fervent exclamations of its praise team leader. Because of the multicultural praise team and their leading, many Hispanics, whites, and blacks lifted their arms up, clapped, shouted, sang, and prayed as if they were one.

Cultural Intelligence Training

One key difference between Madison and the three KIM churches in the T-process was whether or not the church had "cultural intelligence training." Rev. Chung of CFC emphasizes the importance of "training people," especially in the small group setting. Through the training, he emphasizes (1) welcoming strangers, people of different ethnic/racial groups and (2) equipping leaders who are able to disciple them. This first approach, to teach and encourage congregants to welcome others of different ethnicities/

---

21. Min Chung, interview by author, January 15.

races, is common in the three KIM churches. Pastors of these KIM churches emphasize Christian identity over their (Korean) ethnic identity with the expectation that everyone can unite and be one in Christ.

Extending beyond this level of training as demonstrated in the KIM churches, however, Madison deals with cultural issues more seriously by creating and providing a specific learning environment for the congregation which may be called "cultural intelligence training." The reason why cultural intelligence training is crucial in the T-process is because the lack of understanding of the role of culture eventually hinders a church to the extent that it simply cannot move toward becoming a multicultural church, no matter what kind of vision it has. Madison's approach gives us insight into how to implement cultural intelligence training in a local church.

In the implementation of cultural intelligence training in the T-process, several things need to be kept in mind. First, a church needs to put a priority on cultural intelligence training. In the case of Madison, it appointed a staff member as its "Director of Diversity" in order to facilitate this training. Additionally, Madison organized an Anti-Racism Team to discuss, plan, and lead the congregation toward the proper understanding of culture. Since cultures and people do not change at one time or through a single event, prioritizing the heightening of cross-cultural sensitivity is necessary. Otherwise, cultural intelligence will fade, and ultimately, the church will return to undermining the culture and withdraw to the status of being a monocultural church.

Second, to maintain this training as a priority, a church has to create an ongoing learning environment. Madison repeatedly provides well-prepared programs such as its Breakfast Club, 2 ½ days Understanding Racism Workshop[22], Understanding Racism Grow Groups, New Community Living Conversations, 8-week Sunday school classes, 8-week sessions of Institutes for Healing Racism, and so on. For this provision, Madison maintains partnerships with several organizations that specialize in this area, and from these partnerships, Madison learns, adopts, customizes, and develops its own curriculum and programs. The variety and frequency of these programs give the whole congregation more opportunities to both recognize the importance of understanding culture and to participate.

Third, this training must include the church's leaders, not only the congregation. Only when the church leaders take part in the cultural intelligence training can the church expect change.[23] At Madison, its Director of

---

22. See Appendix iv and Appendix v: "Congregations Organizing for Racial Reconciliation (CORR)" and "Understanding Racism Workshop (Application)"

23. Rah, *Many Colors*, 147.

Diversity had completed a two-year training program and was then certified to do anti-racism training for Madison and for the CRC denomination.[24] As of 2006, for instance, all of Madison's staff members and most of its Council had attended the Understanding Racism Workshop.[25]

Fourth, one important consideration in the provision of cultural intelligence training is in providing group training. This format is crucial because "an individual may learn lessons the rest of the community is not learning, which can bring about personal change in an individual without any guarantee of significant changes to the entire community."[26] Since the change in an individual alone will not help the congregation as a whole to become a multicultural church, group learning in this training is indispensable.

Fifth, another consideration for this training is in the power of the community as a learning context. Rah emphasizes that "multicultural learning ... must be experienced through the context of community. Learning in the community occurs through shared experience."[27] He then offers the practical advice that "the [learning] process involves journeying together, sharing meals together, multisensory opportunities, and participatory learning."[28] Here are some examples of what such shared-journey programs look like. Journey to Mosaic (J2M) is "a four-day experiential bus trip from Northern California to Southern California that pairs people up with somebody of a different ethnic background. It unpacks portions of the African-American, Asian-American, and Hispanic-American stories in California through tours, films, and partner/large group discussions."[29] J2M was designed by the Evangelical Covenant Church and North Park Theological Seminary in order to address racial and cultural issues in the United States. One of the benefits of this kind of journey is that "site visits, firsthand accounts and stories, videos, cross-cultural pairings, and group discussions all contribute to a holistic experience of learning."[30] J2M helps enormously in raising the understanding of others and their cultures. For successful learning/training, "one of the essential elements of community learning is creating a safe place, which requires all participants to lay down the power. Ground rules from the very beginning should make clear that all participants (no matter their

---

24. Madison Square Church, "Budget 2005–2006," 16.
25. Madison Square Church, "Budget 2005–2006," 16.
26. Rah, *Many Colors*, 147.
27. Rah, *Many Colors*, 148.
28. Rah, *Many Colors*, 148.
29. Pacific Southwest Conference of the Evangelical Covenant, "A Multiethnic Partnership of Covenant Churches."
30. Rah, *Many Colors*, 149.

status or preexisting authority) ultimately stand on equal footing during the journey."[31] Such training is particularly important for pastors coming from a strongly hierarchical culture.

Having Multicultural Worship Teams

One of the differences between Madison and the three KIM churches is in their multicultural worship teams and their music. The worship teams of all three KIM churches I visited play Anglo-style contemporary music that is the most common and effective for young generations in the United States. In contrast, Madison has multiple multicultural worship teams which serve the Sunday worship services in a scheduled rotation. Even though the teams are ethnically-mixed and try to have a multicultural flavor, each team has its own unique cultural style, based on the leaders and the songs. What helped Madison to really become multicultural was the different styles of its multiple worship teams. Mosaic Church of Central Arkansas also has multiple worship teams for developing a variety of multicultural flavors, because "DeYmaz [senior pastor] recognized that "one size fits all" doesn't work in worship. So there is no dominant style."[32] Instead, seven different worship teams lead Sunday services in rotation. This is how Mosaic becomes more multicultural through having intentionally multicultural worship teams.

In contrast to these examples, another example shows how *the lack* of such multicultural flavors in worship teams can also have an impact. One visitor left the following reflective comment regarding the worship team after visiting Wilcrest Baptist Church (a congregation that was sixty percent white, but also had others of twenty-five different national backgrounds at the time):

> The choir was diverse. It looked to me to be about 1/3 to 1/2 non-white. But the music was not only "white," but rather slow and traditional. I wondered why the non-white people are a part of the choir. Who selects the music? Are there non-Whites who have input into the song and music selection? . . .
>
> Overall, the church struck me as a WHITE church! Except for the pastor and recently ordained deacons making a note of the church being a multiracial church, thereby telling me the church identifies as a multiracial church, I would not have considered it a multiracial church . . .

---

31. Rah, *Many Colors*, 157.
32. Kennedy, "Big Dream in Little Rock," 43.

Personally, I was disappointed, even sad about the disconnect that I saw between what the church claims to be and what, from my visit, it was. People who are non-White are welcome, I am sure, but they don't seem to be appreciated for what they can uniquely bring to the church or really included at every level. Given what I saw and experienced, I would not be able to invite other African Americans to Wilcrest.[33]

Even though Wilcrest was multicultural in terms of its total membership, leadership, and the composition of its worship team members, being culturally insensitive in its music selection gave this visitor the impression that it was not a multicultural church that he or she could be a part of. After receiving the note from this African-American visitor, Rodney Woo, the senior pastor of Wilcrest Baptist Church, recognized that mixed membership alone was not enough to welcome others. This case also shows how using the same worship style from week to week can make an unintended barrier, especially in terms of music style.[34]

The Windmill T-process and Its Explanation

Now it is pertinent to ask how these two groups of steps in the model T-process can work together and help a mono-ethnic/monocultural church to transition toward becoming a multicultural church. The illustration of the "Windmill T-process" in Figure 3 helps to explain the applicable transition process.

---

33. Emerson and Woo, *People of the Dream*, 132.
34. Kennedy, "Big Dream in Little Rock," 43.

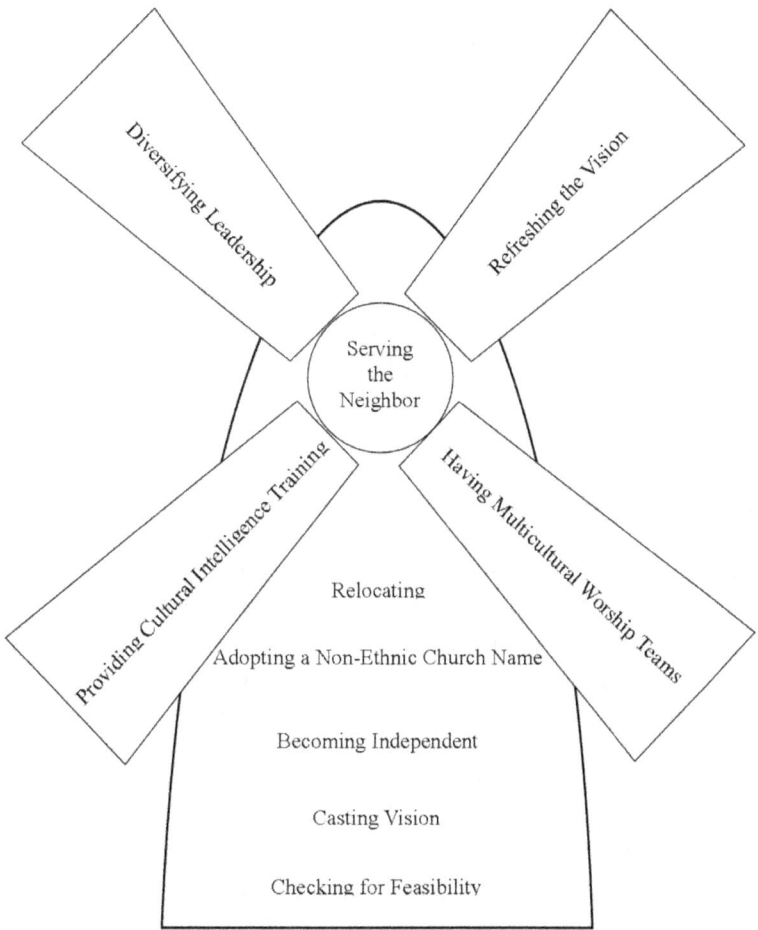

Figure 3. Windmill T-Process

The windmill as a whole represents a local church. The five steps on the windmill's body provide the base which is needed for the windmill to be sustained and to work properly. These steps are important, but this metaphor implies that the body itself cannot produce anything—in this case, the energy for the T-process. The windmill's blades, on the other hand, provide motion, and their efforts make it possible to produce the power to move a church toward becoming multicultural. The central shaft labeled as "serving the neighbor" acts as a bridge between people in the neighborhood and the work of the church. If a church makes an effort to become multicultural in isolation, the T-process will be hard or even impossible; as it engages in service to its neighbors, though, the T-process of change is facilitated. Lastly, this model implies that a multicultural church is not static but must be continually moving in order to be multicultural. In other words, the four efforts represented by the blades should be ongoing in the T-process. Otherwise, the church will lose its multicultural energy.

Two Optional Steps

In addition to the steps contained in the Windmill T-process, I also found two other steps which can be beneficial, but they are not necessary, only optional: facilitating ethnic group meetings and launching multisite campus(es).

Facilitate Ethnic Group Meetings: When a church's membership includes first-generation ethnic groups, providing specific meetings for each ethnic group is beneficial to attract new people from those ethnic groups and to retain them in the church. CFC has several ethnic group meetings, mainly for international students. It may seem awkward for a multicultural church or a church pursuing becoming a multicultural church to encourage people to have ethnic group meetings, but these ethnic group meetings are mainly for first-generation international students who are most comfortable using their own languages. DeYmaz writes of his experience of the power of ethnic ministries, especially for first-generation immigrants.

According to DeYmaz, Mosaic Church decided to provide ethnic ministries for two reasons. First, Mosaic considers this to be the most accessible way for first-generation immigrants to hear the gospel; it is necessary for the sake of evangelism. Second, it is beneficial to provide "an initial level of comfort for internationals coming into the church who are not yet fluent in the language or culture of the United States."[35] DeYmaz says this both/and approach through cross-cultural ministry is beneficial for the entire congregation in terms of its evangelism, discipleship, and leadership development.[36]

Supporting DeYmaz' approach, Christerson and Emerson, as a result of their in-depth sociological studies, concluded that successful multiethnic (multicultural) congregations tend to cater specific sub-populations like ethnic groups. It is because the presence of internally homogeneous groups reduces the personal costs of belonging to multicultural religious congregations. They state, "Thus, internally homogeneous congregations more often provide what draws people to religious groups for a lower cost than

---

35. DeYmaz and Li, *Ethnic Blends*, 109.
36. DeYmaz and Li, *Ethnic Blends*, 109.

do internally diverse congregations." In other words, providing ethnic subgroups in the multicultural church is a natural and effective way to increase the extent of multicultural character while making it easier for people to feel culturally at home.

Starting Multicultural Campus(es): In my case studies, three churches—Lakeview, Renewal, and Madison—employed the strategy of becoming a multisite church in order to pursue becoming a multicultural church. The common experience among those three churches was that they started a multicultural second campus when the main campus was full and was unable to grow any more due to a lack of space. When their church buildings were full, the pastors found that people of the non-majority group were less likely to come than those from the majority ethnic group. Therefore, for the purpose of evangelism and for the sake of pursuing becoming a multicultural church, those three churches prepared to plant a second campus with prayer, planning meetings, and a lengthy communication process with the congregation.

In the case of Lakeview, the church held a "vision night" to discuss planting a second campus in another Chicago suburban area as part of the vision of becoming a multicultural church. At the end of the meeting, about 25 Asians and 25 Caucasians volunteered to participate in the planting of the second campus. Also, Lakeview started fundraising for the new campus that night, and it finished about six months later. Lastly, Lakeview then sent 40,000 mailers to all of its neighbors within a 5-mile radius on four occasions before its grand opening. With a Caucasian campus pastor and racially-mixed founding members, Lakeview's Vernon Hills campus has since then been able to reach to diverse people continually.

In Renewal's case, as it, too, grew and became full on Sundays, it also dreamed of planting the second campus, for them on a different side of Philadelphia. With the vision of expanding to a multicultural congregation, the church gathered a group of voluntary founding members and hired a Caucasian campus pastor, Rev. David Skinner. Unlike Lakeview, Renewal's Devon campus started with ethnically-mixed founding members and having both a Korean-American senior pastor, Rev. Kim, and a Caucasian, Rev. Skinner, working together.

Lastly, when Madison's building was getting too full, even with its having three Sunday morning worship services, the church elected its "2014 Vision Team" in 2006 to find out what to do about this problem. The number 2014 came from the 100th anniversary of the church, and this 2014 Vision Team consisted of 10 members—Rev. Beelen (Caucasian), five blacks, two whites, and one Chinese-American. For several months, the 2014 Vision Team worked through a process that included 1) listening to God's Spirit and Word, 2) gathering information from the congregation, the leadership, and the community, and 3) interpreting and evaluating. In addition, Madison set aside one particular Sunday evening for the congregation to listen to the Holy Spirit for the direction of the church. As a result of this process, the 2014 Vision Team proposed a recommendation, which was then approved by the council and submitted to the staff. It included both purchasing the building which was next to Madison and also beginning a multi-site expansion. In relation to the multi-site campus, Madison began to put an effort into leadership development for both the main and the new sites, looked for a possible location for the first new site, and strengthened its relationships with pastors from other churches, community leaders, and future site leaders. Madison communicated this process and its contents not only through announcements but also by means of mailings and church publications. Madison then had a Vision Casting Sunday in November 2006, where the lead pastor and other church leaders shared the vision's requirements, challenges, and future possibilities, and answered questions for about an hour after each service. For the people who missed one of these three Vision Casting Sunday meetings, Madison provided a written report with common questions and answers which came up in them. After the Vision Casting Sunday, the church council decided to take a step toward becoming multi-site—it held a congregational meeting and then had a vote through a mass mailing. At the conclusion of the process, Madison appointed an African-American pastor as its first new campus pastor and gathered and trained more than 100 members to launch this second campus. Finally, Madison launched its Madison Ford campus in January 2008.

As shown in these three cases, launching a new campus can be a beneficial way of pursuing becoming a multicultural church if the church is growing and is in need of making space for newcomers. All three of these churches started a new campus with a pastor who reflected the target population's race—white and black. Also in all three cases, this step involved a great deal of preparation and thorough communication with the congregation as a whole. In the cases of Lakeview and Renewal, both churches planted their new campuses when they had reached about 300 to 400 members. Since a large proportion of non-Asians joined the new campus, the main campuses of both Lakeview and Renewal then became more Asian-dominant churches again. This effect tells us that planting a new campus for the pursuit of becoming a multicultural church also requires thorough preparation and a backup plan for how the main campus will maintain and increase its own cross-cultural members. A few months after my field research, Renewal West Philly (main) campus and Renewal Devon (second) campus became two independent churches. Even though they are still in good relationships with

Renewal, because the former senior pastor left Renewal, and because the characteristics of both campuses are different in terms of size, ages, culture, and location, the West Philly and Devon campuses decided to become two separate churches. This shows that when a church becomes multi-site for the sake of its multicultural vision, much more effort, with strong leadership, will be required for the campuses to walk together once it happens.

Conclusion

Based on the analyses of four multicultural churches and the findings of this study, I proposed the "Windmill T-process," which includes ten steps in two groups. First is the fixed part, which includes 1) checking for feasibility, 2) casting vision, 3) become independent, 4) adopting a non-ethnic church name, and 5) relocating. The second group involves the moving parts, which are the shaft and blades that produce the power needed for the transition: serving the neighbors, refreshing the vision, diversifying leadership, providing cultural intelligence training, and having multicultural worship teams. There are two more optional processes that can also be beneficial: facilitating ethnic group meetings and starting a multisite campus. In this model, five steps (serving the neighbors, refreshing the vision, diversifying leadership, providing cultural intelligence training, and having multicultural worship teams) are ongoing and revolving parts of the Windmill T-process. Within these five steps, providing cultural intelligence training is a step that is easy to miss but which is indispensable in this model. No multicultural church can say, "Now we are done with the transition process." Since a church is like an organism, which can grow or die, it takes continuous care and effort to maintain and develop the multicultural aspect of a church. The last two steps (facilitating ethnic group ministry and starting a multicultural campus) are optional, based on the church's situation.

7

Conclusion

DUE TO THE INFLUENCE of globalization, multiculturalism in the United States has increased in recent years, and this will in all likelihood only grow in the coming decades. According to the 2010 census, minorities constituted 36 percent of the United States' total population, a percentage which is projected to gradually increase, while the white percentage will decrease to below 50 percent by 2042.[1] In addition, along with the decline of most mainline Christian denominations which have traditionally been predominately white and homogeneous, the Christian portion of the total population is similarly becoming more multicultural. The church in this context has a mission to respond to the call of the Lord to love and serve its increasingly culturally diverse neighbors. To be faithful to that mission, some have transformed themselves into multicultural churches, while others have planted new multicultural churches. Members of the white majority in the United States who were historically the dominant race, and thus in many ways the oppressors of others, and the black minority, who experienced slavery and have been at the receiving end of racism, have both been at the leading edge of this multicultural church movement. Today this movement is expanding more broadly in terms of its participants and leadership, and Korean-American Christians are now facing both the challenges and opportunities which this period of history provides.

Even though a relatively small number of Korean immigrants live in the United States, they have experienced phenomenal growth in terms of the number of Korean immigrant churches. Two main reasons for this are: 1) the high percentage of Christians among the Koreans in the United States, compared to other ethnic/racial groups, and 2) their extremely high commitment to church activities and ministries;[2] in 2018, the number of

---

1. CNN, "Minorities expected to be majority in 2050."; U.S. Census Bureau, "Overview of Race and Hispanic Origin: 2010," 17–18.

2. The Pew Forum, *Asian Americans*. According to a survey, 71 percent Koreans are

Korean churches in the United States was 4,454, a growing trend that is slowing but still continuing. Because of this growth, it is now easy to find Korean churches in most major cities.³

In addition, unlike in the past, language and cultural barriers are now decreasing due to the growing number of English-speaking, second-generation Korean-Americans and their contributions to church development in the United States. Because of the opportunities which the reduction of these barriers brings, the key question arises as to how first and second generation Korean-Americans can work together for the purpose of shifting Korean-American churches in the direction of the multicultural church movement. There can be various stances on ethnic churches, as Miriam Adeney observed:

> What about "the most segregated hour in America, 11:00 a.m. on Sunday"? Is cultivating distinct ethnic churches a sin against the unity of the Body of Christ? Must our aim be multicultural churches (and therefore multicultural missions)? "Yes," says Stephen Rhodes in *Where the Nations Meet: The Church in a Multicultural World* (1998). "No," says Eric Law in *The Wolf Shall Lie Down with the Lamb* (1993). "Yes and No," say Soong Chau Rah in *The New Evangelicalism: Freeing the Church from Western Cultural Captivity* (2009) and Edward Gilbreath in *Reconciliation Blues: A Black Evangelical's Inside View of White Christianity* (2006).⁴

Among these three different stances on the questions, this study shows that the "Yes and No" position must be taken by the first and second-generation Korean-Americans with the consideration of their limitations as well as abilities. Whereas first-generation Korean-Americans have limitations in terms of cultural and language barriers, with their extraordinary zeal for missions, second-generation Korean-Americans' bicultural experience and bilingual ability make them more missional than many other ethnic groups. Consequently, it is important to leverage their potential as emerging leaders in the development of American Christianity.

Christians (Protestant 61 percent, Catholic 10 percent), whereas Chinese (31 percent), Vietnamese (36 percent), Japanese (38 percent), and Indian (18 percent) are much less in the United States in 2012.

3. Suh, "*Mijunkuk Haninkyohoi 4,544* [4,544 Korean Churches in USA]." For instance, in 2018 the number of Korean churches in major states are like this: California (1,375), New York (461), New Jersey (263), Texas (236), Virginia (212), Georgia (208), and Washington (205).

4. Adeney, "Colorful Initiatives," 14.

Although this study pays attention to the changed situation of the globalized multicultural United States and proposes a strategic practical transition model, the Windmill T-process, the driving force behind it is not methodological but is rather theological in motive. In other words, the multicultural church movement is rooted in ecclesiology, the complementarity between particularity and universality, and an understanding of the church's nature—being sent, being contextual, and being incarnational—in the missional church movement. Furthermore, it is important to incorporate new perspectives on the HUP, not as a main principle for pursuing the multicultural church model but as a tool for substantiating a common phenomenon that at times even exists in a multicultural church. Since homogeneous churches constitute the vast majority of American churches and because most people believe that the HUP and multiculturalism are opposites and cannot coexist within a multicultural church, a fresh approach to the HUP enables church leaders to disprove this common myth and even to see its applicability for a multicultural church. In this study, the various applications of the HUP in three churches—Mosaic Churches of Central Arkansas, Mosaic Churches in Los Angeles, and Covenant Fellowship Church—exemplify its validity in a multicultural church setting.

I believe that one of the main roles of theology is to serve the church and Christians by revealing God's will so that the church and its members can faithfully obey his call in its given context. How, then, can a monoethnic/monocultural Korean church work towards becoming a multicultural church, if this is the theologically sound model? What is the most effective and applicable transition-process that Korean immigrant churches can undertake?

Through my field research at four multicultural churches—three KIM churches and one Dutch-initiated church—I discovered several distinctive and significant steps for this transition. These steps serve as the components of my proposed "Windmill T-process" model for the transformation of monoethnic/monocultural churches into multicultural churches. The Windmill T-process model provides ten steps in two groups. The first group includes checking for feasibility, casting vision, becoming independent, adopting a non-ethnic church name, and relocating, while the second includes serving the neighbor, refreshing the vision, diversifying leadership, providing cultural intelligence training, and having multicultural worship teams. This Windmill model leads church leaders to a deeper knowledge of the T-process and its implications.

The Windmill T-process and Yancey's 7 Principles

While Yancey's seven principles in *One Body, One Spirit* provided a larger framework for my study, as well as for my understanding of the multicultural church more broadly, I believe that a comparison and contrast between his seven principles and the Windmill T-process will give readers clarity in understanding the T-process I propose and its application.

"Checking the Feasibility" vs. "Personal Skills"

Before this research, I believed if any Christian or any church lived in a multicultural society like most cities of the United States, they should be multicultural. I believed this because I considered that "context" meant only the setting outside of the church. However, as a result of the case studies, I have come to realize the importance of Christians as carriers of the mission. In other words, we Christians are part of the context. This does not mean that if we are not comfortable in multicultural ministry, it is okay not to participate in it. Rather, I believe this understanding encourages us to develop our multicultural lifestyle as a preparation for multicultural ministry.

In this sense, my step of "checking the feasibility" can be understood as a way of assessment, not only to decide whether we are ready to move on the T-process, but also to provide knowledge of what areas we need to improve and develop in ourselves as a part of the context. In this regard, evaluating church leaders' lifestyles is similar to Yancey's discussion of "personal skills." Though both "checking the feasibility" and "personal skills" focus on church leaders' readiness for multicultural ministry, they differ in that "personal skills" focuses on church leaders' problem-solving abilities in multicultural ministry, rather than on their lifestyle. Yancey emphasizes "personal skills" because a multicultural church's leaders can have more conflicts and interpersonal problems than a monocultural church.[5] However, the evaluation of leaders' lifestyles within my step of "checking the feasibility" asks if a church leader has multicultural human relationships not only in work situations but also in friendships. If these friendships are going well, we can assume that he/she is better able to deal with issues in the church with people from different ethnic/racial backgrounds.

---

5. Yancey, *One Body*, 68.

"Relocating" vs. "Location"

Yancey pointed out the importance of "location" as a principle in multicultural ministry. Since the multicultural church develops from the incarnational nature of the church, being united with multicultural neighbors is important if a church wants to become multicultural; thus, location in a multicultural neighborhood becomes important. The difference between "relocating" in the windmill model and Yancey's "location" is the degree of aggressiveness in its application. Yancey suggests, "What encouragement can I offer churches that want to become multiracial but are already located in neighborhoods that are not integrated? The most obvious possibility for such churches is to move to a more integrated area."[6] That is too radical in my opinion. What we need in the United States is for churches to dare to decide to stay where they are, even when neighborhood demographics are changing or feel threatening, as in the cases of Madison and ECP. In the cases of Lakeview and Renewal, relocating was necessary because their Korean church buildings could not physically accommodate both Korean-speaking and English-speaking congregations. The suggestion of moving into a multicultural neighborhood is therefore meaningful if a church has to move or when a church launches or plants a second campus or daughter church for this purpose. Otherwise, it is also important to emphasize the multicultural value that can exist in staying, when the neighborhood surrounding one's church is involved in a cultural transition.

"Having Multicultural Worship Teams" vs. "Inclusive Worship"

In this regard, I do not differ much from Yancey's "inclusive worship" principle, though there are important differences. Under Yancey's principle, he addresses diversity in music, rotation of worship leaders of different racial backgrounds, offering styles, the length of the worship time, different preaching styles, and so on.[7] In my model, some of these elements can be found in "having multicultural worship teams" and sharing the pulpit under the "diversifying leadership" steps. However, my step of "having multicultural worship teams" emphasizes having culturally diverse worship team members and having multiple worship leaders of different cultural backgrounds. Yancey, with his principle, points to the importance of having different preaching styles, whereas I found that sharing the pulpit with

---

6. Yancey, *One Body*, 132.
7. Yancey, *One Body*, 72–84.

pastors of different racial backgrounds is the more effective way of producing different preaching styles.

"Diversifying Leadership" vs. "Diverse Leadership"

Yancey correctly points out the importance of "diverse leadership" in multicultural ministry. Since I focus much more on the transition process from monoethnic to multicultural rather than maintaining an existing ministry, this idea is named "diversifying leadership" in my process. Nevertheless, it does not overlook the necessity of its being maintained as an ongoing process, even after becoming a multicultural church. This characteristic of "diversifying leadership" is intended to emphasize the effectiveness and need for sharing the pulpit with other pastors of different race(s) or ethnic backgrounds. Sharing the pulpit should be seriously considered not only because of different preaching styles but also because of its symbolic message that all people groups are equally qualified and important in the church. However, caution must be given to the fact that, while promoting and maintaining multiculturalism is important in multicultural churches, we should not prioritize it over the quality of the preaching; many people who came to Madison because of its multicultural character said that they stayed because of the excellent preaching.

"Cultural Intelligence Training" vs. "Intentionality"

One important thing that I found but which is easy to miss in the Windmill T-process is "providing cultural intelligence training." While I anticipated seeing more Korean immigrant churches seeking to become multicultural to reach out to diverse people, I never thought that cultural intelligence training, such as providing activities for anti-racism and racial reconciliation, would be necessary in the shift from monoethnic to multicultural churches. Through this study, however, I found that this was the biggest difference between the three KIM churches and Madison which caused the remarkable degree of multicultural character in its atmosphere. This is because embracing diverse people in a church is only possible when members accept others' whole beings, including their pain and histories. No matter what kinds of cultural backgrounds are present in the congregation, learning through cultural intelligence training can help church members have a deeper understanding of others and eventually help the church to move toward being a multicultural church.

Somewhat analogously, Yancey proposes "intentionality" as a core principle of multicultural ministry. The reason why he offers intentionality as a core principle is because "there is a powerful tendency among Christians to believe that if they just welcome people of other races then such individuals will eventually join their churches and an integrated congregation can develop."[8] But the truth is "multiracial churches do not just spring up."[9] It needs special effort. I agree. Nevertheless, I did not include intentionality as a separate process in the windmill T-process because it is included in all steps in my windmill model.

Overall, Yancey's seven principles are more theoretical and much broader than my steps. In contrast, what I have attempted to do with the windmill T-process is make it more specific and methodological in its approach. Nevertheless, as the image of the windmill symbolizes, the model is more than a method. I believe that ongoing application of the windmill T-process will bring many of the same results that Yancey intended through his seven principles, though articulated more narrowly, specifically, and practically.

Evangelism in the Multicultural Church

In addition to proposing the Windmill T-process, this study helps readers that a church's multicultural status does not in and of itself lead to evangelism and growth. Instead, in most churches, human networks such as those of friends and family are essential in the evangelism undertaken by multicultural churches. Evangelism takes place when the church intentionally provides multiple points of entry. Furthermore, I found that multicultural churches grow not necessarily because of their multicultural characteristics but because of vitality and strengths such as excellence in preaching and strong small group ministry. This finding does not lead us to ignore the importance and need for the multicultural church in the United States. Rather it reminds us to be intentional in our pursuit of becoming and maintaining a multicultural church, because the purpose of its existence is to obey God's call to reach out to *panta ta ethne* (all nations) in the multicultural context.

The Significance of the Study

The significance of this study can be found in several ways. First, this study provides the Windmill T-process model designed specifically for mono-ethnic/monocultural churches who wish to become multicultural. The

8. Yancey, *One Body*, 109.
9. Yancey, *One Body*, 109.

Windmill T-process model highlights the needed steps in the transition process for monoethnic/monocultural churches. In addition, this model can also be applicable for churches which are non-ethnic but still mono-cultural who wish to move toward being multicultural. In that case, most steps in the first group of the model, such as becoming independent, adopting a non-ethnic name, and relocating, would not be needed. Second, the Windmill T-process model which is provided is simple and easy to understand in the way it depicts how to become a multicultural church. As a whole, the Windmill T-process is clear and simple to apply because each step is specific and neither abstract nor too broad. Furthermore, this model's use of the image of a windmill can help people understand and remember it for practice. Also, unlike other models, the small number of required ongoing steps, four blade parts and a shaft, can encourage church leaders to apply this model without confusion because of its straightforward nature. Fourth, the windmill model gives a clear but practical criterion to determine if the church is ready to take on the T-process before moving into praxis. The assessment step, "checking for feasibility," can help examine the possibility of a successful transition; in addition, it can give church leaders an idea of what to do if the church is not ready yet but sincerely wants to transition from being monocultural to becoming multicultural.

Fifth, this study is meaningful because it shows how first-generation immigrant churches can participate in the multicultural church movement. By supporting the second-generation EM congregation, first-generation Korean immigrant churches and especially first-generation senior pastors can catalyze the multicultural church movement, which in turn is also significant for the general church in the United States. The first and second generations are at different points on the continuum of cultural adaptation in the new country. Even though the first-generation immigrants are still struggling with the new environment and its cultural and language barriers, they still play a crucial role. They lay the foundation for church life and mission for the following generations. By investing their emotional, financial, and spiritual resources, they also can maximize the second generations' bicultural and bilingual abilities in the multicultural church movement.

Sixth, this study is also important in that it helps to remove the traditional understanding of the HUP as contradictory to the multicultural church model, by supplementing and enriching DeYmaz's new perspective on it. The examples shown by the three churches in the study give a practical approach as well as a rationale for church leaders not to hesitate but to accelerate their transitions.

Suggestions for Further Study

There are two suggestions for further research. First, it would be beneficial to study and examine non-English-speaking minority-initiated multicultural churches among non-Koreans to see if the Windmill T-process model can be found in their T-processes. Since this study and the Windmill T-process is a product of studying mainly KIM churches, a further examination of non-Korean minority-initiated multicultural churches would give credit to others who want to apply this model.

Second, I would like to suggest evaluating the 80/20 rule for the multicultural (including multiracial/multiethnic) church movement to see if there is a better standard. Most multicultural church movement leading scholars and advocates, including me, use the 80/20 rule as the sole measurable criterion for examining whether a church is multicultural or not. In this rule, if a church has a minority population of over twenty percent, it is considered a multicultural church. However, I feel there must be a better standard, and this rule needs further examination.

As a result of this study, I feel the need to define and discuss a "multicultural church" again as *a heavenly-local church that reflects the heavenly gathering of Christians by obeying the divine call of the Great Commission through serving its diverse neighbors; it is finding the value and beauty of God's creation in the diversity of people and their cultures by embracing others of different ethnicities, races, and cultures in it.*

A heavenly-local church that reflects the heavenly gathering of Christians: the expression of "heavenly-local" indicates the dual-characteristic of the multicultural church that can be found in both 1) locality, which implies that the multicultural church is neither the universal church nor an ideal church in our minds, but one that finds its *raison d'être* in its location *vis-à-vis* its neighborhood, and 2) its diverse gathering reflects the Christian community in heaven as revealed in Revelation 7:9. *By obeying the divine call of the Great Commission*: the multicultural church is a church that focuses on the Great Commission in being and doing. Otherwise, there is no reason for church leaders and the congregation to take the risk of becoming multicultural and give up their comfort zone. Regarding the call, which is divine, the multicultural church does not dare try to "accomplish" God's call, because God is the initiator, sender, performer, and accomplisher of the mission; rather, the multicultural church is a local church that faithfully "obeys" the call with honor and rejoices in its participation. *With its neighbors*: the multicultural church is a local church that exists for its neighbors and which exercises obedience from the neighborhood to all as described in Acts 1:8. *It is finding*: the tense of the expression "is finding" reveals that the multicultural church is not an accomplished or fixed form of a church but is a growing (in character) church with an ongoing T-process until the new heaven and the new earth come. *The value and beauty of God's creation in diverse people and their cultures*: the objects of the ongoing T-process in the multicultural church are the value and beauty in diverse people and diverse cultures which God intended and created. Many churches pursue the Great Commission without recognizing the value and beauty of human beings in diversity, which was created in God's image. The Christians' ultimate gathering in heaven will not wash away the uniqueness of each people group and the different cultures they possess; rather, the heavenly gathering will sing the glory of God in diversity within harmony. *By embracing others of different ethnicities, races, and cultures in it*: the multicultural church is a local church that pursues "finding the value and beauty of God's creation in diverse people and their cultures" not in theory but in action. The multicultural church is intentional in its acceptance of others from different ethnic/racial backgrounds.

Appendix A
Interview Questions for Pastors/Staff of the Case Study Churches[1]

- Can you tell me about your background?
- How did you end up as a pastor here?
- How did this church start?
- What kind of primary impetus made this church become multicultural?
- To become a multicultural church, what kind of decision-making process did your church have?
- In the transition process, who was/were the key person(s)?
- What kinds of methodologies did this church use for the transition from monocultural to multicultural?
- When this church decided to become multicultural, what were the congregation's reactions?
- Please describe the changes in these areas: 1) demographics of the congregation, 2) budget usage, 3) structure, 4) leadership distribution, 5) worship style, 6) congregation's attitude toward other minorities?
- What, if anything, do you do to make sure that the church stays multicultural?
- Do you have any racial or cultural issues in your church? What are they? How do you deal with these issues within the church?
- Have you changed anything about your church because of the different people attending? What are some of the difficulties and blessings you've experienced because you are multicultural?

1. These questions are mostly gained from *One Body One Spirit*, which originally used by Michael Emerson, George Yancey, and Karen Chai Kim. See Yancey, *One Body*, 166. The researcher added few questions based on the purpose of this study.

- Do you think your church should be multicultural? Why? Does it matter?
- Theologically, do you think churches should be multicultural, monocultural, doesn't matter, or depends on the situation? Why?
- If others felt God was calling their church to be multicultural but didn't know how to go about getting started, what advice would you give them?
- What have you learned by being part of this type of congregation? What did you wish you knew that you now know? What, if anything, do you feel like you still need information about?
- Is your church growing? Why?
- Which ethnic group is the fastest growing in your church? Why?
- Do you think that the multicultural churches like your church are more effective and better able to win ethnic minorities than monoracial/ethnic churches? If so, tell me why.
- How does your church directly or indirectly utilize its multicultural characteristics to reach out to unchurched non-Koreans (or non-Anglos)?

Appendix B
Interview Questions for Long Term Members of the Case Study Churches

- How did this church become multicultural? (Impetus, Decision making process, Key person(s)'s role, Methodologies, Congregations' reaction)
- Please describe the changes in these areas: 1) demographics of the congregation, 2) budget usage, 3) structure, 4) leadership distribution, 5) worship style, 6) congregation's attitude toward other minorities?
- What do you think are the characteristics of this church? What three words would you use to describe your church to a friend?
- If you experienced the transition from an EM congregation of a monocultural church to independent multicultural church, what are the main differences?
- What were the main reasons why you visited this multicultural church for the first time instead of another church? What made you want to visit this church? What made this church attractive to you?
- What was happening in your life that made you more receptive to this multicultural church?
- What do you think this church offers that encourages you or other people to visit this church?
- If you were a member of this church before it became multicultural, did you want your church to become a multicultural church? Why or why not?
- When you decided to stay in this church, what were the main reasons/factors? Were they the same as the reasons of the first visit? If they are different, how are they different?

- Tell me the story of how you became involved with Christ and this church.
- What are the merits of this church?
- What are the advantages of this church for reaching out to non-Christian Asian minorities?
- How has this church affected your life? Do you have an example of how this church has affected your life in an important way?
- How did/does this church help you/unchurched minorities grow in Christ?
- Since this church is multicultural, are there any hindrances or difficulties in your church?
- What are the disadvantages of being a Korean-initiated (or Dutch-initiated) multicultural church?
- In relation to evangelism, what are the disadvantages of this church?
- What do you think is the main goal of this church?
- What do you think are the emphases of this church?
- How much does your church focus on evangelism for unchurched non-Koreans (or non-Anglos)?

Appendix C

Interview Questions for New Converts of the Case Study Churches

- What do you think are the characteristics of this church? What three words would you use to describe your church to a friend?
- Did you attend other churches before coming to this church? If you came from another church, why?
- What were the main reasons you first visited this church? What made you want to visit this church? What made this church attractive for you?
- Were you able to find a church where the majority of the members share your ethnicity? If yes, why did you choose not to attend that church?
- How did you know/hear about this church? (friends, internet, mail, etc)
- Before coming to this church, did you know that this church was multicultural? Did it matter? Why or why not?
- What was happening in your life that made you more receptive to this multicultural church?
- What were the main reasons/factors that made you decide to stay in this church? Were they the same reasons you had when you visited this church for the first time? If they are different, how are they different?
- Tell me the story of how you became involved with Christ and this church.
- Your church is multicultural. What are the merits of this church?
- How has this church affected your life? Do you have an example of how this church has affected your life in an important way?
- How did this church or church members help you have faith in Christ?

- How did this church help you grow in Christ?
- If you have a non-Christian friend or family member you want to bring to your church, what are the advantages of this church?
- Since this church is multicultural, are there any hindrances or difficulties for you?
- What are the disadvantages of being in a Korean-initiated (or Dutch-initiated) multicultural church?
- In relation to evangelism, what are the disadvantages of this church?
- What do you think is the main goal of this church?
- What do you think are the emphases of this church?

Appendix D
Multicultural Leadership

THE AIM OF THIS statement is information. We wish to *inform* the people of Madison Square Church (and others who are interested) as to why and how Madison considers ethnic and racial diversity in nominating council members and in hiring pastors and staff.

Note: 'Multicultural' can include such descriptors as age, class, customs, education, economics, ethnic or national origin, gender, language, race, and the like. In this statement, multicultural refers especially to ethnic and racial diversity

WHY Madison Seeks a Multicultural Leadership Team

Our rationale for lifting up multicultural leadership is closely tied to our conviction that God has called us to be a multicultural (i.e., a racially and ethnically diverse) church.

1. We believe that God has called us to remain in this racially and ethnically diverse Madison Square neighborhood and community, in order to faithfully love, serve, welcome and embrace all our neighbors in all their God-given diversity.

2. A multicultural congregation reflects more fully God's creative work of making people of all races and ethnicities in his own image (Genesis 1:27), and his saving intent of uniting people of all races and ethnicities in Christ. "There is *neither Jew nor Greek*, there is neither slave nor free, there is no male and female, for you are all one in Christ Jesus" (Galatians 3:28).

3. A multicultural congregation exhibits more compellingly the aim and power of Christ to "reconcile us both to God in one body through the cross, thereby killing the hostility" (Ephesians 2:16), and the

blood-bought destiny of the church to be "from every tribe and language and people and nation" (Revelation 5:9).

4. A multicultural congregation expresses more forcefully the work of the Spirit to unite us in Christ. "For in one Spirit we were all baptized into one body—Jews or Greeks, slaves or free—and all were made to drink of one Spirit" (1 Corinthians 12:13).

Our commitment to multicultural leadership is tied directly to God's call upon us as a multicultural church. One of the most strategic behaviors of a multicultural church is to ensure multicultural leaders. This is true for council, for staff, and for worship leadership as well as for other service opportunities.

There also is Biblical precedent. When the Grecian Jews complained about being under-served, the apostles with the other believers chose seven assistants, all with Greek names (Acts 6). When Paul and Barnabas were sent from Antioch as missionaries, this diverse young congregation was left in the hands of a diverse leadership group: Simeon called Niger, Lucius of Cyrene, and Manaen who had been brought up with Herod the tetrarch (Acts 13).

HOW Madison Seeks a Multicultural Leadership Team

In these ways:

- *Praying*: The leadership of the church prays in private and in public that God will have mercy on us and bless us with increased ethnic diversity as a church community.

- *Preparing*: We preach the Gospel on these things, we read and recommend books and videos, we offer conferences and training, we encourage relationships across ethnic lines, we worship in different cultural expressions, and more.

- *Probing*: We search for candidates for staff and council leadership who are from various ethnicities. We pursue the web of relationships that we have. We make the positions known in all appropriate ways.

- *Preferring*: We intentionally take ethnicity into account when making choices about who we will nominate for council, call as pastors, and appoint to staff.

- *Persisting:* We confess that oppression and privilege are embedded in our psyche and our structures, and we resolve to grow an anti-racist organization that fosters ethnic minority leadership and expects cross-cultural competence of everyone.

As explained on the previous page, we are called to experience and display the divine gift of ethnic and racial diversity through reconciliation with justice. Therefore, it is not only reasonable and warranted but *strategic and essential* to consider race and ethnicity as part of the criteria for nominating, calling, and hiring.

This is not to say that race and ethnicity are the only and absolute considerations. There also are theological and philosophical and personal considerations. And none of these considerations can be decisive by themselves; many considerations factor into most decisions. However, we are intentional and committed to developing and maintaining policies, practices, mentoring and training that ensure as fully as possible a leadership community that faithfully reflects the culture, gifting, and needs of our congregation and surrounding community.

We pray that the God of grace and wisdom will humble us, give us discernment, and lead us into greater gospel-centered diversity and unity for the glory of Christ and the good of all people.

Bibliography

Adeney, Miriam. "Colorful Initiatives: North American Diasporas in Mission." *Missiology* 39.1 (January 2011) 5–23.
Anderson, David. *Multicultural Ministry: Finding Your Church's Unique Rhythm.* Grand Rapids: Zondervan, 2004.
Arias, Mortimer. "Centripetal Mission or Evangelization by Hospitality." *Missiology* 10.1 (January 1982) 69–81.
Bernard, H. Russell. *Research Methods in Anthropology: Qualitative and Quantitative Methods.* Walnut Creek, CA: AltaMira, 2002.
Bevans, Stephen B., and Roger P. Schroeder. *Constants in Context: A Theology of Mission for Today.* Maryknoll: Orbis, 2004.
Blagg, Deborah. "The Culture of Counseling," October 20, 2010. https://www.gse.harvard.edu/news/uk/10/10/culture-counseling.
Blauw, Johannes. *The Missionary Nature of the Church: A Survey of the Biblical Theology of Mission.* London: McGraw-Hill, 1962.
Blum, Edward J., and W. Scott Poole. *Vale of Tears: New Essays on Religion and Reconstruction.* Macon: Mercer University Press, 2005.
Boles, John B., ed. *Masters & Slaves in the House of the Lord: Race and Religion in the American South: 1740-1870.* Lexington: University of Kentucky Press, 1988.
Bosch, David J. *Transforming Mission: Paradigm Shifts in Theology of Mission.* Maryknoll: Orbis, 1991.
Carson, D. A. *Becoming Conversant with the Emerging Church: Understanding a Movement and Its Implications.* Zondervan, 2005.
Choy, Bong Youn. *Koreans in America.* Chicago: Nelson-Hall, 1979.
Clark, Charles Allen. *Religions of Old Korea.* Seoul: Christian Literature Society of Korea, 1961.
Conde-Frazier, Elizabeth, et al. *A Many Colored Kingdom: Multicultural Dynamics for Spiritual Formation.* Grand Rapids: Baker, 2004.
Covenant Fellowship Church. "2012–13 CFC Census: One Day Servants Retreat," January 2013.
———. *Covenant Fellowship Church 2010 Annual Report.* Champaign: Covenant Fellowship Church, 2011.
———. *Go! Covenant Fellowship Church 2011 Annual Report.* Champaign: Covenant Fellowship Church, 2012.
DeYmaz, Mark. *Building a Healthy Multi-ethnic Church: Mandate, Commitments and Practices of a Diverse Congregation.* San Francisco: Jossey-Bass, 2007.

———. *HUP: Should Pastors Accept or Reject the Homogeneous Unit Principle?* Little Rock, AR: The Mosaix Global Network, 2011. PDF e-book.

DeYmaz, Mark, and Harry Li. *Ethnic Blends: Mixing Diversity into Your Local Church*. Grand Rapids: Zondervan, 2010.

DeYoung, Curtiss Paul, et al. *United by Faith: The Multiracial Congregation as an Answer to the Problem of Race*. New York: Oxford University Press, USA, 2003.

Emerson, Michael O. "The Gift of Our Changing Culture." *Outreach Magazine*, July 8, 2012. http://www.outreachmagazine.com/features/4793-the-gift-of-our-changing-culture.html.

Emerson, Michael O., and Christian Smith. *Divided by Faith: Evangelical Religion and the Problem of Race in America*. New York: Oxford University Press, USA, 2001.

Emerson, Michael O., and Rodney M. Woo. *People of the Dream: Multiracial Congregations in the United States*. Princeton and Oxford: Princeton University Press, 2006.

Engen, Chuck Van. "Is the Church for Everyone?: Planting Multi-ethnic Congregations in North America." *Global Missiology* 1.2 (October 2004). http://ojs.globalmissiology.org/index.php/english/article/viewFile/122/353.

Flett, John G. *The Witness of God: The Trinity, Missio Dei, Karl Barth, and the Nature of Christian Community*. Grand Rapids: Eerdmans, 2010.

Frost, Michael. *The Road to Missional: Journey to the Center of the Church*. Grand Rapids: Baker, 2011.

Garces-Foley, Kathleen. "Comparing Catholic and Evangelical Integration Efforts." *Journal for the Scientific Study of Religion* 47.1 (March 2008) 17–22.

Gelder, Craig Van, ed. *The Missional Church and Denominations: Helping Congregations Develop a Missional Identity*. Grand Rapids: Eerdmans, 2008.

Gibbs, Eddie. *ChurchNext: Quantum Changes in How We Do Ministry*. Downers Grove: InterVarsity, 2000.

Glaser, Barney G., and Anselm L Strauss. *The Discovery of Grounded Theory: Strategies for Qualitative Research*. London: Aldine Transaction, 2008.

Guder, Darrell L., ed. *Missional Church: A Vision for the Sending of the Church in North America*. Grand Rapids: Eerdmans, 1998.

Haynes, Stephen R. *Noah's Curse: The Biblical Justification of American Slavery*. New York: Oxford University Press, USA, 2002.

Hays, J. Daniel. *From Every People and Nation: A Biblical Theology of Race*. Downers Grove: Apollos, 2003.

Hirsch, Alan. *The Forgotten Ways: Reactivating the Missional Church*. Grand Rapids: Brazos, 2009.

Hopler, Thom. *World of Differences: Following Christ Beyond Your Culture Walls*. Intervarsity, 1981.

Hunter, George G. *Church for the Unchurched*. Nashville: Abingdon, 1996.

———. *The Apostolic Congregation: Church Growth Reconceived for a New Generation*. Nashville: Abingdon, 2009.

———. *The Celtic Way of Evangelism: How Christianity Can Reach the West . . . Again*. Nashville: Abingdon, 2000.

———. *The Recovery of a Contagious Methodist Movement*. Nashville: Abingdon, 2012.

Hurh, Won Moo. *The Korean Americans*. Westport: Greenwood, 1998.

Hurh, Won Moo, and Kwang Chung Kim. "Religious Participation of Korean Immigrants in the United States." *Journal for the Scientific Study of Religion* 29.1 (March 1990) 19–34.

Hutchinson, John, and Anthony D. Smith, eds. *Ethnicity*. New York: Oxford University Press, USA, 1996.

Kang, Byung Moon, and Cameron Lee. "Differentiation of Self and Generational Differences in the Korean Immigrant Church." *Journal of Family Ministry* 14.4 (December 2000) 22–31.

Kang, S. Steve. *Unveiling the Socioculturally Constructed Multivoiced Self: Themes of Self Construction and Self Integration in the Narratives of Second-Generation Korean American Young Adults*. Lanham: University Press of America, 2002.

Kim, John T. *Protestant Church Growth in Korea*. Belleville, Ontario: Essence, 1996.

Kim, Jung Ha. *Bridge-makers and Cross-bearers: Korean-American Women and the Church*. Atlanta: Scholars, USA, 1997.

Kim, Rebecca Y. *God's New Whiz Kids?: Korean American Evangelicals on Campus*. Annotated edition. New York: NYU Press, 2006.

———. "Second-Generation Korean American Evangelicals: Ethnic, Multiethnic, or White Campus Ministries?" *Sociology of Religion* 65.1 (2004) 19–34.

Kim, Rebecca Y., and Sharon Kim. "Revival and Renewal: Korean American Protestants Beyond Immigrant Enclaves." *Studies in World Christianity* 18.3 (December 2012) 291–312.

Kim, Sharon. *A Faith of Our Own: Second-Generation Spirituality in Korean American Churches*. New Brunswick: Rutgers University Press, 2010.

Kim, Sinyil. "Korean Immigrants and Their Mission: Exploring the Missional Identity of Korean Immigrant Churches in North America." DMiss Diss., Asbury Theological Seminary, 2009.

Kim, Sung Won. "*Pyongsindosayeok Kimtaepyongmoksa* [Lay Ministry Rev. Tae Pyong Kim]." *Kookmin Ilbo*, July 9, 2010. http://missionlife.kukinews.com/article/view.asp?page=1&gCode=all&arcid=0003901787.

Kim, YoungJae. *Hankook Kyohoisa [History of the Korean Church]*. Seoul: Jireh, 2008.

Kosmin, Barry A., and Ariela Keysar. *American Religious Identification Survey (ARIS 2008) Summary Report*. Hartford: Institute for the Study of Secularism in Society & Culture, 2009. http://commons.trincoll.edu/aris/files/2011/08/ARIS_Report_2008.pdf.

KWMA. "*2012 Hankuk-Sunkyosa PasongHyunHwang* [2012 Korean Missionary Statistics]." https://kwma.org/cm_stats/33979.

Kwon, Ho-Youn, et al., eds. *Korean Americans and Their Religions: Pilgrims and Missionaries from a Different Shore*. University Park: Pennsylvania State University Press, 2001.

Lausanne Committee for World Evangelization. "LOP 1: The Pasadena Consultation –Homogeneous Unit Principle." Lausanne Committee for World Evangelizaiton, 1978. http://www.lausanne.org/en/documents/lops/71-lop-1.html.

Lee, Gil Pyo. "From Traditional to Missional Church: Describing a Contextual Model of Change for Ingrown Korean Diaspora Church in North America." DMiss Diss., Asbury Theological Seminary, 2010.

Lee, Helen. "Silent Exodus." *Christianity Today* 40 (August 1996) 50–53.

Lee, Jung Young. *Marginality: The Key to Multicultural Theology*. Minneapolis: Fortress, 1995.

Lee, Robert G. *Orientals: Asian Americans in Popular Culture*. Philadelphia: Temple University Press, 1999.

Lee, Yur-Bok, and Wayne Patterson. *One Hundred Years of Korean-American Relations, 1882–1982*. University: University of Alabama Press, 1986.

Lindner, Eileen, ed. *Yearbook of American and Canadian Churches 2010*. Nashville: Abingdon, 2010.

Lopez, Angelina. "Hispanics See Security in Citizenship." *Des Moines Sunday Register*. November 17, 1996.

Marti, Gerardo. *A Mosaic of Believers: Diversity and Innovation in a Multiethnic Church*. Bloomington, IN: Indiana University Press, 2005.

McGavran, Donald A. *How Churches Grow*. New York: Friendship, 1965.

———. *Understanding Church Growth*. Grand Rapids: Eerdmans, 1980.

———. *Understanding Church Growth*. 3rd ed. Grand Rapids: Eerdmans, 1990.

McIntosh, Gary L., and Alan McMahan. *Being the Church in a Multi-Ethnic Community: Why It Matters and How It Works*. Indianapolis: Wesleyan, 2012.

McKenzie, Steven L. *All God's Children: A Biblical Critique of Racism*. Louisville: Westminster John Knox, 1997.

McPhee, Arthur. "The Missio Dei and the Transformation of the Church." *Vision (Winnipeg, Man.)* 2.2 (2001) 6–12.

"Michael Oh Becomes New Lausanne Chief Executive." *Christian Today*, February 7, 2013. http://www.christiantoday.com/article/michael.oh.becomes.new.lausanne.chief.executive/31599.htm.

Min, Kyung Bae. *Hankook Gidok Kyohoisa [The Church History of Korea]*. Seoul, Korea: The Christian Literature Society of Korea, 1972.

Min, Pyong Gap. "Immigrants' Religion and Ethnicity: A Comparison of Indian Hindus and Korean Protestants." 2003 Annual Meeting of the American Sociological Association, no date.

———. *Koreans' Immigration to the U.S: History and Contemporary Trends*. New York: The Research Center for Korean Community, Queens College of CUNY, January 27, 2011. http://www.qc.cuny.edu/Academics/Centers/RCKC/Documents/Koreans%20Immigration%20to%20the%20US.pdf.

Min, Pyong Gap, and Dae-Young Kim. "Intergenerational Transmission of Religion and Culture: Korean Protestants in the U.S." *Sociology of Religion* 66.3 (September 2005) 263–282.

Min, Pyong Gap, and Young Oak Kim. "Ethnic and Sub-ethnic Attachments among Chinese, Korean, and Indian Immigrants in New York City." *Ethnic and Racial Studies* 32.5 (June 2009) 758–780.

"Minorities Expected to Be Majority in 2050." *CNN*. August 13, 2008. http://edition.cnn.com/2008/US/08/13/census.minorities/.

Moon, Steve Sang-Cheol. "Missions from Korea 2019: Support Raising." *International Bulletin of Mission Research* 43.2 (2019) 188–195. doi:10.1177/2396939319826836.

Mulder, Alfred E. *Learning to Count to One: The Joy and Pain of Becoming a Multiracial Church*. Grand Rapids: Faith Alive Christian Resources, 2006.

Murabayashi, Duk Hee Lee. "Korean Ministerial Appointments to Hawaii Methodist Churches." Center for Korean Studies of University of Hawaiʻi, 2001. http://www.korean-studies.info/pdf/methmin.pdf.

Neill, Stephen. *A History of Christian Missions*. London: Penguin, 1986.

Newbigin, Lesslie. *The Open Secret: An Introduction to the Theology of Mission.* Revised. Grand Rapids: Eerdmans, 1995.

O'Shaughnessy, Lynn. "10 Most Popular Universities for Foreign Students." *CBS News*, November 28, 2012. http://www.cbsnews.com/8301-505145_162-57555122/10-most-popular-universities-for-foreign-students/.

Okoye, James Chukwuma. *Israel and the Nations: A Mission Theology of the Old Testament.* Maryknoll: Orbis, 2006.

Olson, David T. *The American Church in Crisis: Groundbreaking Research Based on a National Database of over 200,000 Churches.* Grand Rapids: Zondervan, 2008.

Ortiz, Fernando A., and Gerard J. McGlone. *To Be One in Christ: Intercultural Formation and Ministry.* [n.p.]: Liturgical, 2015. EPUB e-book. http://search.ebscohost.com.ezproxy.asburyseminary.edu/login.aspx?direct=true&db=nlebk&AN=1072876&site=eds-live.

Ortiz, Manuel. *One New People: Models for Developing a Multiethnic Church.* Downers Grove: InterVarsity, 1996.

Overseas Koreans Foundation. "2007 Jaewoi Hangulhakkyo Hyunhwang [2007 Overseas Korean School List]," n.d. http://www.korean.net/portal/PortalView.do.

———. "*Jaewoi Dongpo Hyunhwang* [Status of Overseas Koreans]," n.d. http://www.ekosta.org/entry/.

Park, Yong-Kyu. *Hankook Gidok Kyohoisa I [History of the Korean Church I].* Seoul, Korea: Word of Life, 2004.

Payne, Buckner H. "Ariel". *The Negro: What Is His Ethnological Status?* 2nd ed. Cincinnati, 2011. Kindle edition.

Peart, Norman Anthony. *Separate No More: Understanding and Developing Racial Reconciliation in Your Church.* Grand Rapids: Baker, 2000.

Priest, Josiah. *Bible Defense of Slavery.* Glasgow, KY: W. S. Brown, 1853.

———. *Slavery, as It Relates to the Negro, or African Race: Examined in the Light of Circumstances, History and the Holy Scriptures; With an Account of the Origin of the Black Man's Color, Causes of His State of Servitude and Traces of His Character as Well in Ancient as in Modern Times: With Strictures on Abolitionism.* Reprint. Albany: C. Van Benthuysen, 1843.

Priest, Robert J., and Alvaro L. Nieves, eds. *This Side of Heaven: Race, Ethnicity, and Christian Faith.* New York: Oxford University Press, USA, 2006.

Rah, Soong-Chan. *Many Colors: Cultural Intelligence for a Changing Church.* New Edition. Chicago: Moody, 2010.

———. *The Next Evangelicalism: Freeing the Church from Western Cultural Captivity.* Downers Grove: IVP, 2009.

Rambo, Lewis R. *Understanding Religious Conversion.* New Haven: Yale University Press, 1995.

Reimers, David M. *Still the Golden Door: The Third World Comes to America.* New York: Columbia University Press, 1992.

Rynkiewich, Michael. *Soul, Self, and Society.* Eugene: Cascade, 2011.

Ryu, Tongshik. *A History of Christ United Methodist Church, 1903-1988.* Seoul, Korea: Christ United Methodist Church, 1988.

Schaefer, Richard T. *Racial and Ethnic Groups.* 12th ed. Upper Saddle River: Prentice Hall, 2010.

Scupin, Raymond, ed. *Race and Ethnicity: An Anthropological Focus on the United States and the World.* Upper Saddle River: Prentice Hall, 2003.

Sine, Christine. "Where Is Jesus in Your Neighbourhood?" *Godspace*, March 4, 2010. http://godspace.wordpress.com/2010/03/04/where-is-jesus-in-your-neighbourhood/ (accessed February 18, 2013).

Smith, H. Shelton. *In His Image, But . . . : Racism in Southern Religion, 1780-1910*. Durham, NC: Duke University Press, 1972.

Stafford, Tim. "The Tiger in the Academy." *Christianity Today*, April 1, 2006. http://www.christianitytoday.com/ct/2006/april/33.70.html.

Stark, Rodney. *The Rise of Christianity: A Sociologist Reconsiders History*. Princeton: Princeton University Press, 1996.

Suh, InSil. "*Mijunkuk Haninkyohoi 4,544* [4,454 Korean Churches in the USA]," *Christian Today*, January 21, 2018. http://www.christiantoday.us/sub_read.html?uid=25115&section=section12&section2=.

Takaki, Ronald. *A Different Mirror: A History of Multicultural America*. New York: Back Bay, 1993.

The Pew Forum on Religion & Public Life. *Asian Americans: A Mosaic of Faiths*. Washington, DC: The Pew Forum on Religion & Public Life, 2012.

———. *U.S. Religious Landscape Survey*. Washington, DC: The Pew Forum on Religion & Public Life, 2008. http://religions.pewforum.org/pdf/report-religious-landscape-study-full.pdf.

Turner, Terence. "Anthropology and Multiculturalism: What Is Anthropology That Multiculturalists Should Be Mindful of It?" *Cultural Anthropology* 8.4 (November 1993) 411–29.

U.S. Census Bureau. *Overview of Race and Hispanic Origin: 2010*, n.d. http://www.census.gov/prod/cen2010/briefs/c2010br-02.pdf.

———. "Statistical Abstract of the United States 1961," n.d. http://www2.census.gov/prod2/statcomp/documents/1961-02.pdf.

United States. Department of Homeland Security. *Yearbook of Immigration Statistics: 2016*. Washington, DC: U.S. Department of Homeland Security, Office of Immigration Statistics, 2017.

University of Illinois at Urbana-Champaign. "On-Campus Fall 2011 Statistical Abstract of Ten-Day Enrollment (revised)," n.d. http://www.dmi.illinois.edu/stuenr/abstracts/FA11_ten.htm.

Vander Schaaf, Douglas "'Square Roots': The Story of a Changing Church in a Changing Community." Paper submitted to History 395 at Calvin Theological Seminary, December 11, 1978.

Volf, Miroslav. "Exclusion and Embrace: Theological Reflections in the Wake of 'Ethnic Cleansing.'" *Journal of Ecumenical Studies* 29.2 (1992) 230–48.

Walls, Andrew F. *The Missionary Movement in Christian History: Studies in the Transmission of Faith*. Maryknoll: Orbis, 1996.

Warner, R. Stephen, and Judith G. Wittner, eds. *Gatherings in Diaspora: Religious Communities and the New Immigration*. Philadelphia: Temple University Press, 1998.

Whitford, David. "A Calvinist Heritage to the 'Curse of Ham': Assessing the Accuracy of a Claim About Racial Subordination." *Church History & Religious Culture* 90.1 (March 2010) 25–45.

———. *The Curse of Ham in the Early Modern Era: The Bible and the Justifications for Slavery*. St. Andrews Studies in Reformation History. Burlington, VT: Ashgate, 2009.

Wolgin, Philip E., and Irene Bloemraad. "'Our Gratitude to Our Soldiers': Military Spouses, Family Re-Unification, and Postwar Immigration Reform." *The Journal of Interdisciplinary History* 41.1 (Summer 2010) 27–60.

Woo, Deborah. "The Glass Ceiling and Asian Americans." University of California, 1994. http://digitalcommons.ilr.cornell.edu/cgi/viewcontent.cgi?article=1130&context=key_workplace.

Woo, Michelle. "Dave Gibbons Is a Church Misfit." *OC Weekly News*, September 8, 2011. http://www.ocweekly.com/2011-09-08/news/newsong-dave-gibbons/2/.

Woo, Rodney M. *The Color of Church: A Biblical and Practical Paradigm for Multiracial Churches*. Nashville, TN: B&H Academic, 2009.

Woodberry, J. Dudley, ed. *Reaching the Resistant: Barriers and Bridges for Mission*. Pasadena: William Carey Library, 1998.

Wright, Christopher J. H. *The Mission of God: Unlocking the Bible's Grand Narrative*. Downers Grove: IVP Academic, 2006.

Yamauchi, Edwin M. "The Curse of Ham." *Criswell Theological Review* 6.2 (March 2009) 45–60.

Yancey, George. *One Body, One Spirit: Principles of Successful Multiracial Churches*. Downers Grove: IVP, 2003.

Ybarrola, Steven. "Anthropology, Diasporas, and Mission." *Mission Studies* 29 (2012) 79–94.

Yin, Robert K. *Case Study Research: Design and Methods*. 4th ed. SAGE Publications, 2008.

Yoon, In-Jin. "A Cohort Analysis of Korean Immigrants' Class Backgrounds and Socioeconomic Status in the United States." *Korean Journal of Population and Development* 26.1 (July 1997) 61–81.

Yu, Eui-Young. "Korean Population in the United States as Reflected in the Year 2000 U.S. Census." Paper presented at the Population Association of Korea Annual Meeting, Seoul, Korea, 1 December 2001.

Yu, Eui-Young, Peter Choe, and Sang Il Han. "Korean Population in the United States, 2000." *International Journal of Korean Studies* 6.1 (2002) 71–107.

Zhou, Min, and J. V. Gatewood, eds. *Contemporary Asian America: A Multidisciplinary Reader*. New York: NYU Press, 2000.

www.ingramcontent.com/pod-product-compliance
Lightning Source LLC
Chambersburg PA
CBHW070319230426

43663CB00011B/2179